• • • • • • • • • • • • •

The
BEST TOYS,
BOOKS
and VIDEOS
for KIDS

★ ★ ★

The 1994 Guide to 1,000 +
Kid-Tested, Classic and
New Products for Ages 0–10

JOANNE OPPENHEIM
and STEPHANIE OPPENHEIM

Illustrations by Joan Auclair

▇ HarperPerennial
A Division of HarperCollinsPublishers

*With thanks to our family and the many other
families who helped us test for the best.*
—Joanne and Stephanie

HarperCollins books may be purchased for educational, business, or sales pro-
motional use. For information please write: Special Markets Department,
HarperCollins Publishers, Inc., 10 East 53rd Street, New York, NY 10022.

FIRST EDITION

Designed by Janet Tingey

Library of Congress Cataloging-in-Publication Data
Oppenheim, Joanne.
    The best toys, books and videos for kids : the 1994 guide to
1,000 + kid-tested, classic and new products : for ages 0–10 / Joanne
Oppenheim and Stephanie Oppenheim.
        p.   cm.
    Includes bibliographical references (p.   ) and index.
    ISBN 0-06-273196-3
    1. Toys—Catalogs. 2. Bibliography—Best books—Children's literature.
3. Children's literature—Bibliography. 4. Audio-visual materials—
Catalogs. I. Oppenheim, Stephanie. II. Title.
GV1218.5.P67 1993
790.1'33'0216—dc20   93-13577

93 94 95 96 97 ◆ 10 9 8 7 6 5 4 3 2

Contents

Introduction

Why a guide to children's media? Anyone who has walked the aisles of a giant toy supermarket or tried to sift through the mountains of books, videos, audios and software designed for children knows how hard it is to know what to buy. That's what this book is all about! *The Best Toys, Books and Videos for Kids* is an easy-to-use consumer guide that will take the guesswork out of choosing products that are not a waste of your money or your child's time.

How We're Different

The Oppenheim Toy Portfolio was founded in 1989 as the only independent consumer review of children's media. Unlike most other groups that rate products, we charge no entry fees and accept no ads from manufacturers. When you see our award seals on products, you can be assured that they are "award-winning" because they were selected by a noted expert in child development, children's literature and education, and then rated by the most objective panel of judges—kids.

How We Select the Best

We shop for children the year round—only we get to do what most parents wish they could do before they buy. We open the toys, run the videos, read the books, play the music and boot up the software. We get to compare all the toys that may look remarkably similar but often turn out to be quite different. For example, we put the toy trains together and find out which ones don't stay on the tracks.

The Real Experts Speak: Kids and Their Families

To get a meaningful sampling we deal with families from all walks of life. We have testers in the city and in the country, in diapers and in blue jeans, in school clothes and in tutus. They have parents who are teachers, secretaries, lawyers, doctors, writers, engineers, doormen, software programmers, editors, psychologists, librarians, engineers, businesspeople, architects, family therapists, musicians, artists, nurses and early childhood educators. In some instances we have tested products in preschool and after-school settings where we can get feedback from groups of children. Since all new products tend to have novelty appeal, we ask our testers to live with a product for a while before assessing it. Among other things we always ask— would you recommend it to others?

Criteria We Use for Choosing Quality Products

- What is this product designed to do and how well does it do it?
- What can the child do with the product? Does it invite active doing and thinking or simply passive watching?
- Is it safe and well designed, and can it withstand the unexpected?
- Does it "fit" the developmental needs, interests and typical skills for which it was designed?
- What messages does it convey? Toys as well as books and videos can say a great deal about val-

ues parents are trying to convey. For example, does the product reflect old sexual stereotypes that limit children's views of themselves and others?

- What will a child learn from this product? Is it a "smart" product that will engage the child's mind or simply a novelty with limited play value?
- Is it entertaining? No product makes our list if kids find it boring—no matter how "good" or "educational" it claims to be.
- Is the age label correct? Is the product so easy that it will be boring or so challenging that it will be frustrating?

Rating System

Outstanding products, selected by our testers, are awarded with one of four honors:

 Platinum Award—These represent the most innovative, engaging new products of the year. See the 1994 Platinum Award Buying Guide.

 Gold Seal Award—Given to outstanding new products that enhance the lives of children. All products selected for this book have received a Gold Seal Award unless they are marked "Mixed Emotions." Those products that receive a Gold Seal during the year are nominated for the year-end's top Platinum Award List.

 Blue Chip Classic Award—Reserved for classic products that should not be missed just because they weren't invented yesterday.

 SNAP Award—Our Special Needs Adaptable Product Award is given to products that can be used or easily adapted for children with special needs. All products reviewed in that section are SNAP Award winners.

1994 PLATINUM AWARD BUYING GUIDE

	Infants	Toddlers
TOYS	**Fold 'n Go Play Around Mat** (Playskool) **Peek a Boo Play Mirror** (Wimmer-Ferguson) **Velveteenie Circus Animals** (North American Bear Co.) **Baby Gumballs** (Playskool)	**Peek a Boo Stacker** (Fisher Price) **Hide Inside** (Discovery) **Duplo Airport** (Lego) **Super Sports Car** (Today's Kids)
BOOKS	**Let's Look At My World** (Witt, Scholastic $5.95) **Let's Eat/Vamos a Comer** (Shirotani, Simon & Schuster)	**Time For Bed** (Fox/Dyer, Harcourt Brace) **The Little Red Hen** (Barton, HarperCollins) **Little Buddy Goes Shopping** (Yee, Viking) **Mother Hubbard's Cupboard** (Rader, Tamborine) **Annabel** (Boland/Halsey, Dial)

Preschoolers	Early School Years
Talking Barney (Playskool)	**Multicultural Puppets** (Learning Resources)
Press N Dress Doll (Pockets of Learning)	**Spaghetti Machine** (Natural Science)
Recycling Trucks (Little Tikes and Nylint)	**Madeline Doll** (Eden)
Air Nikko Remote Control Jet (Nikko)	**Kwanzaa Doll** (Golden Ribbon)
Shape 'N' Color (Anatex)	**Technics with Pneumatics** (Lego)
2- Sided Magna Doodle (Tyco)	**Criss Cross Hot Wheels** (Mattel)

Darcy and Gran Don't Like Babies (Cutler/ Ryan, Scholastic)	**From Sea to Shining Sea** (Cohn, Scholastic)
Goldilocks and The Three Bears (Langley, HarperCollins)	**Garth Pig Steals the Show** (Rayner, Dutton)
I Am Really A Princess (Shields/Meisel, Dutton)	**Honest Abe** (Kunhardt/ Zeldis, Greenwillow)
I Spy Two Eyes—Numbers in Art (Micklethwait, Greenwillow)	**Korean Cinderella** (Climo/Heller, Harper-Collins)
Stop Thief! (Kalan/Abolafia, Greenwillow)	**My New York** (Jakobsen, Little Brown)
When I was Little (Curtis/Cornell, Harper-Collins)	**The Sweetest Fig** (VanAllsburg, Houghton Mifflin)
Margaret and Margarita (Reiser, Greenwillow)	**I'll See You In My Dreams** (Jukes/ Schuett, Knopf)
Plane Song (Siebort/Nasta, HarperCollins)	**Planes of the Aces** (Moseley/Bowden, Doubleday)
	The Three Little Wolves and the Big Bad Pig (Trivizas/Oxenbury, McElderry)
	Once Upon a Time (Prater, Candlewick)

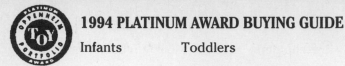

1994 PLATINUM AWARD BUYING GUIDE

	Infants	Toddlers
VIDEO		**Sesame Street 25th Birthday** (Random House) **See How They Grow: Pets** (Sony) **Spot** (Disney)
AUDIO	**'Til Their Eyes Shine— The Lullaby Album** (CBS)	**Good Night Moon** (Caedmon) **Bethie's Really Silly Songs** (Discovery)

1994 Special Needs Adaptable Product Awards

Ramp and Wheel Chair Dollhouse Accessories (Little Tikes)
Press 'N Dress Doll (Pockets of Learning)
Sponge Painters (Alex)
Motor Tracks (Kapable Kids)
Watch Me Talk Mirror (Mattel)
Barney Keyboard (Playskool)
Hal's Pals (Hal's Pals)
Hot Tot Wrist and Ankle Rattles (Eden)
Bumble Ball (Ertl)
Air Nikko Remote Control Jet (Nikko)

Preschoolers	Early School Years
Peter, Paul, and Mommy, Too (Warner)	**John Henry** (Rabbit Ears)
Harold & The Purple Crayon (CC Studios)	**The Wild Swans** (Lightyear)
The Tale of Peter Rabbit and Benjamin Bunny (Goodtimes)	**Ira Sleeps Over** (Family Home Entertainment)
Millions of Cats and Blumpoe the Grumpoe Meets Arnold the Cat (MCA)	**Aladdin** (Disney)

Preschoolers	Early School Years
Peter, Paul, and Mommy, Too (Warner)	**The Cat In the Hat** (El Gato Ensombrerado) (Dr. Seuss, Random House)
Winnie the Pooh Storytime Giftset (Disney)	**I Got Shoes** (Sweet Honey in the Rock/ Music for Little People)
Put On Your Green Shoes (Sony)	

COMPUTERS

Preschoolers	Early School Years
Kiddesk (Edmark)	**The New Grolier Multimedia Encyclopedia** (Software Toolworks)
Grandma and Me (Brøderbund)	**The Treehouse** (Brøderbund)
Mickey's ABC's (Disney)	**Dinosaur Adventure/ Space Adventure** (Knowledge Adventure)
Millie's Math House (Edmark)	**Arthur's Teacher Trouble** (Brøderbund)
Rodney's Funscreen (Activision)	**Mario Paint** (Nintendo)

TOP-RATED GREEN PRODUCTS '94

Heightened concern for the environment has translated into a flood of "ecology" products targeted for kids. In children's products, eco-mania has inspired legions of eco-action figures, piles of pro-planet plush, and books with trendy eco-slogans. But ecology needs to be more than a fad. Meaningful involvement for kids begins with active, immediate experiences that connect them to the natural world. The products here are chosen to engage kids curiosity and sense of wonder. Before we can expect kids to save the planet, we need to help them learn to love it.

TOYS

Recycling Trucks (Little Tikes/Nylint)

Paper Making Kits (Chasley/Galt)

Oh Grow Up Plant Kit (Creativity for Kids)

Endangered Species Puzzle (Schaffer)

3-D Rainforest Jigsaw Puzzle (Binary Arts)

BOOKS

Animals in Danger (McCay/Moseley, Alladdin)

The Big Book for Our Planet (Durell et al, Dutton)

Dinosaurs to the Rescue! (Brown, Little Brown)

Where's That Insect? (Brenner et al, Scholastic)

VIDEOS

Look What I Grew (Intervideo)

My First Green Video (Sony)

Sing Along Earth Songs (Random House)

This Pretty Planet (Tom Chapin, Sony)

AUDIO

Anarctica (Cowcher, Soundprints)

Put On Your Green Shoes (Sony)

Big, Big World (A & M)

COMPUTER SOFTWARE

The San Diego Zoo Presents the Animals! (Software Toolworks)

TOP-RATED MULTICULTURAL PRODUCTS '94

Never before have so many products reflected our cultural diversity. What do we mean by muliticultural? Some products introduce kids to cultures beyond their own and expand their view of the world. Others reflect more familiar settings. The best of these products capture our differences along with the universal feelings that connect us.

TOYS
Multicultural Career Puppets (Learning Resources)
Multicultural Family Puppets (Constructive Playthings)
Ring Around the Rosy Board Game (Ravensburger)
Kwanzaa Doll (Golden Ribbons)
Eskimo Art (Patail)
Multicultural Crayons & Markers (Crayola)
Walk-Along Drum (Music for Little People)

BOOKS
Bamboo Hats and a Rice Cake (Tompert/Demi, Crown)
Brown Angels (Myers, HarperCollins)
Hue Boy (Mitchell/Binch, Dial)
Grandfather's Journey (Say, Houghton Mifflin)
Magical Tales from Many Lands (Mayo/Ray, Dutton)
Margaret & Margarita (Reiser, Greenwillow)
Happy Birthday, Martin Luther King (Marzollo/Pinkney, Scholastic)

AUDIO
The Cat In the Hat/(El Gato Ensombrerado)(Seuss, Random House)
Joining Hands with Other Lands (Kimbo)
I Got Shoes (Sweet Honey in the Rock)

VIDEO
The Song of Sacajawea (Rabbit Ears)
We All Sing Together (Random House)
John Henry (Rabbit Ears)

There are reviews of classic green and multicultural products throughout the book. These are just among the newest for '94.

Using This Book

Each section begins with a developmental play profile that tells you what to expect during each stage and what "basic gear" will enhance learning and play. We also give you suggestions for best gifts for your budget and, perhaps most important of all, a stage-by-stage list of toys to avoid.

Because we know how busy people are these days, our reviews are purposefully short and provide information on how to get your hands on the product.

A word about prices: Our award-winning products are not all high-ticket items. We have selected the very best products in toy supermarkets, as well as those that you will find in specialty stores, museum shops and quality catalogs. We have listed the suggested retail prices, but they will vary tremendously depending on where you shop.

Telephone numbers: Where available, we have given a customer service number if you have difficulty locating the product in your area. For some educational products, you'll find a catalog number for ordering.

Child's Play—More Than Fun!

For children, playing is more than a fun way to fill the day. It's through play that children learn and develop all sorts of important physical, intellectual and social skills. Like musicians, children use well-chosen toys, books and music to orchestrate their play. As they grow and develop, so does their need for more complex playthings that challenge and enhance their learning. Toys and stories with the right developmental fit help create a marvelous harmony for learning and fun. *The Best Toys, Books and Videos for Kids* is a resource book you can use to make that kind of mix.

1 ★ TOYS

1 ★ Infants
Birth to One Year

What to Expect Developmentally

LEARNING THROUGH THE SENSES. Right from the start babies begin learning by looking, listening, touching, smelling and tasting. It's through their senses that they make sense of the world. In this first remarkable year babies progress from gazing to grasping, from touching to tossing, from watching to doing. By selecting a rich variety of playthings, parents can match their baby's sensory learning style.

REACHING OUT. Initially you will be the one to activate the mobile, shake the rattle, squeeze the squeaker. But before long baby will be reaching out and taking hold of things and engaging you in a game of peekaboo.

TOYS AND DEVELOPMENT. As babies develop so do their needs for playthings that fit their growing abilities. Like clothes, good toys need to fit. Some of the toys for newborns will have short-term use and then get packed away or passed along to a new cousin or friend. Others, such as the crib-rail activity center, may become a favorite floor toy. Still others will be used in new ways. During this first year babies need toys to gaze at, listen to, grasp, chomp on, shake, pass from one hand to another, bang together, toss, chase and hug.

YOUR ROLE IN PLAY. No baby needs all the toys listed here. In fact, to your new baby no toy will be more interesting than your smiling face, the sound of your voice and the touch of your hands. Playing with your baby is not just fun—it's one of the most important ways babies learn about themselves and the world of people and things!

• •

Basic Gear Checklist for the horizontal infant

★ ★ ★

- ✔ Mobile
- ✔ Musical toys
- ✔ Crib Mirror
- ✔ Soft fabric toys with differing sounds and textures
- ✔ Fabric dolls or animals with easy-to-grab limbs

• •

Basic Gear Checklist for the vertical infant

★ ★ ★

- ✔ Rattles and teething toys
- ✔ Manipulatives with differing shapes, sounds and textures
- ✔ Washable dolls and animals
- ✔ Busy box
- ✔ Musical toys
- ✔ Soft fabric-covered ball
- ✔ Rolling toys or vehicles
- ✔ Plastic containers for filling and dumping games
- ✔ Cloth blocks
- ✔ Bath toys
- ✔ Cloth or sturdy cardboard books

🚫 Toys to Avoid 🚫

These toys pose choking and/or suffocation hazards:

- Antique rattles
- Foam toys
- Toys with elastic
- Toys with buttons, bells and ribbons
- Old wooden toys that may contain lead paint
- Furry plush dolls that shed
- Any toys with small parts

These toys are developmentally inappropriate:

- Shape sorters and ring-and-post toys call for skills that are beyond infants

THE HORIZONTAL INFANT

Time was when infants' rooms and products were pastel only. Not any more. Research has shown that during the early weeks of life babies respond to the sharp contrast of black-and-white patterns. But does that mean your whole nursery needs to be black and white? Not at all. In no time your baby is going to be responding to bright colors, interesting sounds and motion.

CRIB TOYS: MOBILES, MIRRORS AND MORE

A musical mobile attached to crib rail or changing table provides baby with fascinating sights and sounds. During the first three months infants can focus only on objects that are relatively close. Toys should be between 8" to 14" from their eyes. Before you buy any mobile, look at it from the baby's perspective. What can you see? Many attractive mobiles are purely for decoration and do not have images that face the baby in the crib. Here are our favorites.

INFANT STIM-MOBILE

(Wimmer Ferguson $19.95) New baby will be fascinated with the black-and-white, high-contrast patterns of the ten vinyl 3" discs and squares that dance and dangle on this nonmusical mobile for the crib or changing table. Ten colored discs and squares ($7.95) can be added for new visual interest, or you can buy the whole set for $24.95. May not look as cute as other mobiles, but babies do react to the visual stimulation of this early crib toy. (800) 747-2454.

LASTING PLAY MUSICAL MOBILE

(Fisher Price $29.99) New this year, Fisher Price's updated classic mobile with a music box lights up and can be used after your baby has outgrown the mobile. Our testers liked being able to set the music for 30 minutes. Some objected to the light switch and the need for batteries. (800) 432-5437.

PANDA DOMINO MOBILE   PLATINUM AWARD

(Dakin $50) Our favorite mobile, with playful black-and-white pandas dressed up with primary-color collars around their necks. Spins to the tune of "Twinkle, Twinkle, Little Star." A consistent winner with infants, who enjoy the sounds, sights and motion, and parents who want something decorative as well as functional. Primary-colored circus theme also a favorite. (800) 227-6598.

> **SAFETY TIP:** Mobiles should be removed by five months or whenever baby can reach out and touch them to avoid the danger of strangulation or choking on small parts.

DOUBLE-FEATURE CRIB MIRROR   BLUE CHIP

(Wimmer Ferguson $26.95) A truly distortion-free crib mirror. Comes with mirror on one side and high-contrast graphics, including a face and a boat, on the other side; the latter will be of greatest interest to younger babies. Unlike many crib toys, this mirror ties at all four corners, so it can't be used as a lift-and-bang toy like many other crib mirrors. Has no moving parts for older babies to manipulate. (800) 747-2454.

COW OVER THE MOON TAG-ALONGS BLUE CHIP

(Dakin $15) Attractive fabric cow, stars and moon dangle from soft-fabric ring. Attaches with Velcro fastener to crib, car seat or stroller. A good gazing toy for the early months that your baby can safely reach out to touch. A new Humpty Dumpty version is also available. (800) 227-6598.

CRIB CENTER

(Little Tikes $22) Baby can begin to investigate nine different activities on this bright-yellow combination crib mirror/activity center, which can be used later as a carry-about toy. The spinner and color wheel provide early lessons in cause and effect. One toy tester family raved that this toy bought them an extra twenty minutes of sleep in the morning! (800) 321-0183.

> **SAFETY TIP:** The first run of these crib centers was recalled because of an unsafe level of lead paint on the barbershop roller, which was red. The current model has a purple roller.

SPIN-AROUND BUSY BOX

(Playskool $18.75) A house-shaped busy box with seven activities, including dials to turn, peekaboo mirror with sliding door cover and a roller and ball that spin and rattle. Designed for both crib and floor play. Labeled 3–24 months but of greatest interest to sitting-up stage and beyond. (An updated musical busy box with seven tunes looked good but was not available for testing.) (800) 752-9755.

FRIENDLY FRAME PLATINUM AWARD

(TOT $18.50) Strap this white-and-black vinyl picture frame to crib rail, stroller or car seat, and fill with one of several attention-getting graphics or family photos. Recognizing that infants respond to novelty, this is a clever idea that fills the bill for providing an ever-changeable view. (203) 448-6705.

MUSICAL TOYS

Few toys are as soothing to newborns as a music box with its quiet sounds. Today most musical toys for infants don't come in boxes, but rather in plush toys. We prefer some of the newer pull-down musicals to soft plush dolls with hard metal wind-up keys that older babies may chew or get poked with by accident. When baby starts turning over, use musical wind-up plush dolls with supervision, not as crib toys.

FORGET-ME-NOT BLUE ELEPHANT MUSICAL PULL

(Gund $20) Pull the handle at the end of this blue elephant's trunk to activate the music. Eventually baby will be able to do it herself. (908) 248-1500.

MUSICAL PILLOW   BLUE CHIP

(Eden $20) You can tie this 4 1/2" × 6" musical pillow embroidered with Peter Rabbit onto a newborn's bassinet, crib or stroller. It's also a small and comforting take-along for nap time or overnights away from home. A perfect baby shower gift. (212) 947-4400.

> **SAFETY TIP:** Pillows and stuffed animals left in cribs present a suffocation hazard.

WRINKLES GIRAFFE

(Dakin $25) An unusual musical giraffe in yellow plush with orange spots, tufted tail and mane. Pull the head and the giraffe's long neck extends and plays "Brahms Lullaby" as its head moves slowly back into resting position. Interesting textures to feel, action to watch and sound to hear. (800) 227-6598.

EQUIPMENT FOR PLAYTIME

BEST IN ITS CATEGORY:
FUNTIME SOFT BOUNCER SEAT

(Summer $49.95) This fabric chair provides the perfect perspective for young infants who are ready for a little elevation but are not able to sit up. Comes with bright-colored toys on a bar that baby will first gaze at and later reach out and spin. Also available with a canopy to keep the bright sun out of baby's eyes. Use with adult supervision only. Up to 25 pounds. (800) 926-8627.

● ●

ACTIVITY TIP:
Free-standing activity gyms can also be pulled up to an infant seat for new interest. Note: Activity gyms are greatly enjoyed but should only be used with total supervision. We looked at several. One of our testers got a hand caught and another almost kicked a lightweight gym over. Century's version rated the best but we recommend cutting off the string attachments.

● ●

> **SAFETY TIP:** Never place any type of baby carrier on a table, bed or counter. Even though the baby has never done it before, there's no way of predicting when he will make a move that can tip the carrier.

FOLD 'N GO PLAY AROUND ✦'94 **PLATINUM AWARD**

(Playskool $34) This cheerful, primary-colored circular play mat with bright-red polka dots looks perfect for very young babies at home or on the go. Attached to the soft wraparound bumper are five textured activities for baby to explore with all of her senses. Looks like many higher-priced mats. You may want to remove the big button closure under the mat, which might be a problem with older babies who are exploring or teething. (800) 752-9755.

> **SAFETY TIP:** Some of the most beautiful baby blankets and play mats on the market are adorned with ribbons, pearls and other decorations—all of which pose a choking hazard to a baby. Save these quilts for decoration.

STROLLER MATES
(Summer $19.95) Attach these three squeezable characters to stroller for baby to manipulate and enjoy on outings. Plenty of textures, sounds and activity for baby to investigate. (800) 926-8627.

> **SAFETY TIP:** Many parents find the back-and-forth action of a swing a soothing diversion for a restless infant. However, we find it difficult to recommend any infant swings because they can entrap limbs and necks or even collapse. If you choose to use one, we urge you not to leave the room. Use it with constant supervision.

FIRST LAP & FLOOR TOYS: RATTLES, SOUND TOYS & MORE

Infant toys can help adults engage and interact with newborns. A bright rattle that baby tracks visually, a quiet music box that soothes  or an interesting doll to gaze or swipe at are ideal for beginning getting-acquainted games. These toys can be used at the changing table or for lap games during playful moments after a feeding, before a bath or whenever.

RATTLES

Many rattles are too noisy, hard and heavy for newborns. While some will be used by adults to get baby's attention, the best choices for newborns are rattles with a soft sound that won't startle and a soft finish that won't hurt. During the first months an infant's arm and hand movements are not yet refined. Here are some of the best rattles for early play times.

COCK-A-DOODLE ZOO SHAKE ME DOLL

(Eden $9.95) Bold black-and-white patterns for visual interest, stitched features for safety, velvety velour head and hands for texture and a rattle inside for sound appeal all add up to a just-right first doll for infants. Also new and top-rated with our testers are Eden's velour and brightly-colored Hot Tots ($9.95). (212) 947-4400.

KINDER RATTLE

(Gund $6) Attention-getting bright-red or yellow terry rattles come in bear or giraffe shape with a hole in the middle for easy grasping. (908) 248-1500.

LINKY DINK GEOMETRICS

(Gund $8) Velour circle, triangle and square are interlocked and have a quiet rattle stitched inside. This soft machine-washable toy is available in bold black, white and red combo or in pastel or primary colors. An excellent rattle for two-handed play. (908) 248-1500.

PATTERN PALS   PLATINUM AWARD

(Wimmer-Ferguson $19.95 set of three) A new line of multisensory soft toys that are just right for early lap games. There's a fish, a boat and a caterpillar that are easy to grasp. Each has a black-and-white design on one side and a different primary color on the other. All have a unique sound and texture. A best bet for newborns. (800) 747-2454.

STAR RINGS   BLUE CHIP

(Parents Child Development $10) Smiling star face has four easy-to-grab rings that swing and clatter and can eventually be used to chomp on. Ideal for grabbing baby's attention. (201) 831-1400.

TINKLE, CRINKLE, RATTLE AND SQUEAK

(Gund $10) Just as the name says, this long, easy-to-grasp velour worm-shaped toy has varied sounds in each brightly colored segment. It's 17" long and machine washable, and responds to baby's touch with interesting sounds. (908) 248-1500.

• •

ACTIVITY TIP:

When baby is flat on her tummy, play a little tracking game that strengthens neck and arm muscles. Shake a rattle just above eye level but to her right. Slowly move rattle to the left and gently help baby turn.

• •

FIRST HUGGABLES

Newborns often receive tons of soft dolls that are too big, too fuzzy and even unsafe for now. Although they may be decorative and fine for gazing at, fuzzy plush dolls with ribbons, buttons, plastic features that may pull out or doodads that may be pulled off are better saved for preschool years.

When shopping for huggables look for:

- Washable fabric such as velour, terry or cotton
- Stitched-on features
- Easy-to-grasp legs or arms
- Sound effects sewn safely inside
- No long ribbons or bells
- Interesting textures
- Small enough size for infant to hold with ease

FLATOPUP

(North American Bear Co. $23) This friendly 12" black-and-white velour dog is just right for small hands and made of safe, nonfuzzy velour. Cat lovers will enjoy Flat-cat. (800) 682-3427.

LULLABY BEAR   PLATINUM AWARD

(Gund $21) An 11" honey-colored bear with embroidered features and almond-colored paws that comes with a special lullaby tape by popular children's singer Joanie Bartels. (908) 248-1500.

POOKY PENGUIN

(Gund $8) With bold-yellow beak and red flipper feet, Pooky is a chunky little black-and-white velour penguin with a soft body and a special squeaky sound to grab an infant's interest. (908) 248-1500.

THE VERTICAL INFANT

Many of the toys from the horizontal stage will still be used. By now, however, the mobile should be removed from the crib, and new, interesting playthings should be added gradually. As new toys are introduced, put some of the older things away. Recycle toys that have lost their novelty by putting them out of sight for a while; then reintroduce them or give them away. A clutter of playthings can become more of a distraction than an attraction.

RATTLES AND TEETHERS

Now is the time for manipulatives that encourage two-handed exploration as well as providing interesting textures, sounds and safe chewable surfaces for teething.

CAR TEETHER

(Battat $4) A flat car that's red on one side and blue on the other. Has soft-plastic yellow wheels to teethe on and

an easy-to-grab rooftop window that acts as a handle.
(518) 562-2200.

FUNSHINE MIRROR BLUE CHIP

(Ambi $9) A hand-held yellow plastic
sun with mirror on one side and picture of a teddy bear on the other
makes for great looking, licking and
games of peekaboo. Outer edges will
also be used for teething. (201) 831-1400.

HAND AND FOOT TEETHERS BLUE CHIP

(Chicco $6.95) Easy-to-grasp, with a pleasant vanilla
scent to smell and just right to chomp on, this set of
hand- and foot-shaped vinyl teethers is soft enough to be
safe, hard enough to chew on. (800) 336-8697.

SHINY RATTLES

(Fisher-Price $4.70 each) Two partially see-through rat-
tles with metallic insides reflect the colorful beads,
which make interesting sounds and motion. Come in
easy-to-grasp dumbbell and flower shapes. Great for the
price. (800) 432-5437.

SPIN, RATTLE & ROLL

(Discovery Toys $9.98) Our testers really enjoyed hold-
ing onto this mini-activity center with hoops to teethe
on, a ball to spin and a fish to move back and forth. Good
for two-handed action. (800) 426-4777.

TWIN RATTLE

(Ambi $6.50) Two sunny-yellow cogwheels with happy
faces rattle and turn as they are held or passed from
hand to hand. (201) 831-1400.

FLOOR TOYS
FIRST BLOCKS

SOFT PICTURE CUBES

(Battat $15.50) Four fabric-covered soft blocks with bold graphics of familiar go-together objects to know and name, such as an apple and a tree in primary colors. Some cubes contain jingly bells, and all are ideal to toss, stack and mostly knock down. (518) 562-2200.

SQUEAK BLOCKS

(Chicco $17) Set of six squeezable, squeaky vinyl blocks are lightweight, easy to grasp and fun to stack and knock down (mostly the latter). Embossed with numerals and objects to count. For now the numbers are purely decorative and add interesting textures to nibble and explore. (800) 336-8697.

• •

ACTIVITY TIP:

Make a stack of soft blocks and give baby a demo in knocking them down. Encourage baby to do an instant replay. Provide "boom diddy boom" sound effects!

• •

FILLING AND SPILLING GAMES

With their newly acquired skills of grasping and letting go comes the favorite game of filling and dumping multiple objects in and out of containers.

BABY GUMBALLS
PLATINUM AWARD

(Playskool $10) Older babies will enjoy dropping three giant "gumballs" in the dome-shaped gumball dispenser. Push the big lever (which squeaks) and a gumball drops out. An interesting toy for learning about cause and effect as well as providing repetitive fill-and-spill action and sound. (800) 752-9755.

BABY'S FIRST BLOCKS　　BLUE CHIP

(Fisher Price $8) Technically this is a shape-sorter, but the 12 blocks (circles, squares and triangles) will be used to fill, spill and throw long before baby can fit them into the three-place shape-sorter lid of the container. Put the lid away for now. A nongimmicky classic that is neither complicated nor expensive. (800) 432-5437.

SNAP-LOCK BEADS　　BLUE CHIP

(Fisher Price $4) These lemon-sized plastic beads are basic gear for developing fine motor skills and the ability to litter the floor. Long before baby can pull them apart or put them together they're great fun for chomping on, humming into, picking up, tossing and little games of fill and dump. (800) 432-5437.

TOYS FOR MAKING THINGS HAPPEN

Some of the best infant toys introduce babies to their first lessons in cause and effect. Such toys respond with sounds or motion that give even the youngest players a sense of "can do" power—of making things happen!

ACTIVITY POTS AND PANS　　BLUE CHIP

(Fisher Price $13.75) These won't replace the "heavy metal" kind for banging, but this five-piece set includes a pot with a peekaboo mirror, one with a rattle, a lid with a squeaker and a whistling spoon. A toy to manipulate, for pretend play. Older kids will like nesting and stacking pieces together. (800) 432-5437.

DISNEY COLOR SPIN　　BLUE CHIP

(Mattel $10) Here's a fascinating floor toy: Brightly colored Ping Pong–sized balls are enclosed under a dome and activated by turning a large, round spinning ball. Adults will need to activate this for starters. It's hard to keep your hands off this hypnotic and slight mysterious lesson in cause and effect. (800) 524-8697.

LIGHTS 'N' SOUND PIANO   PLATINUM AWARD

(Fisher Price $30) Three oversized musical keys light up and chime when touched. A spinning roller plays one of three classic nursery tunes. This easy-to-activate musical toy empowers your baby to make things happen! (800) 432-5437.

PEEK-A-BOO PLAY   PLATINUM AWARD

(Wimmer-Ferguson $12) This soft-vinyl product features a safety mirror that is behind two cushioned doors that open and close for peekaboo fun. The mirror also has high-contrast graphics with a "mommy face" on the back of the product. Just the right size for lap play and two-handed investigations. (800) 747-2454.

PEEK-N-SQUEEK EGG

(Century $17) A wonderful interactive toy for peekaboo lap games. Put your hand in the fuzzy egg and—surprise!—a baby chick puppet pops ups. A built-in squeaker in the beak produced smiles of delight with our testers. Also available in a bright-red apple with a pop-out worm. (216) 468-2000.

POP 'N' SPIN TOP
PLATINUM AWARD

(Playskool $9) An easy-to-activate top with big colorful hopping-popping balls and a barbershop-like post that twirls inside a see-through dome. Baby just pushes a big red button to activate. Very satisfying toy for a baby who is just discovering the fun of making things happen. One of our favorite new toys in this category. (800) 752-9755.

• •

FREEBIE:

Play "Buzzing Bees." Hold your fist in the air and say, "Here is a bee hive, but where are the bees?

Hiding inside—watch and see!" Wiggle your fingers and make buzzing sounds as you tickle the baby.

• •

TEETER TOTTER BEARS

(Tomy $8.99) This happy-looking chime ball, in the shape of a bright-yellow Mama Bear, rocks and chimes in response to baby's purposeful or accidental swipes. She holds a little bear that spins. An easy-to-activate toy with sound and motion payoffs. (714) 256-4990.

FIRST ROLLING TOYS AND VEHICLES

Rolling toys such as small vehicles and balls can match babies' developing mobility. Toys placed slightly beyond baby's reach can provide the motivation to get moving. But make it fun. Avoid turning this into a teasing time. Your object is to motivate, not frustrate. Games of rolling a ball or car back and forth make for happy social play between baby and older kids as well as adults.

BABY'S FIRST CAR   BLUE CHIP

(Ambi $13) This chunky little yellow car has a red squeaker on the roof and a smiley face with eyes that move as it's pushed along the floor. Scaled just right for small, chubby hands. (201) 831-1400.

CHIMEY CHUM GIRAFFE

(Tomy $8.99) Grab the handle of this bright-yellow giraffe on chunky red wheels and it will rattle as it's rolled along. Fun for crawling baby to push along or for rolling-back-and-forth floor games. (714) 256-4990.

HEDGEHOG

(Kouvalias $25) Bright-blue smiley hedgehog with yellow wheels. Cut-on on back of hedgehog makes it easy for baby to grasp and roll. Makes a noisy sound as it's moved along. (201) 633-5090.

HUMPTY DUMPTY COME-BACK ROLLER
PLATINUM AWARD
(Ambi $15) A jolly-looking Humpty Dumpty sits in a red roller wheel. Push it forward and it "magically" rolls back gently. Nice for sitting-up babies and beginning crawlers because it won't frustrate them by going too far. Works best on bare floors. (201) 831-1400.

• •

FREEBIE:
Put five or six interesting small toys and baby books in a paper bag or box for baby to explore. This is one way to help baby establish short independent playtime. Small boxes with toys inside motivate exploration and make happy surprises.

• •

PEEK 'N POP TURTLE
(Playskool $10) This friendly white turtle with a green peekaboo head is ideal for encouraging baby's own locomotion. Enclosed beads make a pleasing popping sound when car is pushed. (800) 752-9755.

• •

ACTIVITY TIP:
Before they can really stand solo, babies enjoy holding on and standing. Try a slow dance of "Ring Around a Rosy." Making a game of falling down helps take the sting out of the inevitable.

• •

SQUEEZ'EMS
(Tomy $5) A chubby little vinyl vehicle has fat round wheels and built-in squeaker. A nice first car for floor play because it is soft and safe for teething crawlers. (714) 256-4990.

First Tub Toys

BALLS IN A BOWL   BLUE CHIP

(Parents Child Development Toys $17)
For filling and spilling games, this big see-through bowl
has three little balls with spinners that are fun to take
out and put back in. Can be used for floor and tub play.
(201) 831-1400.

> **SAFETY TIP:** The Consumer Product Safety
> Commission reports 11 deaths and 17 injuries
> associated with baby bath "supporting rings,"
> devices that keep baby seated in the bath tub.
> Never rely on such devices to keep baby safe.
> Going to answer the door or phone can result in
> serious injury or worse to babies and toddlers.

ERNIE'S RUBBER DUCKIE
BLUE CHIP

(Playskool $2.99) A perfect bath
pal. A squeezable floating bath toy
for the littlest bathers. (800) 752-
9755.

FLOATING FAMILY

(Fisher Price $11) Two jumbo Little People figures will fit
into a floating turtle, blue boat or red life ring. Can be
used for floor or tub play. (800) 432-5437.

First Balls

KINDERGUND COLORFUN BALL
BLUE CHIP

(Gund $7–$12) Lightweight, bright-colored velour ball
that jingles and is easy to grasp, toss and roll. A perfect
toy for crawlers to chase and for early back-and-forth
roly-poly social games. 4 1/2" and 6 1/2". Comes in primary
colors and red, black and white. (908) 248-1500.

MY FIRST FOOTBALL

(Bantam $10) A terry-cloth football with jingly bell inside.
Encourages social and physical action. (212) 564-6750.

SAFETY TIP: While at first glance foam balls may seem like a safe bet, they are not for infants, as small pieces may be chewed off and ingested. This is also true of Nerf-type balls that have a plastic cover that can be chewed through.

SHAKERBALL

(Chicco $9.95) An interesting see-through ball with many little marbles sealed safely inside. Baby will enjoy watching and hearing the marbles tumble through the slotted dividers inside the ball. A good choice for floor or tub. (800) 336-8697.

ACTIVITY TIP:

Where's the ball? As well as rolling the ball back and forth to baby, try this hide-and-seek game. Cover most of the ball with cloth and ask, "Where's the ball?" If your baby doesn't uncover the ball, lift the cover and hide it again. Eventually you can cover the object completely. This game helps baby learn that even if an object can't be seen, it still exists.

MORE HUGGABLES

MY VERY SOFT BABY

(Playskool $9.99) An ideal first doll with pliable vinyl face and totally soft, washable pink terry-cloth body. Makes pleasant giggly sound when squeezed. African-American version available. (800) 752-9755.

TINY LOVES

(Century $19) Huggable fuzz-free 17" velour bunny or bear with all stitched features. Makes a soft jingly sound and has squeezably soft arms and legs for little hands to grab. An ideal choice for older babies and toddlers. (216) 468-2000.

VELVETEENIE CIRCUS ANIMALS ⭐94⭐ **PLATINUM AWARD**
(North American Bear Co. $14–$31) Choose from a
menagerie of brilliantly colored velour circus animals
with stitched features for safety. A hot-pink monkey with
long legs and tail is a favorite. Lions, elephants and seals
all available. (800) 682-3427.

TODDLERS-IN-TRAINING TOYS

Some of the early walking toys found in the next
chapter may be ideal for infants who are seriously
working on walking before their first birthday.

BEST TRAVEL TOYS FOR INFANTS

Having a supply of several
small toys can help divert and
entertain small travelers
whether you're going out for a
day or away for a week. Select
several very different toys, for
example:

- Key-ring teether
- Hand-held mirror
- Suction-cup rattle to attach to a table
- Small huggable
- Familiar quilt to rest on
- Musical toy

BEST NEW BABY/ SHOWER GIFTS

Big Ticket $50 or more	Domino Musical Mobile (Dakin) or Infant Seat (Summer)
Under $25	Crib Center (Little Tikes) or Musical Pillow (Eden)

Under $20	Cow Over the Moon Tag-Along (Dakin) or Squeak Blocks (Chicco)
Under $15	Peek-a-Boo Play (Wimmer Ferguson) or Colorfun Ball (Gund)
Under $10	Tinkle, Crinkle, Rattle, Squeak (Gund) or Peek 'n Pop Turtle (Playskool)
Under $5	Snap-Lock Beads (Fisher Price) or a Lullaby Tape

LOOKING AHEAD: BEST FIRST BIRTHDAY GIFTS FOR EVERY BUDGET

Big Ticket $50 or more	Child-size Raggedy Ann or Andy (Applause)
Under $25	Push 'n Ride Walker (Little Tikes) Good Night Moon Book and Doll Set (Eden)
Under $15	Pop 'n Pals (Playskool) or Play 'n Pop (Mattel)
Under $10	Pop Corn Popper (Fisher Price)
Under $ 5	Cardboard Book (see Books chapter)

2 ★ Toddlers
One to Two Years

What to Expect Developmentally

ACTIVE EXPLORATION. Anyone who spends time with toddlers knows that they are active, on-the-go learners. They don't visit long because there are so many places and things to visit and explore. Toys that invite active investigation are best for this age group. For toddlers, toys with doors to open, knobs to push and piccces to fit, fill and dump provide the raw material for developing fine motor skills along with language and imagination.

BIG-MUSCLE PLAY. Toddlers also need playthings that match their newfound mobility and their budding sense of independence. Wheeled toys to push, ride on and even ride in are great favorites. So is equipment they can climb, rock and slide on. In these two busy years toddlers grow from wobbly walkers to nimble runners and climbers.

LANGUAGE AND PRETEND POWER. As language develops, so does the ability to pretend. For beginners, games of make-believe depend more on action than story lines. Choose props that look like the things they see in the real world.

TOYS AND DEVELOPMENT. Some of the toys in this chapter, such as those for beginning walkers, will have short-term use. However, many of the best products are what we call "bridge toys," playthings that will be used now and for several years ahead. While no toddler needs all the toys listed here, one- and two-year-olds do need a good mix of toys that fit varying kinds of play modes—toys for indoors and out, for quiet, solo sit-down times, as well as social run-and-shout-out-loud times. A rich variety of playthings (which may include a plain paper shopping bag or some pots and pans) gives kids the learning tools they need to stretch their physical, intellectual and social development.

YOUR ROLE IN PLAY. Playing (and keeping up) with an active toddler requires a sense of humor and realistic expectations. In order to satisfy their growing appetite for independence, select uncomplicated toys that won't frustrate their sense of "can do" power. For example, if your toddler does not want to sit down with you and work on a puzzle now, she may be willing in an hour, or she may be telling you that it's too difficult and should be put away and tried again in a few weeks.

A WORD ON SHARING. It's prema-  ture to expect a toddler to share. While you can introduce the concept, do not be chagrined if your toddler screams "It's mine!" Reassuring a toddler that she will get her toy back or perhaps reminding her that her friend shares his toys when you visit are gentle ways of teaching a very difficult concept that will be much easier as she reaches the next stage.

● ● ● ● ● ● ● ● ● ● ● ● ● ● ● ● ● ●
Basic Gear Checklist for Ones
★ ★ ★

✔ Push toys
✔ Pull toys
✔ Ride-on toy
✔ Small vehicles
✔ Musical toys
✔ Huggables
✔ Manipulatives with moving parts
✔ Toy phone

✔ Lightweight ball
✔ Fill-and-dump toys

● ● ● ● ● ● ● ● ● ● ● ● ● ● ● ● ● ● ●
Basic Gear Checklist for Twos
★ ★ ★

✔ Ride on/in toy
✔ Push toy
✔ Big lightweight ball
✔ Shovel and pail
✔ Climbing/sliding toy
✔ Art supplies
✔ Big blocks
✔ Table and chair
✔ Props for housekeeping
✔ Huggables
✔ Simple puzzles/shape-sorters

🚫 Toys to Avoid 🚫

The following toys pose choking and suffocation hazards:

- Foam toys
- Toys with small parts (including small plastic fake foods)
- Dolls and stuffed animals with fuzzy and/or long hair
- Toys labeled 3 and up (no matter how smart toddlers are! The label almost always indicates that there are small parts in or on the toy)
- Latex balloons (Note: The Consumer Product Safety Commission reports that latex balloons are the leading cause of suffocation deaths! Since 1973 more than 110 children have died from suffocation involving uninflated balloons or pieces of broken ones. They are not advised for children under age six)

The following toys are developmentally inappropriate:

- Electronic educational drill toys
- Shape-sorters with more than three shapes

- Battery-operated ride-ons
- Pedal toys

ACTIVE PHYSICAL PLAY

PUSH WALKERS/RIDE-ONS
FOR BEGINNING WALKERS

Beginning walkers will get miles
of use from a low-to-the-ground,
stable wheeled toy. The products
on the market are not created
equal. Here are some basic things
to look for:

- The wobbly toddler may use
  the toy to pull up on, so you'll
  want to find one that is
  weighted and won't tip easily.
- Try before you buy. Some ride-
  ons are scaled for tall kids, others for small kids.
- Toddlers do not need battery-powered ride-ons!
  Encourage foot power, not push-button action!
- Toddlers are not ready for pedals. Four wheels
  and two feet on the ground are best.
- Toys with loud and constant sound effects are
  appealing in the store but can become annoying
  in tight spaces.

ACTIVITY ROCKER

(Today's Kids $40) Toddlers enjoy the gentle motion of
this low-to-the-ground rocker with adjustable contour
seat. Its dashboard has nine activities for developing
dexterity and plain old fun. Has a seat belt for security
but should be used with supervision. (800) 258-8697.

PUSH CART   BLUE CHIP

(Galt $79.95) This classically styled wooden push cart is
pricer than any of its plastic counterparts but can be
passed down to younger siblings and perhaps even their
kids! Very stable for early walkers and a perfect first
wagon for carting treasures. (800) 899-4258.

BEST IN ITS CATEGORY:
PUSH 'N RIDE WALKER
PLATINUM AWARD

(Little Tikes $20) For wobbly begin-
ning walkers who still need to hold
on, this low-to-the-ground yellow car
can be pushed about and later easily
straddled for ride-on action. With
working steering wheel and quiet
beep-beep horn for pretend play,

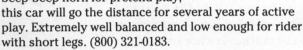

this car will go the distance for several years of active
play. Extremely well balanced and low enough for rider
with short legs. (800) 321-0183.

RIDE-ONS AND RIDE-INS FOR OLDER TODDLERS

DOUBLE FUN WAGON

(Today's Kids) This innovative wagon is cleverly
designed to double for hauling or as a ride-in vehicle.
The floor of the wagon can be opened halfway to the
ground so toddlers can sit in it and "ride" along or they
can pull cargo with the handle. Mattel is also working on
a convertible kiddie car, but it was not yet ready for test-
ing. 1–5. (800) 258-8697.

MINI-VAN   PLATINUM AWARD

(Little Tikes $85) A perfect
vehicle for pretend travel. A
blue van with working doors,
a mobile phone, sun roof, keys
that turn, a horn and a back
seat for cargo. Runs on foot
power. A real hit with our
testers. 2–5. (800) 321-0183.

TODDLER SCHOOL BUS

(Flexible Flyer $69.99) School's open and here's a bus big
enough for a driver and passenger. This big yellow ride-
in has a pop-out stop sign and a steering wheel with
horn. Getting this put together is no easy task, but once
assembled it is a great favorite for active pretend. (601)
494-8456.

★ COMPARISON SHOPPER—PLASTIC CARS

You can't go wrong with either the **Super Car** (Today's Kids $45) or the **Cozy Coup** (Little Tikes $50). Our testers found them to be a toss-up. Both are brightly colored and have no licensed characters to make them trendy or gender-specific. Both built to last! An ideal choice for pretend and physical play. 2 & up. Little Tikes (800) 321-0183/Today's Kids (800) 258-8697. For those looking for a convertible with a trunk, **Super Sports Car** (Today's Kids $45) is a good choice. ❀ Platinum Award.

TRIKES: SEE PRESCHOOL SECTION.

PUSH AND PULL TOYS

Push comes before pull. Instead of holding on to someone's hand, young toddlers often find sheer joy in the independence of walking while holding on to a push toy. Some of the best of these toys will also be used for pretend play. Pull toys are for older tots who are sure-footed and can look over a shoulder without tripping.

CORN POPPER   BLUE CHIP

(Fisher Price $9) A favorite for young toddlers who are steady on their feet. Lightweight, inexpensive and satisfying noisemaker with colorful beads that safely pop in see-through dome. (800) 432-5437.

> **SAFETY TIP:** Avoid pull toys with springs and beads that many toddlers will try to eat. Old pull toys from the attic may have dangerous levels of lead paint. The law also now requires that pull strings be no longer than 12".

CLICKITY CRICKET PULL TOY   BLUE CHIP

(Kouvalias $45) Jaunty green bug with yellow hat, eight yellow legs, green body and red wheels. Looks a lot like the star of the book *The Very Hungry Caterpillar*. A four-legged version is available for $30. Kouvalias makes some of the most charming wooden pull toys. They are pricey but can be passed along, maybe even to grand-children. 2 & up. (201) 694-5006.

• •

FREEBIE:

Your toddler's favorite toy may be a big shopping bag to fill, dump and tote around. Empty plastic soda bottles with lids and rings removed make big but lightweight cargo.

• •

BALLS

Big, lightweight balls for tossing, kicking, chasing or social back-and-forth, roly-poly games are favorite pieces of basic gear. Soft-fabric balls or slightly deflated beach balls are the best choice for now. Avoid foam and balloon-filled balls that are a chok-ing hazard if nibbled.

CLIMBERS AND ROCKERS FOR INDOORS AND OUT

JUNIOR ACTIVITY GYM
BLUE CHIP

(Little Tikes $95) Four walls, a platform and a gentle slide lock together to form a wonderful play space where tots can climb, crawl through openings, hide out and slide. This all-purpose activity center will be used for physical and pretend play for several years. Can be used indoors or out. No hardware needed. 1 1/2 & up. (800) 321-0183.

TIKE TREEHOUSE   BLUE CHIP

(Little Tikes $90) This is for older toddlers who are sure-footed. Active climbers will enjoy using big muscles and imagination with this combo slide, climber and play-house. Compact enough for indoor use. Will provide years of play. Also available in green and tan to blend more into the backyard. 2 & up. (800) 321-0183.

THREE TOT ROCKER

(Flexible Flyer $29.95) One, two or three kids can rock on this sturdy red rocker. Has a broad base for stability and handgrips to grab. 1 1/2 & up. (800) 521-6233.

STRICTLY OUTDOORS: WADING POOLS, SANDBOXES, PROPS FOR THE SANDBOX, GARDENING TOOLS, TOP-RATED LAWN MOWER AND SNOW FUN

★ COMPARISON SHOPPER—WADING POOLS

Our testers preferred inexpensive hard-vinyl wading pools to those that had to be blown up or filled with water to hold a shape (most of these had sides that were too high for younger toddlers to climb in and out of by themselves). Pre-

fab wading pools are also easier to lift, dump and clean. You'll find an adequate no-frills pool for under $20. Our testers also enjoyed these pools, which cost more money:

COOKIE MONSTER SLIDE 'N SPLASH POOL

(SLM $24) A mini-slide and a hook-up that turns the back-yard hose into a sprinkling fountain make this 60" diameter × 10" high wading pool extra fun. Cookie's arms and legs make nice seats. (800) 645-1174. For a more generic pool, try the **Whale Wading Pool** (Flexible Flyer $55) This big blue whale has a spout that sprinkles water and a small slide inside. Made of more substantial plastic than the SLM model. Use either with adult supervision. (800) 521-6233.

SANDBOXES

MICKEY MOUSE SANDBOX

(SLM $35) Now the leader of the band is also holder of the sand—a big 50" diameter blue sandbox molded in the shape of Mickey's head—à la Oldenberg! Mickey's big ears make great seats for mud-pie bakers. Comes with smiling Mickey cover. (A companion red wading pool is available for those who find two Mickeys better than one.) 2 & up. (800) 645-1174.

TUGGY SANDBOX

(Step 2 $80) You'll need tons of
sand for this big tugboat-shaped
sandbox. But there's plenty of
room for several kids to play
together and built-in pretend
power with a captain's wheel for
steering the jolly boat anywhere!
2 & up. (800) 347-8372. Almost identical in design, but different in color, Little Tikes' tropically colored **Island
Cruiser** ($90) is also a good choice. Really depends on
your color preference.

Sandbox Props: A basic bucket from any
toy store will do—just be sure to check
for smooth edges. If you're looking for
something with a little more interest,
these are good choices.

SEE-THRU BUCKET AND WATER MILL

(Brio $1.80 and up) This well-known wooden train maker
has introduced a wonderful line of sand and water toys.
A see-through bucket ($5.50) can be accessorized with
water/sand mill ($3) or pump ($4), each of which fit into
the rim of the pail. (800) 558-6863.

• •

FREEBIE:

Many of the best props for the sandbox are in your
kitchen: a plastic colander, an empty margarine
container, strainers, squeeze bottles, etc.

• •

THE YOUNGEST GARDENER

GARDEN TOOLS

(Little Tikes $12) Every season of the
year will be covered with a rake for
falling leaves, a hoe for weeding summer gardens and a shovel that can
dig snow or soil. Made of bright plastic that won't rust
when they are inevitably left outside. 2–5. (800) 321-0183.

BEST IN ITS CATEGORY:
BUBBLE LAWN MOWER   BLUE CHIP

(Fisher Price $22) Tots are thrilled with this red-and-black lawn mower that blows bubbles when pushed! A grand combination of early pretend play, action and making things happen. (800) 432-5437.

WATERING CAN SET

(Little Tikes $10) Watering can, trowel and cultivator for young gardeners-in the-making. These are working tools that can go from garden to sandbox without rusting when left outside. 2 & up. (800) 321-0183.

• •

FREEBIE:

Painting with water is a neat outdoors activity for older toddlers. A paintbrush and bucket of water produce satisfying but temporary effects—early lessons in evaporation or magic: take your pick!

• •

SNOW FUN

DELUXE TODDLER SLEIGH
BLUE CHIP

(Flexible Flyer $30) Ready for dashing through the snow, this bright-red toddler sled has high sloping sides, molded side runners, safety seat belt and strong yellow towrope. A great way to get about in snow. (800) 521-6233.

• •

SHOPPING TIP:

A child-sized snow shovel can provide great pretend and active play. Any toy supermarket will have one. Just be on the lookout for sharp edges.

• •

SIT DOWN PLAY

FIRST PUZZLES AND MANIPULATIVES

Toddlers enjoy toys that invite investigation but don't demand too much dexterity. Toys with lids to lift, buttons to push and dials to turn give them satisfying feedback along with playful ways to develop fine motor skills and eye/hand coordination. Many of these are for older toddlers with greater dexterity.

FIRST PUZZLES

BEST IN ITS CATEGORY: SIMPLEX WOODEN PUZZLES

(Battat $6–$15) Toddlers need puzzles with easy-to-grasp knobs connected to whole objects rather than multiple-piece jigsaw puzzles. This company makes storybook-quality graphics with smooth, splinter-free wood. Newest boards include a farm family and their animals or a smaller puzzle with three playful sailor mice on their boat. 2 & up. (518) 562-2200.

DRESS-UP OR BUGS PUZZLE

(Ravensburger $5.95) These single-piece puzzles are fine for older toddlers. But since they do not have knobs, they may pose a dexterity problem for some children. Choose whichever theme appeals most to your toddler. 2 & up. (201) 831-1400.

FIRST PUZZLES

(Playskool $4) For toddlers, stick with the single-piece puzzles with knobs from this series. Less beautiful than the Simplex puzzles, but the price is right and they are widely available. 2 & up. (800) 752-9755.

MANIPULATIVES

BEADS ON WIRE TOYS   BLUE CHIP

(Anatex and Educo $20 and up) Both of these companies make wonderful tracking toys with colored beads of different shapes and sizes that can be moved up, down and around curved and twisted wire mazes. Beads are tethered down so the young child can handle them safely. These abstract toys develop eye/hand skills, language, counting and pretending. Educo's 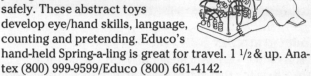 hand-held Spring-a-ling is great for travel. 1 1/2 & up. Anatex (800) 999-9599/Educo (800) 661-4142.

HIDE INSIDE 🌟 PLATINUM AWARD
(Discovery $16.98) Six fabric toys with different shapes and textures are perfect to explore and fit in and out of a bright fabric cube with big enough opening for little hands to use with ease. 1 & up. (800) 426-4777.

> **SAFETY TIP:** Toddlers still put things in their mouths. Check the size of small toys with a choke tube from Toys to Grow On. $1. (800) 542-8338.

BUSY GEARS   PLATINUM AWARD
(Playskool $16) A variety of large and small gears and cranks can be arranged in endless spinning combinations on the pegboard base. A hands-on early introduction to simple machines that will be enjoyed by preschoolers, too. 2 1/2 & up. (800) 752-9755.

★ COMPARISON SHOPPER—POP-UP TOYS
Many toy companies have their own versions of this basic pop-up toy that requires kids to discover a variety of manipulative moves to get the different characters to pop up. Our testers liked both Disney **Play 'N Pop**  (Mattel $15) and **Sesame Street Busy Poppin' Pals** (Playskool $15). Both have a handle for toting about that toddlers love. A satisfying toy that develops eye/hand coordination, memory and the delight of making things happen! 1 1/2 & up. Mattel (800) 524-8697/Playskool (800) 752-9755.

TELEVISION
(Battat $16) A handy little portable TV with chunky green button to push and change the pictures on the screen. Turn the yellow knob for cranking sound. Matches toddlers' fascination with push buttons that make things change. 1 ½ & up. (518) 562-2200.

TODDLER KITCHEN
(Fisher Price $22) With plenty of doors to open and close, a switch that makes a pan spin, a shape-sorter and a toaster that goes boing—this is an interesting floor toy for young toddlers that has more to do with manipulative action than typical toy kitchens for dramatic play. 1 & up. (800) 432-5437.

FIRST CONSTRUCTION TOYS

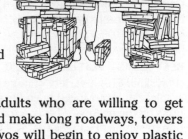

For the youngest toddlers, knocking down blocks will still be more typical than building. But twos and up will begin to use and enjoy big cardboard blocks with adults who are willing to get down on the floor and make long roadways, towers and bridges. Older twos will begin to enjoy plastic blocks such as Duplo and Mega Blocks. See the Preschool section's descriptions of construction toys.

FIRST NESTING, STACKING AND SHAPE-SORTER TOYS

COUNT AND MATCH PEGBOARD   PLATINUM AWARD
(Battat $10) Little hands will be busy with the 25 easy-to-grasp, brightly colored chunky pegs that can be sorted

by color or shape on the 10" square base. Pegs can also be stacked and eventually strung like beads. A handsome toy made of sturdy plastic. Would cost three times more in wood. 2 & up. (518) 562-2200.

PEEK-A-BOO STACKER   ★'94★   PLATINUM AWARD

(Kiddicraft $7.99) Unlike most ring-and-post stacking toys, this has no post. Any one of the color "cups" fits on the base. As each piece is added to the stack a smiling face pops up like a magical peek-a-boo surprise. No need to put it together in size order, so there is no right or wrong way that would frustrate toddlers. 1 1/2 & up. (800) 432-5437.

SORT AND STACK SET   PLATINUM AWARD

(Battat $14.95) A stack of learning and fun in this set of ten nesting cups. The largest is also a pail with a lid that doubles as a shape-sorter. Comes with four geometric shapes to fit in slots and stickers to decorate cups with numerals from 1 to 10. Develops hand/eye coordination, size-order concepts and counting. 1 1/2 & up. #2312 One Step Ahead (800) 274-8440.

PRETEND PLAY

As language develops, older toddlers begin their early games of pretend. So much of the real equipment tots see adults using is off-limits to them. Child-sized versions can (sometimes) offer a satisfying alternative and fuel the imagination of little ones who love to mimic what they see you doing. Never again will sweeping and cleaning be more fun than to a toddler!

DOLLS AND HUGGABLES

Both boys and girls enjoy playing
with dolls and soft animals. Toddlers
like oversized but lightweight huggables to love and lug about. Since
they are still likely to chew on their
toys, select uncomplicated huggables
without small decorations, long hair
or accessories that can be pulled off.

BABY DOLLS

(Madame Alexander $30) Dressed in pajamas, this sweet
little hairless doll is ready for a bedtime story and lots of
hugs. Nothing complicated here. A good first doll. 2 & up.
Available in specialty stores. (Balica/Tiger $15 & up) A
less-pricey bald choice with eyes that open and close for
beginning pretend play is named Baby Kate. Available in
most toy supermarkets.

CABBAGE PATCH DOLLS   BLUE CHIP

(Hasbro $15 & up) Select one of these lightweight clas-
sics made with vinyl heads and soft, huggable bodies.
Clothes are easy on/off with Velcro closings. Choose
boys or girls, with bald heads or yarn hair, and none with
small add-ons such as pacifiers or bottles that may be
mouthed. Once again, less is more! (800) 752-9755.

FLATJACK OR FLATAPUS

(North American Bear Co. $22 &
up) Toddlers love oversized huggables to lug about, but they need
to be lightweight and uncomplicated. A blue-velour hippo or
white rabbit with stitched-on features and floppy body will fill the

job description and your toddler's arms. Looks a lot like
Margaret Wise Brown's *Runaway Bunny*. (800) 682-3427.

MY BUDDY   BLUE CHIP

(Playskool $20) A relatively big, hefty and elaborate tod-
dler boy doll is dressed in overalls and cap. Has vinyl

face and fabric body. African-American version available. For older, bigger toddlers of 2 & up. (800) 752-9755.

SNUFFLES

(Gund $25 & up) For this age, chose a huggable that's not too fuzzy. This lovable, white pot-bellied polar bear is a perfect companion. (908) 248-1500.

RAGGEDY ANN & ANDY   BLUE CHIP

(Applause $25 & up) A classic soft doll with yarn hair, stitched features and floppy body. Perfect guest for tea parties and other adventures. Specialty stores.

DOLL ACCESSORIES

Most toddlers will try to get into whatever baby furniture you buy. It's better to wait until the next stage for more elaborate and delicate baby beds, high chairs and strollers. See Preschool section for best bets.

VEHICLES

BABY BUBBLE CAR

(Ambi $14) A sleek little yellow car with red wheels and a driver who turns inside the see-through bubble window as the car is rolled. Push the red button on the roof and it squeaks and wheels click. (201) 831-1400.

BUSY DRIVER

(Playskool $20) An update of a classic floor toy. This dashboard is complete with clicky steering wheel, squeaky horn, keys that click, great roaring gear shift and glove compartment to open and close. No wheels needed to take off on imaginary travel. (800) 752-9755.

PUSH 'N' GO TRAIN

(Tomy $4.99) Push the little conductor's red hat and send this little train on its way. Ideal for toddlers who will enjoy making this little choo-choo go. Works best on hard floors. 18 mos. & up. (714) 256-4990.

STACK AND DUMP TRUCK
BLUE CHIP

(Parents Child Development Toys
$22) Sturdy green truck comes with a
cargo of round and square chunky
chips that fit into slots, over hub
caps and into the storage area. Great for sorting, matching and pretending. Can be used as a pull toy. 18 mos. &
up. (201) 831-1400.

TODDLE TOTS DUMP TRUCK AND LOADER

(Little Tikes $10 & up) These two plastic trucks are per-
fect for toddlers building with sand and water. The dump
truck holds big loads and tips easily to empty. Loader
has scoop to lift, carry and dump. Both come with play
people for extra pretend power. Either truck will fit in a
large beach bag! (800) 321-0183.

HOUSEKEEPING PROPS

Older toddlers, both boys and girls,
adore imitating the real work they see
grown-ups doing around the house.
Sweeping the floor, vacuuming, cooking, caring for the baby—these are
thrilling roles to play. Many of the
props for this
sort of pretend will be used for several years. They
are what we call "bridge toys" that span the years.

BROOM

(Fisher Price $4.25) Few toys will be enjoyed more by
toddlers than a broom. Part push toy, part cleaning tool,
this is a winner you'll find in most toy supermarkets.
(800) 432-5437.

MAGIC VAC   BLUE CHIP

(Fisher Price $18) Terrific push toy for pretend clean-up.
Having their own machine helps some tots overcome
their anxieties about the loud sound of the real thing.
Requires no batteries. Lights up and makes popping
sound when pushed. 2 & up. (800) 432-5437.

CORDLESS PLAY PHONE

(Little Tikes $10) For pretend calls to Grandma, this has buttons to push, an antenna, a base with directory dial to spin and no cord for no-worry, safe play. 2 & up. (800) 321-0183.

TALKING PHONE

(Playskool $20) Turn the big dial to a picture, press the easy-to-activate arrow and there are eight different messages on this brand new phone. Designed for safety, there is no cord in the rattling receiver. Has a carry handle for tote-along talking toddlers. 9–24 mo. (800) 752-9755.

> **SAFETY TIP:** An old real phone may seem like lots of fun, but the cord and small parts pose a choking hazard to toddlers.

TOY DISHES AND POTS

Finding a sturdy, gender-free set of dishes isn't easy! Many sets we tested cracked, were too small for little hands and were very, very pink!

Battat's primary-colored sets rated high in all categories. **The Tea Set** ($14.50) comes with a teapot that really pours (surprisingly, not true of most!) and four simple cups and saucers with serving tray, sugar and creamer. The 13-piece **Cooking and Baking Set** ($12.95) will appeal to junior chefs. Remove cutlery for kids who still mouth toys. (518) 562-2200. Little Tikes' **Kitchen Partyware Set** ($17) comes in retro colors from the '40s instead of pastels. We wish the colors were brighter like Battat's, but both fill the bill for safety and are big enough to use for snacks. 2 & up. (800) 321-0183.

> **SAFETY TIP**: Toddlers do not need fake food! Since they mouth most toys, you'll want to avoid phony food that's especially tempting to "eat" and may be a choking hazard.

TOY KITCHENS

KIDS KITCHENETTES
(Today's Kids $30 each) For toddlers in apartments where space is tight, this company's low-to-the-ground Sizzling Stove (11" × 12"), Fun Fridge (11" × 17") and Magic Dishwasher (11" × 12") are good choices separately or in combination. 2 & up. (800) 258-8697.

PARTY KITCHEN BLUE CHIP
(Little Tikes $80) Here's a big all-in-one combo kitchen for junior chefs. Unit is 20" W × 40 1/2" H and includes a combo stove, oven, sink, built-in coffeemaker, cordless phone and drop side table for small eaters to use. For smaller spaces, the Compact Kitchen (Little Tikes $60) is only 13 1/2" W × 34" H. Has sink, stove top, oven and microwave oven. Both white with yellow trim. Will be used well into the preschool years. 2 & up. (800) 321-0183.

WOODEN KITCHENS
(Back to Basics $162) An all-wooden kitchen is going to cost considerably more than the average plastic job. Most are made for the school market, where they are used for years and years by dozens of kids. If you're willing to make this kind of investment we suggest this all-in-one compact sink, stove and cupboard built of maple. It measures 35"H × 24"W × 12"D. It has a removable sink pan for water play, two "burners," an oven/storage space and a scrolled high back with shelf for dishes. 2 & up. #73. (800) 356-5360.

MINIATURE PRETEND SETTINGS

LITTLE PEOPLE FARM
(Fisher Price $30) At last Fisher Price has updated their Little People line and made the figures larger and safe enough for toddlers. The barn door "moos" when it's opened and closed. Our toy

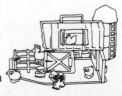

tester loved putting all the creatures in the barn and saying goodnight! We removed the bale of hay; although it does not fit in the choke tube, our toy tester kept mouthing it. 1 1/2 & up. (800) 432-5437.

LITTLE PEOPLE GARAGE

(Fisher Price $30) Place the car in the open-air elevator, turn the crank and the car is on the top floor of the garage ready to speed down the ramp. Comes with two cars, two drivers, gas pump and a car lift for repairs. 2 & up. (800) 432-5437.

> **SAFETY TIP**: Fisher Price Little People made before 1991 pose a choking hazard to children under three. The company has since enlarged the product.

NOAH'S ARK

(Little Tikes $20) Eight chunky animals can be put in and out of ark, which has a lift-up roof and carrying handle. Fun for tub and floor play. Not a work of art like T. C. Timber's wooden ark (see Preschool section), but safe for toddlers who still put things in their mouths. (800) 321-0183.

• •

FREEBIE:

Empty, staple-free boxes are among the best toys known to toddlers. Great for sitting in, climbing out of, coloring on, lugging around or loading up.

• •

ART AND MUSIC

ART SUPPLIES

Encourage your toddler to explore colors and textures. This is not the time for coloring books and drawing within the lines. Scribbling comes before drawing, just as crawling

comes before walking! You can give your toddler a sense of "can do" power by providing big, easy-to-grasp crayons and blank paper, bright tempera paint with thick brushes, or play-dough and finger-paints for lively hands-on fun!

You'll need to supervise and establish a place where art materials can be used. If your toddler persists in eating supplies or spreading them on floors or walls, put them away for a while and try again in a month or two.

WASHABLE SO-BIG CRAYONS

(Crayola $2.99) Little crayons will snap in toddlers' hands, and the fancy-shaped variety are dangerously small (and don't color very well either). These oversized crayons are just right for easy grasping and scribbling, and they have the added perk of being washable. For convenient storage and toteablity look for the Crayola Big Bucket ($7.99). 1 1/2 & up. (800) CRAYOLA.

MAKING DOUGH

Playing with pre-made or home-made dough is marvelous for twos who love pounding, poking, rolling, crumbling and hands-on exploring. At this stage the finished product is unimportant. The focus is on smashing a lump flat or pulling it apart into small pieces or mixing blue and yellow to get green. Dough should be used with supervision in an established place for messy play. Beginners will try to taste: It's nontoxic but not for eating. Put it away if they insist on mouthing and try again in a few weeks.

PLAY-DOH

(Playskool $5.59) Imagine a 12-pack with a 2-ounce lump of a dozen different colors. One generation's wish is another's reality with this set that includes grape, lime and even brown! Don't let them see all the tubs; open one or two at a time at most. Add plastic dishes for added pretend! 2 & up. (800) 752-9755.

• •

FREEBIE:

Save money by making your own dough with this homemade play-dough recipe. Kids will enjoy getting their hands into the bowl and helping to mix up dough, which can be stored in a covered container. Mix together 1 cup of flour, 1/3 cup salt, a few drops of vegetable oil and enough water to form a dough. Food coloring or a splash of bright tempera paint can be added.

• •

PAINTS AND EASELS—SEE PRESCHOOL SECTION

MUSICAL TOYS

ACCORDION

(Battat $16.95) Squeezing the handles makes a happy sound and sets balls whirling in a see-through enclosure. Cause and effect in action. 1 1/2 & up. (518) 562-2200.

BEST IN ITS CATEGORY: EASY-TOUCH TAPE PLAYER   PLATINUM AWARD

(Mattel $30) At last, an innovative tape player designed especially for the littlest music lover! Has just two big on and off buttons toddlers can work independently. All other controls are set by an adult. Has big handle and bumper to protect against thuds. We do wish it could take rechargeable batteries. Some testers complained about the number of batteries they used. (800) 524-8697. The new Playskool Electronics version has three volume levels but requires a screw driver to adjust, which our testers felt was inconvenient.

MARACAS AND TAMBOURINE

(Little Tikes $17) Shake, rattle and feel the beat. These safe, chunky rhythm instruments are perfect for the youngest music makers. Maracas in bright orange have see-through dome so tots can see the marbles inside.

Yellow tambourine is easy to play and makes a pleasant-
enough sound. (800) 321-0183.

MUSIC BOX RADIOS   BLUE CHIP
(Fisher Price $13) Toddlers like to wind the knob and
watch the pictures turn as they sing along with this classic music maker that plays "Somewhere Over the Rainbow." Built-in handle satisfies toddlers' love of toys to
tote. (800) 432-5437.

MUSICAL BOOM BOX
(Fisher Price $16.99) Push the big red
antenna and the animal graphics spin
to the music; hit the pretend cassette
and it "boings"; spin the speaker and
colors whirl; and there's a handle for
toting. There are lots of ways to get
feedback from this easy-to-activate
toy that looks like a miniature boom
box. 1 & up. (800) 432-5437.

★ COMPARISON SHOPPER—XYLOPHONES
Rock 'n Roll Xylophone (Fisher Price $13) 1 ¹/₂ & up, or
Xylophone (Little Tikes $15) 1 ¹/₂ & up. If you have a very
good ear, neither of these musical pull toys will please it.
Fisher Price's version is tinny and the Little Tikes is
slightly flat but has a fuller sound. Both require supervision since the mallets are likely to be put in the mouth. In
the end our testers preferred Little Tikes, but we found
that the better product in this category is the **Tap-a-Tune
Piano** (Little Tikes $23), which is designed for an older
toddler and has no mallet. 2 & up.

BATH TOYS

FISHY FRIENDS
(Ambi $10.50) A four-piece set of floating friends for tub
play. Open the big yellow-and-blue fish with red fins and
you'll find a green turtle, a blue-and-white penguin and a
chubby yellow fish. Each of the small creatures floats
and stores away when tub fun ends. (201) 831-1400.

BEST IN ITS CATEGORY: PLAY BUCKETS
BLUE CHIP

(Kiddicraft $6.99) A set of three small
buckets, each with a different action.
One has sprinkling holes in bottom,
one has a pouring spout and one has a
hole on the side. Great for bath and
beach. (800) 432-5437.

SAFETY TIP: Foam bath toys are a choking hazard to toddlers, who may bite off pieces. Unfortunately, many of the age labels on such products are in very small print.

BASIC FURNITURE

TABLES AND CHAIRS

Now's the time for a child-
scaled table and chairs. Will
be used for years for real and
pretend eating, art work, puzzles and sit-down fun. Look for
a surface that can take soap
suds, finger paints, clay and

other messy substances like peanut butter and
jelly. Chairs need to be built for stability. Your
choice will depend on personal taste and budget
considerations. Most of the plastic toy makers'
tables are practical but very plastic!

Some basic safety and design questions you may
want to check:

- Can your child get on and off chairs/bench easily?
- Is this a set that will work when your child gets a
  little bigger?
- If you're looking at a wooden set, are there
  exposed screws or nuts (check the underside)
  that can cut your child?
- Is the surface washable and ready for abuse? (A
  beautiful painted piece will be destroyed by
  paint, play-dough, crayons, etc.)

SELECTING BACKYARD GYM SETS

Backyard swings, slides and climbers can provide years of active fun. Having such equipment right outside your own door is more than just convenient. It's an open-ended invitation to get outside and use those muscles and that endless energy.

Although the primary attraction may be the swing and slide, often these hold less long-term interest than the climber, which is used for exercising both body and imagination. If your family is still very young, find a set that can be fitted with toddler swings that surround and support little ones. A good gym set can be upgraded with standard swings and still later be expanded with a climber, which is often the best part of a gym as children get older. Here are some tips on choosing equipment and installing and supervising its use.

Shop where you can see and compare gym sets that are set up. Ask yourself:

- Is the set sturdy?
- If it's wooden, is it smooth or likely to turn splintery? Is it made with pressure-treated wood. If so, you should know that the chemicals used are hazardous when ingested. Children must wash their hands after playing on such sets, especially before eating.
- Whether it's wood or metal, are there any sharp or rough edges?
- Are the swing seats like soft straps that conform to a child's body? These are safer and easier to get on and off.
- If there are swings hung on chains, are they sealed in vinyl so they won't pinch fingers?
- Are the spaces between ladder rungs wide enough so a child's head can't get caught?

- Are nuts and bolts embedded so they can't snag fingers and clothing?
- Is the set scaled to your child's physical and developmental needs? Many sets come with climbers and slides that are not really appropriate for preschoolers.
- Will you be able to add on as children grow?
- What's the weight capacity recommended by the manufacturer? How many kids can safely play on it together?
- Who will install the set and how will it be anchored? Sets should be installed with stakes or in concrete "footings" so they won't tip, and on surfaces such as grass, sand or rubber matting to cushion falls.
- Do you really have room for it? Equipment should be at least 6' from fences, buildings or anything that could endanger kids.
- What's your budget? Most of the wooden sets start at $500, but that's just for the basic unit. By the time you're finished adding the slide, climber and/or playhouse you can be talking about $1,000 to $1,500 and up.

Here are the names of several major gym set companies:

- Childlife. Top-rated. Distinctive wooden green finish is smoother and less likely to splinter than any other sets we looked at. Wooden sets from $450 and up. (800) 462-4445.
- Creative Playthings. Wooden sets from $449 and up. (800) 444-0901.
- Yards of Fun. Wooden sets from $455 and up. (800) 348-5400.
- Hedstrom. Metal sets from $149 and up. Available from Sears and many toy supermarkets.

BEST TRAVEL TOYS FOR TODDLERS

- Familiar huggable
- Big washable crayons and pad of paper in a travel sack small enough to fit into a glove compartment
- Inflatable ball
- Small cardboard books they can handle themselves when in their car seats
- Musical toy or tape player and tapes
- For extended stays: a small set of big plastic blocks or the "favorite toy of the week," one you know she'll be happy to play with while you're unpacking!

BEST SECOND BIRTHDAY GIFTS FOR EVERY BUDGET

Under $100	Mini-Van (Little Tikes) or table and chairs
Under $75	Toy Kitchen (Little Tikes)
Under $50	Sandbox or Clickity Cricket Pull Toy (Kouvalias)
Under $30	Three Tot Rocker (Flexible Flyer) or Easy-Touch Tape Player (Mattel)
Under $25	Magic Vac (Fisher Price) or *Good Night Moon* book (HarperCollins) and Bunny (Eden)
Under $20	Duplos (Lego) or Busy Gears (Playskool) or giant cardboard blocks
Under $15	Sort and Stack Set (Battat) or puzzle
Under $10	Cordless Phone (Little Tikes) or Crayola Big Bucket or video
Under $5	Pop 'N' Go Train (Tomy) or Play-Doh (Playskool) or Broom (Fisher Price)

3 ★ Preschool
Three to Four Years

What to Expect Developmentally

LEARNING THROUGH PRETEND. Preschoolers are amazing learning machines! Watch and listen to them at play and you can hear the wheels of their busy minds working full tilt. From sunup to sundown, preschoolers love playing pretend games. Playing all sorts of roles gives kids a chance to become big and powerful people. Providing props for such play gives kids the learning tools to develop language, imagination and a better understanding of themselves and others.

SOCIAL PLAY. Your once happy-to-be-only-with-you toddler has blossomed into a much more social being. She enjoys playing with other kids. Sharing is still an issue, but there's a budding understanding of give and take.

SOLO PLAY. Unlike the toddler who moved from one thing to another, preschoolers become able to really focus their attention on building a bridge of blocks, working on a puzzle or painting pictures.

TOYS AND DEVELOPMENT. Although preschoolers love to play at counting and singing or even trying to write the alphabet, informal play is still the best path to learning. Building a tower with blocks, they discover some very basic math concepts. Digging in the sand or floating leaves in puddles, they make early science discoveries.

BIG MUSCLES. Threes and fours also need time and space to run and climb and use their big muscles to develop coordination and a sense of themselves as able doers.

YOUR ROLE IN PLAY. A child who has shelves full of stuffed animals or every piece of the hottest licensed character may seem to have tons of toys, but the truth is that, no matter how many Turtles or Trolls a kid has, such collections offer just one kind of play. Every now and then, take an inventory of your child's toy clutter to see what's really being played with and what needs to be packed away or donated.

● ●

Basic Gear Checklist for Preschoolers

★ ★ ★

- ✔ Set of blocks and props (small vehicles, animals, people)
- ✔ Trike
- ✔ Doll and/or soft animals
- ✔ Dress-up clothes
- ✔ Housekeeping toys
- ✔ Transportation toys
- ✔ Art materials, crayons, paints, clay
- ✔ Simple puzzles (8 pieces and up)
- ✔ Matching games
- ✔ Picture books
- ✔ Tape player and music and story tapes
- ✔ Sand and water toys

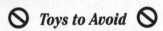 **Toys to Avoid** 🚫

These toys pose a safety hazard:
- Electric toys or those that heat up with light bulbs that can burn
- Toys with projectile parts that can injure eyes
- Toys without volume control that can damage ears
- Two-wheelers with training wheels
- Latex balloons

These toys are developmentally inappropriate:

- Complex building sets that adults must build while children watch
- Teaching machines that reduce learning to a series of right or wrong answers
- Coloring books that limit creativity

PRETEND PLAY

This is the age when pretend play blossoms. Some kids pretend with blocks, trains and miniatures they move about as they act out little dramas. Others prefer dressing up and playing roles with their whole bodies. Either way, such games are more than fun. They help children learn to stretch their imaginations, try on powerful new roles, cope with feelings and fears, and develop language and social skills.

HOUSEKEEPING TOOLS

Props for cleaning, cooking and child care are used by both girls and boys. Kitchen toys will be used for playing house and running restaurants. As children's experiences broaden, so does the scope of their games of make-believe.

BROOM AND MOP SET

Few toys will get more use by both boys and girls than a mini-broom or mop. This is an inexpensive winner you'll find in most toy supermarkets. Just check for smooth finish. Or you can order a child-sized set (Back to Basics $12) with corn broom, dust mop, cotton wet mop, squeeze mop, dust pan and feather duster. #79. (800) 356-5360.

BEST IN ITS CATEGORY:
MAGIC VAC　BLUE CHIP
(Fisher Price $18) Our testers rated this pretend cleaner tops. Requires no batteries. Lights up and makes popping sound when pushed. (800) 432-5437.

PRESS 'N' PLAY IRONING SET
(Little Tikes $20) Never again will ironing clothes be so much fun! This set is scaled right and designed for safe play. Irons with pretend cords or those that actually heat up are not appropriate because they are dangerous. (800) 321-0183.

KITCHENS AND TOY DISHES—SEE TODDLER SECTION.

DOLLS AND HUGGABLES

Preschoolers love soft animals as huggable playmates. In addition to large stuffed animals, a baby doll is the perfect play companion for trips away from home and for at-home tea parties.

BATHBABY GIRL OR BOY　PLATINUM AWARD
(Corolle/Brio $70) There's been a lot of media attention to dolls and the birthing process. Oddly enough, genderspecific dolls that reflect children's anatomies are rare and often very homely. These anatomically correct dolls are the exception. Totally tubable for water play preschoolers love. A good choice for new big brothers and sisters who like having a baby to care for, too. (800) 558-6863.

BABY DOLL
(Pleasant Co. $54) This mail-order-only 15" babydoll, with a soft, huggable body dressed in a lace-trimmed sleeper, undershirt and diaper is adorable and is available as Caucasian or African- or Asian-American. This

company makes gorgeous but expensive accessories. The catalog is worth a look. (800) 845-0005.

CABBAGE PATCH KIDS   BLUE CHIP

(Hasbro $15 & up) Also less pricey but always a hit with this age group are these once-hotter-than-hot soft-fabric dolls that come with easy on/off clothes in both boy and girl models as well as African-American and Caucasian. (800) 752-9755.

CHRISTINA

(Balica $35) For a less expensive, genderless, but well-made vinyl babydoll with soft cloth body, consider Christina, a solid choice that's widely available in toy supermarkets.

CURIOUS GEORGE

(Gund $24) This storybook, full-bodied hand puppet can double as a huggable doll and would make a great gift, along with a Curious George book or video (CC Studios; see Videos section). (908) 248-1500.

HUGGY BEAN DOLL

(Golden Ribbon $25) This soft-fabric African-American doll comes with easy on/off clothes. She's a bit like a Cabbage Patch Kid but cuter. The same company makes other family members, but this is the one you'll find in most toy supermarkets. (800) 722-8285.

MUSICAL PAWS

(North American Bear Co. $34 & up) Choose one of these adorable 12" musical dolls. Whiskerina is a cuddly cat in a tutu who plays "Waltz of the Flowers" and Rodeo Cub is a bear in chaps who plays "Old Suzanna." (800) 682-3427.

TALKING BARNEY '94 PLATINUM AWARD

(Playskool $34.99) The popularity of this purple dinosaur has meant a flood of licensed products. Unlike the pull-toys of yesteryear, this one says hundreds of Barney-

type expressions. There are also a number of plush but
silent Barneys that will fill the bill for less.

★ COMPARISON SHOPPER—DOLL STROLLERS AND FURNITURE

Budget and taste will go into
making the choices here. Just
like the real equipment, there
are doll carriers for the silver-
spoon set and more practical
models for your average doll.

DOLL BUGGY

(Little Tikes $25) Here's another gender-specific pink
plastic carriage that can hold a doll up to 18". Has big
wheels that can't be removed and a low-to-the-ground
sturdiness. 2 & up. (800) 321-0183.

DOLL STROLLER

(Tudor TOT $45) This is the sturdiest of the tubular, real-
istic-looking strollers that we found in most toy supermarkets. It's mid-priced and lightweight enough for walks
to the park. Will fit a full-sized babydoll. 3 & up.

DOLL STROLLER

(Pleasant Co. $65) This stroller looks like the real McCoy.
It is made with bright-red denim and has an adjustable
seat so baby can sit up or lie down. The stroller col-
lapses for the doll that travels. 3 & up. #22200. (800) 845-
0005.

LULLABY BASKET

(Pleasant Co. $78) For the pam-
pered doll, this beribboned
wicker basket, designed for dolls
up to 15", has carrying handles
and is lined in blue-and-white
gingham. There's a ruffled pillow
and blanket and a musical heart
that plays "Brahms Lullaby." 3 &
up. #21700. (800) 845-0005.

WICKER STROLLER

(Marshall Baby $129) Who wouldn't love putting their doll in this white wicker carriage that looks like it rolled out of a picturebook. Lined with cotton cushion and ready for rolling, strolling pretend. A larger and pricier bassinett was just introduced. Either of these will be an extravagant dream gift! 3 & up. Back to Basics (800) 356-5360.

WOODEN DOLL CRADLE   BLUE CHIP

(Community Playthings $72) A solid-maple cradle designed for schools and built to last. The large 29" model is big enough so kids can climb in and play baby or put a family of dolls to sleep. This company has been making wooden toys for years, mostly for the school market. Sturdy enough to become a family heirloom. 2 & up. (800) 777-4244.

PUPPETS AND PUPPET STAGES

Through the mouths of puppets kids can say things that they might not otherwise speak about. So puppets are a way of venting feelings and developing imagination and language skills. Young puppeteers replay stories or create original ones, developing skills that link directly to reading and writing.

BUG PUPPETS

(Folkmanis $12 & up) Our toy testers loved these plush hand puppets that fit like a glove. Choose from ladybugs, butterflies and insects for developing "pesty" language skills. The same company makes more elaborate and higher-priced puppets from friendly dogs to a bald eagle. 4 & up. (510) 658-7677.

FAMILY SETS

(Constructive Playthings $31 per set) For more realistic role-playing try this four-piece family with mom, dad, brother and sister. Caucasian, Hispanic, Afro- and Asian-American sets available. All-fabric heads and bodies. Company will customize families! FPH721L. (800) 832-0572.

PICK A PUPPET

(Creative Education of Canada $14) Here's a versatile
puppet set with two hand puppet bodies and Velcro features that can be used to create an ever-changing cast of
players. We like the royal set with crowns and gowns for
storybook dramas. (800) 982-2642.

SESAME STREET PUPPETS

(Applause $15 & up each) Since most beginning pup-
peteers know Bert, Ernie and other Sesame Street characters, it's easy for them to step into familiar roles.
These plush puppets come in hand and full-body sizes.
(800) 777-6990.

PUPPET STAGES FOR ALL BUDGETS

Childcraft's $125 wood
stage (45"W × 51"H) is top
of the line, with chalkboard
front for announcing show-
time, a curtain and shelves
in back for storage. Can be
reversed and used as a play
store. This is a big-ticket
item, designed for class-
room or home—a toy that
will be used for years.
#21063. (800) 631-5657.

DOORWAY THEATRE   BLUE CHIP

(Poppet $45) This 29"W × 62"H fabric stage hangs in a
doorway on an adjustable rod! It has a working curtain
and storage pockets to hold puppets and props. (800)
241-1161.

PUPPET STAGE

(Creative Education of Canada $12) This table-top stage
is made of brightly colored corrugated plastic (recycled)
and measures 27"H × 24"W × 10"D. It's lightweight, folds
flat for storage and is indestructible. (800) 982-2642.

• •

FREEBIE:

Do it yourself—a large appliance box can be turned into an excellent puppet stage, and so can a cloth-covered card table that kids can hide behind. Another great option is a spring curtain rod and length of fabric that can be used in any doorway.

• •

DRESS-UP PLAY AND LET'S PRETEND PROPS

There are a lot of dress-up kits around. Truth be told, most kids will enjoy dressing up in real clothes as much as the store-bought variety. Old pocketbooks, briefcases, jewelry, hats and such are treasures to kids. For very specific role-playing a hat, a scarf or a homemade badge is often all that's needed to transform young players. Below are a few specialty items you may want to buy.

ACTION HATS

(Childcraft $ 9.95) This set of six hats includes the following roles: firefighter, construction worker, racer, police, cyclist with goggles and engineer. #50312. (800) 631-5657.

★ COMPARISON SHOPPER—DOCTOR'S KITS

Remember when doctors paid house calls with their little black bags? Younger kids will enjoy the portability of the Fisher Price bag ($15), which includes a pressure gauge, stethoscope (which does not work), thermometer, bandage and other necessities for quick cures. The Little Tike Center ($23) includes a pressure gauge, stethoscope, thermometer and eye chart, which stores in a stand-up case that becomes an "office." Younger testers found the heavy plastic case difficult to close but still enjoyed using the toy again and again.

STETHOSCOPE

(Constructive Playthings $7.95) For a stethoscope that
really works, we found one in a school-supply catalog.
#MTC 261. (800) 448-4115.

TUTOR PLAY COMPUTER   BLUE CHIP

(Tomy $15) No batteries are needed for this toy com-
puter with keyboard that magically reveals letters, numbers and pictures on the little screen. For the youngest
techie in the family. (714) 256-4990.

CORDLESS PLAY PHONE

(Little Tikes $10) Before you buy a play phone with
sound, put the receiver to your ear. We were alarmed by
how loud they were! Testers were also concerned that
the antennas could poke an eye if a child fell while using
the phone. This phone is very young-looking compared
to most but also the safest. (800) 321-0183.

DOLLHOUSES AND PARKING GARAGES

Some of the mini-settings listed in
the Toddlers section will be used
in more elaborate ways now. If you
put them away, try bringing them
out again and see how differently
your child plays with them. Here
are descriptions of recommend
settings that are more complex.

DOLLHOUSE

(Little Tikes $70) Of all the plastic dollhouses for very
young children, Little Tikes Place is the sturdiest and
least complicated. Kids love the fact that many of the furnishings—such as an art easel, table, sandbox and toy
car—look like the pieces of equipment this company
makes in child sizes. Comes with table and four chairs,
cozy coupe car, dog, baby, highchair and a family of five
(available in African-American or Caucasian). More
detailed and elaborate dollhouses are most appropriate
for school-aged kids. (800) 321-0183.

WOODEN DOLLHOUSES

(Plan Toys $99 & $139) If nothing will do but wood, here are two modern-looking A-frames. Both have open roofs for easy access. The pricier one has sliding doors and wallpaper. Rooms enough for a bedroom, bathroom, living room, kitchen and dining room. Furniture all beautifully crafted in wood is about $20 per room. Seen in many catalogs. (212) 689-3590.

CALICO CRITTERS

(Tomy $9 & up) Adorable little families of woodland creatures make charming storybook-like characters for dollhouse play. Many of the furnishings look straight out of the Three Bears! Great miniatures at a sensible price! (714) 256-4990.

PARKING GARAGE

(Back to Basics $99) An exceptional three-level parking garage scaled for Matchbox-sized vehicles. You need space for this 24"L × 16"W × 17"H wooden garage that has a service station, gas pumps and service elevator to take cars to every level. #169. (800) 356-5360.

POWER & SOUNDS GARAGE

(Fisher Price $29.99) This innovative novelty toy combines the fun of a garage and car wash with mechanical play. A power "drill" actually enables kids to change tires and even the chassis of the car. The drill also operates the car lift and drive-through car wash, which can be operated with batteries or manually. 4–7. (800) 432-5437.

TRUCKS AND OTHER VEHICLES

Preschoolers are fascinated with all forms of transportation. The real things are out of reach and on the move, but toy trucks, cars, boats, jets and trains are ideal for  make-believe departures both indoors and out. Choose vehicles with working parts to use with blocks, in the sandbox or at the beach.

★ COMPARISON SHOPPER—DUMP TRUCKS

For hauling stuff and loading, dumping and loading up again, few vehicles are more useful than a dump truck. For a versatile indoor/outdoor job you should look at Little Tikes' **Big Dump Truck** ($23), with articulated cab and great dumping action; (800)321-0183. Or the classic metal **Mighty Tonka Dump Truck** ($17), which is an update of the one you and your parents probably played with in the sand; (800) 752-9755.

MIGHTY TRACTOR TRAILER WITH BULLDOZER

(Tonka $50) Newest in the Mighty Tonka lineup, this authentic-looking bulldozer has a working front-mounted blade that rides on a trailer with removable ramps, all pulled by a tractor with super-wide wheels. Earth-movers are going to get a lot of active play with this in the sand box or playroom. 4 & up. (800) 752-9755.

WATER CANNON FIRE TRUCK

(Tonka $27) This gleaming red pumper comes with extendable ladder, working siren and firefighter. Great realistic details for dramatic play. Or consider some of the smaller Tonka hook-and-ladder and pumper sets that are scaled down and useful as block builders' props. (800) 752-9755.

★ COMPARISON SHOPPER—CEMENT MIXERS

(Little Tikes $30) Little Tikes' bright-yellow plastic cement mixer that spins, lifts and pours "concrete" is best for younger kids of the sandbox set. The cab is articulated to make turns and the back end lifts to pour. (800) 321-0183. Tonka's ($25) big classic metal version is much more realistic-looking and will appeal to older kids who want the real thing. While the back end does not lift to pour, it does spin and will spill the "cement" out the chute. (800) 752-9755.

THE SOUND MACHINE TRUCK

(Nylint $39.95) No ordinary toy truck, this is a gleaming black 18-wheeler with detachable trailer and working door for loading cargo. Turn the key on back of the rig and the motor revs up. Has air-brake sounds when stopped and warning beeps when backing up. Comes loaded with batteries and ready to roll! A sure-fire winner! For indoor use. (800) 397-8697.

RECYCLING TRUCKS 🏅 PLATINUM AWARDS

Right on the mark for the '90s, two recycling trucks for environmentally aware preschoolers. Little Tikes' ($17) version doubles as a shape sorter and has a younger look. (800) 321-0183. Nylint's metal model is likely to appeal to slightly older kids. (800) 397-8697.

REMOTE-CONTROL VEHICLES

AIR NIKKO 🏅 PLATINUM AWARD

(Nikko $38) With real jet sounds and the most amazing flashing lights, this jaunty remote-control jetliner thrilled our preschoolers and their parents. Sound can be turned off—a real plus. Very easy to control with a single button that moves the jet foward or makes it turn. Would be enjoyed by fives and sixes as well. 3 & up. (214) 422-0838.

PRESCHOOL REMOTE CONTROL CAR

(Playskool $30) Push the single button down and the car spins. Push it again and it goes foward. This chunky little car is truly designed for young kids. (800) 752-9755.

FIRST TRAINS AND TRACK TOYS

A nonelectric train is a classic toy that will keep growing in complexity as you add working bridges, roundhouses and other extras. We know many stores display their trains on tabletops with track glued down, but some of the open-ended play value is lost when you do that at home. As kids become more advanced builders, they will enjoy making ever-changing and elaborate settings with track and blocks combos.

TRAIN-BUYING TIPS

- Most starter sets come with just a circle of track that will lose its appeal quickly. Start out with enough track to make it interesting.

- Most wooden track sets are compatible with Brio trains, the best-known line, but stick with one company for track since some sets are thicker than others.
- For economy and multiple choices, add accessories from various makers.
- Preschoolers are not ready for electric trains, except to watch!

TOP-RATED SETS

SUSPENSION BRIDGE TRAIN SET   PLATINUM AWARD

(Brio $69.95) All aboard! Here's an elaborate, top-of-the-line wooden train set with 20 pieces of track (135"), one suspension bridge that looks like the Golden Gate, ascending tracks with supports and a three-piece magnetic train. This company's Circus Train ($25) is one of our favorites. Also a brand new station with ascending tracks. Very neat! (800) 558-6863.

WOODEN TRAIN

(T. C. Timber $63.50) Set comes with enough track to form a figure eight, a pass-through tunnel-bridge and a train that fastens with magnets. This company's track has ridges that look like railroad ties. Many bridges, buildings and other accessories are available for their trains, which are all Brio-compatible. (800) 359-1233.

THOMAS THE TANK ENGINE

(Learning Curve $69) Thomas fans will be thrilled to have this little blue train rolling along their wooden train tracks. A 22-piece starter set includes Thomas, track, an engine shed, RR signs, trees and play figures. The set comes with only two vehicles. Other trains are sold separately ($6 & up). Set is Brio-compatible. (800) 776-6909.

DUPLO TRAIN AND TRACK SET   BLUE CHIP

(Lego $44) Pulled by a stout engine, the train cars carry cargo and passengers and combine nicely with Duplo

blocks. Fitting car couplings and tracks together can be tough for some threes to do solo. (203) 763-4011.

1-2-3 TRAIN SET
(Playmobil $60) Brand-new, this plastic set comes with station, nifty bridge for rolling action and play figures. Extra tracks can be purchased to extend layout. Youngest players will need help to assemble track and couplings. (908) 274-0101.

• •

SHOPPING TIP:
Perfect for pretend adventures, a roadway play mat will define the space kids can use as their own. Can be rolled up and stored or used as a decorative rug. For young children this mat is an early introduction to "reading" and using a pictorial map. Available in catalogs and specialty shops.

• •

CONSTRUCTION TOYS

 If there's one toy no child should be without, blocks are it! Few toys are more basic. Stacking a tower, balancing a bridge, setting up a zoo—all call for imagination, dexterity, decision making and problem solving. Built into the play are early math and language concepts that give concrete meaning to abstract words like "higher," "lower," "same" and "different." Best of all, blocks are wonderfully versatile—they build a space city today, a farm tomorrow. Kids heavily into Turtles and Mermaids can even create their own settings.

Kids will enjoy both wood and plastic types of blocks; each provides different kinds of valuable play experiences. Choosing blocks depends largely on your budget and space. Although many of these sets are pricey, they are a solid investment that will be used for years to come.

WOODEN BLOCKS

Unit blocks come in many shapes and lengths, all carefully proportioned to each other. Many catalogs offer unit blocks in sets of different sizes. Parents are sometimes disappointed when kids don't use the small starter sets they buy. Keep in mind that kids really can't do much with a set of 20 blocks and no props. This is one of those items where the more they have, the more they can do.

JUNIOR UNIT BLOCKS　　BLUE CHIP

(T. C. Timbers $62.50) These smaller-scaled, all-maple hardwood blocks are perfect where storage space is tight. They are also half as expensive as a set of standard-sized blocks, with as many shapes and pieces. This set comes with 140 pieces in 12 shapes, including arches, columns, triangles, ramps and buttresses. (800) 359-1233.

★ COMPARISON SHOPPER—UNIT BLOCKS

No two catalogs have the same number of blocks or shapes in any set, so there's a small difference in all the sets listed. The cost of shipping will vary depending upon where you live. Our best suggestion is that you call around and compare. Here's a sampling of what a good basic set will run:

- Back to Basics set of 82 blocks in 16 shapes (#133). $124 (800) 356-5360.
- Childcraft set of 86 blocks in 12 shapes (#50090). $109.95 (800) 631-5657.
- T. C. Timbers set with 87 pieces in 23 shapes (#50-6674). $200 (800) 359-1233. (Higher price reflects greater number of shapes.)

PROPS FOR BLOCKS

Providing a variety of props, such as small-scaled vehicles, animals and people, enhances building and imaginative play. Here are some props designed to inspire young builders.

HIGHWAY RESCUE FLEET

(Heros/Darda $27) These six wooden vehicles are just the right props for dramatic block-city play. Set includes a fire truck, ambulance, police van, tractor trailer and tow truck with car in tow. (800) 638-1470.

WINDOW/DOORS   BLUE CHIP

(T. C. Timbers $13.50–$17.50 each) Take your choice of a sliding see-through window, overhead garage door or front door, framed to fit the scale of standard unit blocks. (800) 359-1233.

GIANT FLEXIBLE DINOSAUR COLLECTION

(Toys to Grow On $29.50) Eight magnificent dinosaurs made of colorful, pliable plastic. This generous set will thrill any dino enthusiast. While members of the set are not scaled to each other, the stegosaurus is 16" long! You won't be disappointed. Terrific props for blocks or sandbox. #1236 (800) 542-8338.

WILD ANIMAL SET

(Constructive Playthings $19.95) Set of five wild animals includes a 12" tall giraffe, an elephant, a zebra, a lion and a polar bear made of vinyl, with proportioned bodies and accurate coloring for playing zoo, circus and wild fantasy stories. Scaled right for standard unit blocks. #MTC-101L. Also available: Seven Farm Animal Set (MTC-100L). (800) 832-0572.

THE CASTLE

(Educational Concepts $48) A wonderful prop for medieval play. There are five stone-like walls, a red working drawbridge, slotted pillars and parapets! Walls can create a self-contained castle or be used as a facade with other blocks. Add a few Robin Hood action figures and your preschoolers are ready for medieval intrigue. (800) 962-6785.

NOAH'S ARK   BLUE CHIP

(T. C. Timbers $62.50) Thirty-two painted wooden animals and Noah's family come aboard this handsome ark that kids can assemble like an elegant puzzle. Animal pieces will be used for zoo, circus and other pretend play. Some of the pieces are small for kids who are still mouthing things, but this is a classic! (800) 359-6144.

• •

ACTIVITY TIP—PLAYFUL CLEANUP:

Preschoolers often need help cleaning up. You can get some learning in by saying, "I'll find the trucks, you pick up all the cars," or "Let's find all the smallest blocks first." Set up open shelves for blocks and baskets for props to avoid having a constant jumbled mess!

• •

CARDBOARD BLOCKS

GIANT CONSTRUCTIVE BLOCKS   BLUE CHIP

(Constructive Playthings $15.95) These sturdy 12" × 6" × 4" cardboard blocks are printed like red bricks and great for stacking into towers, walls and other big but lightweight creations. Strong enough for kids to stand on, this classic building tool will stand up to years of creative use. Set of 12. #CP-626. (800) 832-0572.

PLASTIC BLOCKS

Plastic building sets call for a different kind of dexterity. Here's what you should look for:

- Beginners are better off with larger pieces that make bigger and quicker constructions.

- Duplo-sized blocks are easier and less frustrating for little hands to manipulate.
- Select open-ended sets rather than model building sets that call for following complex directions. Save those for more experienced builders in the next age group.
- Encourage beginning builders to experiment rather than copy or watch you build.

★ COMPARISON SHOPPER—PLASTIC BRICKS

In the perpetual price war between plastic brick makers here's what you should know:

- Tyco and Mega Block preschool-sized bricks are compatible with Lego's Duplos.
- You will generally get more pieces for less money from Lego's competitors.
  But
- The less expensive sets will have fewer shapes than Lego's.
- Lego's preschool Duplo blocks are compatible with their standard Lego bricks, but the preschool blocks from other makers are not compatible with standard-sized Legos.
- Each maker's preschool bricks are compatible with their own brand of standard-sized bricks. In other words, brand B's preschool blocks will fit brand C's preschool blocks but not brand C's standard-sized blocks.
  The bottom line is:
- For longest use, your best buy is probably to pick one system—high price or otherwise—and build on it.

DUPLO BASIC BUCKET   PLATINUM AWARD

(Lego $29) A tubful of chunky plastic blocks to fill and dump, snap together and take apart, with wheel base for making simple vehicles and big bunny, pup, cat and people faces to use for pretend play and building. Other sets with jungle and zoo animals are also great choices.
1 1/2–5. (203) 763-4011.

DUPLO PULL-BACK MOTORS

(Lego $9) A 4" red block on rubber tread tires has pull-back friction motor inside. Young builders can customize their own vehicles on the bases and have plenty of sound and action. No batteries needed. (203) 763-4011.

DUPLO AIRPORT ★'94 PLATINUM AWARD

(Lego $36) Take off with this wonderful new theme set that includes a control tower, helicopter, airplane, car, gas pump and play figures. 2 & up. (203) 763-4011.

PLAY TABLE   PLATINUM AWARD

(TableToys $85) No more plastic building bricks all over the rug! Here's a terrific play table with storage bag in the center to hold plastic Lego-type blocks. The 26"-square surface of the table acts as a base for building and can be changed from Duplo-style blocks to standard Lego size, so it will be used for many years of creative play. A 31" × 15" wooden-framed table ($99) is also available for those who don't want plastic. (800) 999-8990.

• •

SHOPPING TIP:

Older preschoolers will enjoy mixing their old chunky Duplos with the smaller-scaled Lego bricks. These do demand more dexterity, so don't rush kids into frustration. See Early School Years section for more advanced sets.

• •

OTHER CONSTRUCTION TOYS

MEGA BLOCKS   BLUE CHIP

(Ritvik $10 & up) These oversized plastic pegged blocks are easy for preschoolers to take apart, fit together and assemble into good-sized constructions with a minimum of pieces. A basic set with wheels and angled pieces adds to the variety of vehicles and buildings kids can create. Most sets also include white pieces that make them compatible with Duplo-sized blocks. (800) 465-MEGA.

FLEXIBLOCKS MASTER BUILDER SET

(Flexitoys $35) An interesting variation of plastic blocks that hinge and stack so builders can construct vehicles that roll and gears that turn. Set comes with 192 pieces, wheels, axles and eight bears. 4 and up. (800) 543-2569.

BRIK BLOCKS

(Briks $60 & up) A 72-piece set of really big bricks with wheels and tools for building. Here's what's neat and special about these big plastic bricks: They can be "locked" together so that structures can be built, lifted and moved. More dexterity needed to fasten and unfasten bricks. 4 & up. (800) 438-2745.

KRINKLE BRICKS

(Battat $5 & up) These bristly-textured blocks are different and in some ways easier to stick together than bricks that snap. So these are a satisfying choice for kids who haven't yet got the dexterity for harder-to-handle building toys. (518) 562-2200.

EARLY GAMES AND PUZZLES

Preschoolers are not ready for complex games with lots of rules or those that require serious strategy skills. Your best bet for family fun are games of chance where players  depend upon the luck of the draw rather than skill. The idea of taking turns is often hard, and so is the concept of winning or losing. We've selected games that can be played cooperatively and those that are quick and short so there can be lots of winners. Some of the best games here can also be played as solo solitaire/ matching games.

BUSY GEARS   PLATINUM AWARD

(Playskool $16 & up) A variety of large and small gears and cranks can be arranged and rearranged in endless cause-and-effect spinning combinations on the pegboard base. Meshing the gears calls for both dexterity and problem solving, like a three-dimensional moving puzzle! There's no right or wrong way, but it's a challenge to make working machines that set all the pieces in motion. (800) 752-9755.

CANDYLAND   BLUE CHIP

(Milton Bradley $6) A classic preschool game for learning colors, counting and taking turns. No reading needed, and each round is relatively quick. (413) 525-6411.

FLOOR DOMINOES

(Galt $14) Set of 28 double-sided dominoes with pictures to match on one side and bold color-coded dots on the other side. Ideal for counting, picture and color matching. (800) 899-GALT.

LOTTINO   BLUE CHIP

(Ravensburger $14.95) Illustrator Dick Bruna's colorful graphics make this a beauty of a matching game. Players identify and match lotto cards with pictures on their playing boards. Winner is first to cover board. Develops language as well as matching skills. Also a good choice from Ravensburger: My First Lotto. 3–7. (201) 831-1400.

LYLE, LYLE CROCODILE

(Briarpatch $16) Fans of Bernard Waber's friendly crocodile Lyle will have fun playing this concentration game, which calls for matching pairs while trying to avoid Mr. Grumps. No reading needed. This company also makes a color game with graphics from *The Very Hungry Caterpillar.* 4–8. (800) 232-7427.

MATCH-A-BALLOON   BLUE CHIP

(Ravensburger $14.95) Throw the colorful die and match the bright balloon on the playing board with the color thrown. First to cover all the balloons wins. An easy way to learn matching and colors. 3–6. (201) 831-1400.

MOTHERS & BABIES MATCH-UP

(Ravensburger $14) Instead of competing to win, here's a game that can be used for several cooperative or solo games. There are 18 pairs of animal mothers and babies that fit together in self-correcting, no-reading matching games for children. 4 & up. (201) 831-1400.

ACTIVITY TIPS:

Bandanna Game #1   Choose several
  toys or household items with distinctive shapes and textures. Put
  them in a bag. Cover player's eyes
  with bandanna. Child reaches in,
  picks an item and tries to identify it
  by feel.

Bandanna Game #2   Put four items on a table.
  Cover child's eyes with bandanna. Take one item
  away. Child must tell what is missing. Trains
  kids' power of observation and memory.

SHAPE 'N' COLOR 🏅 PLATINUM AWARD

(Anatex $18) A color-coded sorting board has five bright vinyl posts on which to sort the 50 plastic chips by shape or color. Pattern cards are also included for another kind of challenge for eyes and hands. Comes in a plastic drawstring bag that makes a handsome package but may be dangerous. 3 & up. (800) 999-9599.

TOOLS PUZZLE

(Lauri $10.95) Eight tools (saw,
hammers, wrenches, screwdriver
and drill) fit in and out of this
crepe foam-rubber 11 1/2" square
puzzle frame. A new Kitchen Tool
Set, with pot, rolling pin, spoon
and other cutlery, is also available. Whole pieces are easier for
beginners. 2–5. (207) 639-2000.
Note: This company will replace
lost pieces for 50¢ each.

LACING GAMES

Three favorites: **Jumbo Stringing Beads** (Blue Chip) (T. C. Timbers $16.95) Stringing 27 large wooden beads in different colors and shapes is fun and will develop the refined hand movements needed for writing. (800) 359-1233. **Cotton Reels** (Galt $9) These colorful plastic spools are good for sorting by color or stringing in patterns. (800) 899-4258. **Lacing Shapes** (Lauri $6) Kids love lacing the thread in and out of the holes in these rubbery animal shapes. (207) 639-2000.

SCIENCE TOYS AND ACTIVITIES

Floating a leaf in a puddle, collecting pebbles in the park, making mud pies in the sandbox, watching worms wiggle— these are a few of the active ways children learn about the natural world. Here are our favorites for early science exploration.

MAGNETS AND OBSERVATION TOOLS

MAGNETIC BLOCKS

(Battat $12.95) Playful intro to the power of magnetism. Magnets are safely embedded in 16 brightly colored blocks. Can be built into moving vehicles with wheels. (518) 562-2200.

GIANT SUPER MAGNET

(Marvel $3.95) A 13" horseshoe magnet. Easy to hold and powerful enough to pick up several metal objects. #MTC-405 Constructive Playthings. (800) 832-0572.

• •

ACTIVITY TIP:
Give your preschooler a sheet of peel-off stickers to put on anything they find that the magnet sticks to. Or give kids a bag full of household items to sort in two baskets. Have them put all the things that are attracted to the magnet in one basket and all other things in another.

• •

HARDWOOD GIANT MAGNIFIERS

T. C. Timber's **Wooden-handled Magnifier** ($20) is pricey but beautifully crafted with an extra-big plastic safety lens for close-up looking. (800) 359-1233. (Marvel $19.95) The 11" high, wooden stand holds the large, easy-to-use plastic magnifier, which provides a focused, blown-up view of whatever is put below. #WB-4 Constructive Playthings. (800) 832-0572.

GARDEN WORK

Preschoolers love the magic of seeing things grow. Apartment dwellers can garden on a windowsill. For the backyard set, more elaborate child-sized tools are available.

BUBBLE BLOWER

(Fisher Price $19) Turn the big blue crank to blow bubbles and real leaves: A great hit with our testers. (800) 432-5437.

GARDEN TOOLS

(Little Tikes $12) Every season of the year will be covered, with a rake for falling leaves, a hoe for weeding summer gardens and a shovel that can dig snow or soil. Made of bright plastic that won't rust when they are inevitably left outside. 2–5. (800) 321-0183.

MULCHER MOWER

(Little Tikes $25) If you prefer fake grass clippings to bubbles flying, take home this new mower with a see-through chute where green clippings jump, a turn key, a gas cap that opens to "fill 'er up" and good sound effects. (800) 321-0183.

RED WAGON   BLUE CHIP

(Radio Flyer $45) Perfect for carting plants, tools, imaginary playmates or you name it. This is a classic 36" × 17" × 4 1/2" vehicle for hauling. (800) 621-7613.

GARDEN TRACTOR AND CART

(Little Tikes $68) This pedal-driven bright-green tractor pulls a cart that detaches to become a wheelbarrow. Great for hauling tools and dirt! (800) 321-0183.

SAND AND WATER TOYS

Sand and water are basic materials for exploring liquids and solids, floating and sinking, sifting and pouring. An inexpensive pail and shovel are basic gear and less upsetting to lose than the high-priced spread. A sand mill is also basic for sandbox or beach. Older preschoolers will be delighted with a set of turrets and tower molds for building beautiful sand castles—kids will add moat, imagination and who knows what else! Some other sand tools are also worth considering.

AQUA PLAY CANAL SYSTEM

(Galt $60 & up) Here's a fascinating water toy that's fun for pretend and early science learning. A system of inter-locking blue plastic water-ways provides a hands-on way to investigate how boats, locks, pumps and waterwheels work. Expensive but unique! Can be used in an empty tub with swim suits on cold days. Would be most enjoyed by older fours & up. (800) 899-4258.

• •

SHOPPING TIP:
You can find molds in almost any toy store. Just be sure to check the edges for roughness. Most catalogs offer new combinations every season, some with handy net bags for storage.

• •

DELUXE SAND & WATER SET
(Battat $19.95) The ultimate ten-piece beach set: supersize bucket with hose sprinkler, sandmill, small pail, molds and other tools that fit under the sieve lid. #2702 One Step Ahead. (800) 274-8440.

WATER PISTON
(Galt $5.95) Pump the hand-held piston in the water; when filled, it will squirt a powerful stream. This is a fun way to learn about hydraulics in a tub or wading pool. (800) 899-4258.

SAND AND WATER TABLE
(Playskool $60) This plastic table looks like a picnic table but comes with side-by-side wells for sand and water and a cover that converts the table for art projects or picnics. For indoor playroom or backyard fun. (800) 752-9755.

• •

ACTIVITY TIP:
Give kids empty squeeze bottles, sieves, funnels, different-shaped cups and tumblers for pouring, sprinkling and spilling experiments.

• •

**PORTABLE POOLS AND SANDBOXES—
SEE TODDLERS SECTION.**

ACTIVE PHYSICAL PLAY

Active play builds preschoolers' big muscles, coordination and confidence in themselves as able doers. It  also establishes healthy active patterns for fitness, relieves stress and provides a legitimate reason to run and shout. Agreeing on the rules of the game and taking turns promotes important social and cooperative skills. For tips on buying swing sets, see Toddlers section.

AIRPLANE TEETER TOTTER

(Little Tikes $75) Bright red with white propeller, this three-seater seesaw also turns 360 degrees and banks like a plane. One child can ride alone in the cockpit. Excellent for physical and pretend play as well as cooperative social play. (800) 321-0183.

BOINGO BALL

(OddzOn $18) A silky fabric cover wraps around this partially air-filled foam ball. Lightweight and big enough for preschoolers to enjoy bouncing, chasing and even catching. Made by the same folks who brought you the Koosh Ball. (408) 866-2966.

HYDRANT

(Fisher Price $19.99) If you like doing two things at once, here's a terrific way to water the lawn and help the kids cool off. Providing there's no drought, this is an entertaining piece of equipment. Once connected to your garden hose, it sprays out of the side or through the top. Sprays better than the Mickey Sprayer from Mattel. (800) 432-5437.

LADY BUG JUMPING BALL   BLUE CHIP

(Togu/T. C. Timbers $19.90) A big 17 3/4" inflatable ladybug ball with two built-on handles to hold as child sits on top and bounces along. A bounce-along favorite! (800) 359-6144.

OCTOPUS

(Little Tikes $80) Our toy testers ranging from two to six years found many ways to enjoy this sit, stand and spin toy. Like a mini merry-go-round, this turquoise plastic-molded octopus can be used by several children of mixed ages together. (800) 321-0183.

PLAY TUNNEL

(Back to Basics $42) A real "retro toy" that remains a favorite with preschoolers who love crawling in and out of the 9' long canvas tunnel over and over again. The tunnel is 23" in diameter and folds flat for storage. #53. (800) 356-5360.

TREDS PLAY BALL

(Weiss Twice $5.95) A 7 1/2" sports activity ball that can be used for tossing, kicking and catching. Comes in hot colors with "treads" that make it easy to hold onto or throw even when wet. (212) 532-5359.

• •

ACTIVITY TIP:

Painting with straws is a great outdoors game. Take a large piece of construction paper and pour puddles of tempera paint on the paper. Preschoolers love blowing the paint with a straw to create their own designs.

• •

WHEEL TOYS—TRIKES AND OTHER VEHICLES

Many of the vehicles featured in the Toddlers section will still be used by preschoolers. Vehicles such as the Kiddie Coop, Mini Van and School Bus with no pedals remain solid favorites. Older pre-schoolers are also ready for tricycles and kiddie cars with pedals. The battery-operated vehicles

that go 5 MPH look tempting, but they won't do anything for big muscle action. Here's what to look for
in a three-wheel drive with pedal action:

- Bigger is not better. Don't look for a trike to
  grow into.
- Take your child to the store to test drive and
  find the right size trike. Kids should be able to
  get on and off without assistance.
- Preschoolers need the security of a three-wheeler
  that is more stable.
- A primary-color bike can be reused by younger
  sibs regardless of their gender.

TOP-RATED

COLOR CART

(Hedstrom $30) If you're shopping for a child who is not
too tall, look at Hedstrom's 10" beauty in black with neon
hot trim. Has a padded saddle seat, adjustable handlebar
and cargo carrier on back. Model is also available in red,
white and blue. (800) 934-3949.

KETTRIKE MAXI   BLUE CHIP

(Kettler $79 & up) For a top-of-the-line
trike that will last through several
preschoolers, look at Kettler's, which
come in various sizes and styles. Their
trikes can be used with a detachable push
bar, which is useful not just for beginners
but in the city where tots like to ride to
the park and adults need to stay in control. (804) 427-2400.

SPORT CYCLE

(Little Tikes $45) If you are looking for a plastic trike for a
long-legged preschooler, test drive the Sport Cycle. Its
wide wheelbase makes this plastic bright-red "motorcy-
cle" a solid choice for stability. Has an instrument panel,
clicky key, windshield and gas cap that opens for "fill 'er
up" pretending. Scaled bigger than most. (800) 321-0183.

STAND-ALONE CLIMBERS

Activity Gym (Little Tikes $190) is a durable climber with four colorful panels that lock together to form an all-purpose play environment. Has dominated the market for years because of its sturdiness and reasonable price. 3 & up. (800) 321-0183. Note: As we go to press, several new climbers are in production from both Little Tikes and newcomer Step 2. Both are introducing much taller climbers that we were unable to test, but they will clearly require adult supervision.

CLIMBASAURUS

(Flexible Flyer $80) This is a low-to-the-ground climber, slide and hideaway cave in the shape of a bright yellow and blue dinosaur. Ideal for big muscle play. Can be used indoors or out. (800) 521-6233.

PLAYHOUSES

This is the ultimate toy for pretend play that will be used for several years of solo as well as social play. Kids as young as two love the magic of going in and out of a space that's scaled to child size. Threes and up are thrilled with the "privacy" of a little house of their own, and kids as old as six and seven will use it for all sorts of pretend.

TOP-RATED HOUSES

As in the grown-up housing market, there are a variety of playhouses to fit different tastes and budgets. Little Tikes practically owns this part of the plastic real estate market. The smallest playhouse, 46"H ($150), will be outgrown before the 52"H pastel **Country Cottage** ($200). For still grander, larger and thematic housing, consider the 6'H **Log Cabin** ($260) or their wonderful **Castle** ($275) with hidden escape passages, turrets and towers. If you prefer a wooden structure and price is no object, you'll do best at a roadside fence dealer who also sells prefab sheds.

● ●

FREEBIE:
For temporary indoor housing, don't overlook the charm of a big cardboard box with cut-out windows and door or a tablecloth draped over a table for little campers to use as a tent. A great way to overcome rainy-day cabin fever.

● ●

ART SUPPLIES

Markers, crayons, chalk, clay or paint each provides different experiences, all of which invite kids to express ideas and feelings, explore color and shapes, and develop muscles and control needed for writing and imagination. A supply of basics should include:

- Big crayons
- Washable markers
- Glue stick
- Tempera paint
- Finger paint
- Molding material such as Play-Doh or plasticine
- Colored construction paper
- Plain paper
- Safety scissors

● ●

BUYING TIP:
Our testers were disappointed with fancy-shaped crayons that give less-colorful results than regular wax crayons. Preschoolers' little hands also have better control with fatter crayons instead of the standard size.

● ●

PAINTS AND BRUSHES

Tempera paint is ideal for young children because of its thick, opaque quality. Watercolors are more appropriate for school-aged children. Young children will have more success with thick brushes rather than  skinny ones, which are harder to control. To reduce the number of spills, invest in paint containers sold with lids and openings just wide enough for a thick paint brush. Buying paint in pint-sized squeeze bottles will be more economical than buying small jars of paint that will dry out. Look for both nontoxic and washable labels on any art supplies you buy.

SPONGE PAINTERS

(Alex $3) For bold strokes preschoolers will love this set of three foam painting tools. There are two wide "brushes" made of foam instead of bristles and a small paint roller for long sweeping effects. Great for painting with water, too. (201) 569-5757.

FINGER PAINTS

(Crayola $1.49) Here's a neat new package of fingerpaints in three squeeze tubes. Ideal for out-of-doors fun—let them paint on an outdoor table or cookie sheet. When they're done, use the hose to clean up kids and table. (800) CRAYOLA.

• •

ACTIVITY TIP:

Magic Painting is great fun. Have child draw on paper with a piece of wax or a white crayon. Then water down a bit of tempera and have child paint over invisible drawing. Abracadabra! The drawing appears!

• •

TWO-SIDED MAGNA DOODLE ⭐ PLATINUM AWARD

(Tyco $20) This new variation on the Magna Doodle is quite different from the original. Kids can draw on either side of the magnetic board. One side is white and the other is black, so what you get is a positive and negative image—which our testers found interesting. The "eraser" is tied on rather than built in as it is on the still excellent original. 3 & up.

EASELS

Some say a flat table makes painting easier since the colors won't run. However, having an easel set up makes art materials accessible whenever the mood moves young artists.

If you prefer a wooden easel, our testers gave high ratings to those with chalkboards on one side and write-and-wipe marker boards on the other (Back to Basics $64 & up). Our parents preferred clipping sheets of paper to the easel rather than using paper on a roller, which requires an adult to cut a new sheet for every new work of art. Some of our kid testers couldn't resist pulling too much and creating a real paper trail! (800) 356-5360.

CREATIVE ART CENTER AND DESK

(Step 2 $60) This plastic cen-
ter has two easels and a work
table in between. Good for
families with lots of painters
or solo painters with lots of
play dates. Takes up more
room than the more tradi-
tional easel. 2 & up. (800) 347-
8372.

DOUBLE EASEL

(Little Tikes $60) This easel has a chalkboard on one side and a large clip that holds a pad of 17" × 20" paper on the other side. Has removable trays to hold paint. Bright-blue plastic with white and yellow accents. (800) 321-0183.

MODELING MATERIALS

PLASTICINE

This is an oil-based modeling material that your old "clay" set probably contained. Unlike Play-Doh or clay, plasticine never hardens, though you may need to soften it up by kneading it before your child can work with it. It can be reused again and again.

PLAY-DOH

(Playskool $5 & up) This classic dough is still a favorite for rolling, patting and poking. Some of the tools and kits add their own agenda. This is a self-hardening material that dries out if left uncovered. (800) 752-9755.

• •

FREEBIE:

Cookie cutters, rolling pins, baby bottle rings and other items around your kitchen make great tools for molding.

• •

SELF-HARDENING CLAY

(Adica Pongo, Alex & Crayola $3 & up) Kids can model with this material that dries in the air. It is more responsive to the touch than either Play-Doh or plasticine. Kids will need to learn to use water whenever they join one piece with another. Creations can be painted when clay dries. Found in toy and art supply shops.

MUSIC AND MOVEMENT

BAMBINA RHYTHM INSTRUMENTS

(JTG $4 & up) These brightly colored, eye-appealing rhythm instruments come in the shape of different animals. *Safety note:* Many come with small

bells that are hazardous to kids who still put things in their mouths. (800) 222-2584.

SIX-PIECE RHYTHM BAND SET

(Music for Little People $29.50) Our testers loved this set, which has wonderful sound quality. Six pieces include 5" cymbals, jingle tap, hand castanet, 6" tambourine, 5" triangle and block. Ideal for dance and play-along games that develop physical movement, nonverbal expression and joy of music. #7103. (800) 346-4445.

• •

ACTIVITY TIP:

Use cymbals to beat out someone's first name. For example, Sa-man-tha would get three beats. Take turns guessing whose name is being clanged.

• •

CHIME ALONG   BLUE CHIP

(Woodstock Chime $30) See Early School Years section.

PRESCHOOL FURNITURE BASICS

ALPHA DESK

(Today's Kids $40) Kids can pre-tend to be at work or school when they straddle the seat of this activity desk with wipe-off marker surface. Like an old school desk, the lid lifts to reveal a bristle surface that holds letters and numbers. Has a removable tray to hold supplies. (800) 258-8697.

TABLE AND CHAIRS

These are convenient pieces of basic gear that will be used for art work, puzzles, tea parties and even lunch. You'll find many choices in both plastic and wood. This is a decorating choice as well as a functional one. For safety and buying checklist, see Toddlers section.

BEST TRAVEL TOYS

Top-rated Take-alongs:

- **Doll Carrier/Snuggly** (Pleasant Co. $16) A good travel toy so you don't end up carrying the doll that has to go on all family outings. (800) 845-0005.
- **Fit-a-Face** (Lauri $12.95) Four round puzzles with big easy-to-fit geometric shapes that store in a handy carry-along case. 2–5. (800) 451-0520.
- **No Spill Bubble Tumbler** (Little Kids $6) A spill free bubble container. Turns upside down without a spill! Comes with 2 wands, 4 oz. of solution. Refillable. (800) 545-5437.
- **Tape player and tapes.** There's probably no better toy to make the miles fly than a tape player and a supply of song and story tapes.
- **Travel Magna Doodle** (Tyco $10 & up) This magnetic drawing tool with tied-on "pen" and built-in eraser comes in many different sizes. An ideal travel toy for drawing, tic-tac-toe and even writing letters and numbers.
- **Magnaplay Puzzles** (Darda $6 & up) Our tester loved the Design Maze for Mice, a playful maze that can be arranged in multiple ways on a thin magnetic board. (800) 638-1470.
- **Press 'n' Dress Doll** (Pockets of Learning $29.95) ❀ Platinum Award. Samantha looks like a big paper cut-out doll, but she's made of fabric and has a wonderful wardrobe that attaches

with Velcro. Doll and clothes store in a zip-up carrier. Constructive Playthings (800) 832-0572.

BEST THIRD AND FOURTH BIRTHDAY GIFTS FOR EVERY BUDGET

$100 Plus	Play kitchen or wooden blocks set
Under $100	Table for plastic blocks or easel or ride-on vehicle
Under $50	Doll equipment or nonelectric toy train set
Under $25	Doll or plush animal or truck
Under $20	Puppet or set of toy dishes
Under $15	Picturebook or Busy Gears
Under $10	Puzzles or game or audio tape
Under $5	Crayons or markers

4 ★ Early School Years
Five to Ten Years

What to Expect Developmentally

LEARNING THROUGH PLAY. During the early school years, as children begin their formal education, play continues to be an important path to learning. Now more complex games, puzzles and toys offer kids satisfying ways to practice and reinforce the new skills they are acquiring in the classroom.

DEXTERITY AND PROBLEM-SOLVING ABILITY. School-age kids have the dexterity to handle more elaborate building toys and art materials. They are curious about how things work and take pride in making things that can be used for play or displayed with pride.

ACTIVE GROUP PLAY. These early school years are a very social time when kids long for acceptance among their peers. Bikes and sporting equipment take on new importance as the social ticket to being one of the kids. Children try their hand at more formal team sports where being an able player is a way of belonging.

INDEPENDENT DISCOVERY. Although these are years when happiness is being with a friend, children also enjoy and benefit from solo time. Many of the products selected here are good tools for such self-sufficient and satisfying skills.

Basic Gear Checklist for Early School Age

★ ★ ★

✔ Two-wheeler with training wheels
✔ Sports equipment
✔ Dolls/soft animals
✔ Craft kits
✔ Water paints, markers, stampers
✔ Board games
✔ Musical instrument
✔ Tape player and tapes
✔ Lego, Playmobil and other construction sets
✔ Electronic game/learning machines

 Toys To Avoid

These toys pose safety hazards:
● Chemistry sets that can cause serious accidents
● Plug-in toys that heat up with light bulbs and give kids serious burns
● Audio equipment with volume controls that can be locked
● Projectile toys such as darts, rockets and B-B guns, or other toys with flying parts that can do serious damage
● Super-powered water guns that can cause abrasions
● Toys with small parts if there are smaller children in the house

The following toys are developmentally inappropriate:
● An abundance of toys that reinforce gender stereotypes; for example, hair play for girls and gun play for boys

PRETEND PLAY

School-age kids have not out-
grown the joys of pretending.
They want more elaborate and
realistic props for stepping
into the roles of storekeeper,
athlete or racing car driver.
For some, miniature settings
such as puppet theaters, dollhouses and castles are a

preferable route to make-believe. This is also the
age when collecting miniature vehicles and action
figures can become a passion. Such figures generally reflect the latest cartoon or movie feature.
Nobody needs all the pieces although many kids
want them all. But for kids at this stage, owning a
few pieces of the hottest "in" character represents a
way of belonging.

PROPS FOR PRETEND

PARAPHERNALIA FOR PRETENDING   BLUE CHIP
(Creativity for Kids $13) Here's a mixed pack of para-
phernalia for pretend games of all sorts. There are tickets for show time, checks for taking food orders. (216)
589-4800.

• •

SHOPPING TIP:
You can put together your own props for playing
office or store. Put together a kit with such goodies
as a paper punch, big paper clips, markers, pens,
date stamper, envelopes and blank paper. Store in
an official office folder.

• •

MAGIC FAX MACHINE
(Tyco/Playtime $20) The ultimate office prop for the '90s!
You write on the pressure-sensitive screen, dial the num-
ber, hit the button and out comes the hard copy of your

writing. Works better than this company's Magic Copier. (800) 367-8926.

WALKIE TALKIES   BLUE CHIP

(Fisher Price $24) Great way for hide-and-seek players and super-sleuth detectives to communicate. Each unit has a built-in speaker/microphone for secret messages. Kids can use the Morse code key for signaling. 9-volt batteries required. (800) 432-5437.

DOLLHOUSES AND OTHER PRETEND ENVIRONMENTS AND PROPS

Kids are ready now for finer details in house and furnishings. Specialty dollhouse shops and crafts stores sell prefabs and custom houses to fit all budgets.

VICTORIAN DOLL HOUSE
PLATINUM AWARD

(Playmobil $104 & up) Don't try to set this up before you give it! Putting it together is part of the fun. This is a challenging but well-designed model to construct together. When the deed is done it will be used for dramatic play. Victorian furnishings and figures add to the fantasy and charm. 6 & up. (800) 752-9662.

DUNGEON MASTER'S CASTLE SET

(Lego $72.99) Twelve fearless knights on horseback will guard this fortress. A challenging castle to build and use for dramatic play. Has three towers, a working drawbridge and a secret dungeon with glow-in-the-dark ghost. 8 & up. (203) 763-4011.

WOODEN CASTLE

(T. C. Timbers $57) This 85-piece set of wooden blocks can be used to create a handsome castle with turrets and towers. This is for younger kids in this age group. Easier to assemble than the beautiful Lego and Playmobil castles, which are designed for more advanced builders. 5 & up. (800) 359-6144.

KNIGHTS ACTION FIGURES

(Reeves/Britains $8 & up) These handsome knights in armor come as foot soldiers or mounted on fine steads (some even have friction mechanisms) and are ready for whatever is asked of them! Chiefly found in specialty and museum shops, these highly collectible figures are intended for play, not just display. 5 & up. (201) 633-5090.

PIRATE SHIP

(Playmobil $78) Ahoy mates! Here's another favorite setting for school-age kids to build, play with and display with pride. Younger kids in this age group will need adult help in fitting all the pieces together. 8 & up. (800) 752-9662.

PUPPETS AND PUPPET STAGES

Puppets provide an excellent way for kids to develop language and storytelling skills. Many of the hand puppets as well as the puppet stages listed in the Preschool section will get lots of mileage now. Older kids may also become interested in making shadow, stick or hand puppets of their own. They may also be delighted with learning to pull the strings of marionettes.

CHILDREN'S THEATRE   PLATINUM AWARD

(Peeleman-McLaughlin $19.95) Printed on sturdy cardboard, this charming tabletop puppet stage comes with storybook-style scenery and a large cast of stick puppets for productions of such classics as Cinderella and Red Riding Hood as well as original dramas. A great way to develop language and storytelling skills and explore puppets, without a huge investment. 5 & up. (800) 779-2205.

FANTASY PUPPET THEATERS

(Areton Enterprises $35 & up) Here's a charming piece of Czechoslovakian folk art, a tabletop stage with working curtain, hand-painted stage sets and uncomplicated marionettes for beginners. (800) 453-4018.

FARM ANIMALS

(Folkmanis $14 & up) A mother hen and a little chick make a perfect pair for acting out such classics as Henny Penny or original parent/child dramas. The chick ($14) is very unusual because human fingers go into the feet to do the walking. These are the latest additions to this company's wonderful line of high-quality puppets. (510) 658-7756.

LACE-A-PUPPET KIT

(Lauri $9.95) A package of pre-cut hand puppet forms, with safety needles, yarn, felt pieces and everything needed to create eight original puppets. A new Lace-a-Bunny Kit, with makings for three puppets, is also available. These make a nice craft kit for a birthday party activity kids can make and take as a favor. (207) 639-2000.

MULTICULTURAL CAREER PUPPETS
⭐ PLATINUM AWARD

(Learning Resources $19.95 each set of five) A Hispanic businesswoman, a female African-American doctor and a Caucasian male farmer are just three of the puppets in this wonderful new line that reflects our cultural diversity in the workplace! 4 & up. (800) 222-3909.

PUCKER

(Gund $45) This 25" long full-body green frog prince with a yellow crown is waiting for someone to kiss him and turn him into a royal. An amusing choice for fairy tale dramas. (908) 248-1500.

DOLLS

Now's the time when girls get heavily invested in dolls with tons of paraphernalia. Although five- and six-year-old boys often find ways to play with a cousin's or sister's doll or dollhouse, they are more likely to choose action figures to satisfy this kind of play. Both boys and girls continue to enjoy soft stuffed animals, the zanier the better.

For many years the only kinds of dolls around were blond with blue eyes. Over recent years manufacturers have created wonderful dolls that reflect our cultural diversity. Here are some of the best.

BABY DOLL

(Pleasant Co. $54) A soft-bodied 15" infant with vinyl head comes dressed in a sleeper, undershirt and diaper. Available as Caucasian, Asian or African-American. Beautiful clothes, furniture and accessories can add up to top dollar, but they are beautifully made. (800) 845-0005.

INTERNATIONAL COLLECTION

(Madame Alexandra $50 each) These 8" dolls in authentic costumes from other lands are chiefly for collecting and display. Leaving them alone will be difficult for all but the oldest girls in this group. (212) 283-5900.

KENYA

(Tyco $25) An African-American doll that comes in three skin tones and has a fabulous head of hair that can be styled from curly to straight to cornrows with beads and back to curly. (800) 367-8926.

KWANZAA DOLL PLATINUM AWARD

(Golden Ribbon $25) Dressed in traditional West African clothing, these 12" brown-vinyl girl or boy dolls come with either yarn or rooted hair and have a soft, huggable body. (800) 722-8285.

LITTLE LOVES

(Pauline $70) Charming line of soft-bodied 8" dolls with vinyl faces. Available with Caucasian, Asian or African-American features. This company makes the prettiest Asian dolls. Very special! (201) 831-1400.

SHANI

(Mattel $20) This stylish doll's name means "marvelous" in Swahili. Her two friends are fashion dolls, each with different skin tones, facial features, hair styles and clothes. (800) 524-8697.

OTHER NOTABLE DOLLS

BARBIE

(Mattel $6 & up) This is the age when girls often start collecting Barbie, her friends and all their paraphernalia. They may spend hours acting out small dramas with their collections. Although Barbie has had several careers over the years (doctor, astronaut, office worker), she remains a glitzy fantasy figure. (800) 524-8697.

MY SIZE BARBIE

(Mattel $100) We had some reservations about this, the ultimate Barbie! She's 3' tall and designed to be able to share her outfit with girls sizes 4 to 10. Also comes with jewelry and makeup to share. Our eight-year-old Barbie collector was ecstatic about her. What she loved best was dressing Barbie in her clothes. (800) 524-8697.

CORINNE OR OTHER GIRL DOLLS

(Corolle & other makers $80 & up) One beautiful doll with long silky hair and a wardrobe of stunning clothes is often the last and most memorable doll that a girl of 6 to 9 will cherish. Corinne is 21" tall, with long chestnut hair and hazel eyes. She comes dressed in a pleated skirt, red trimmed jacket, beret and a shoulder purse. 6 & up. (800) 558-6863.

FLIP DOLLS

(Pockets of Learning $20 each) Storybook lovers will adore these fabric dolls. Flip the Three Bears doll with

Mama and Papa holding baby back to back and you'll find Goldilocks! #6304A2 A Red Riding Hood who flips into Granny and the Bad Wolf is also available. (800) 328-8360.

GINNY DOLLS

(Dakin $30) These 8" dolls have been around for years. Unlike Barbie, Ginny is a girl, not a jet-setter who lives the lifestyle of the rich and famous. Her clothes are the sort of things a girl would wear, so they satisfy the collector's bug and moms who see Barbie as a poor model. (800) 227-6598.

MADELINE CARRY-ALONG DOLL ✹ PLATINUM AWARD

(Eden $38) Madeline comes tucked in her bed along with three changes of clothes in a neat fabric carrying case. Nothing, not even her appendix scar, was left out. 5 & up. (212) 947-4400.

MUFFY VANDER BEAR AND HOPPY VANDERHARE

(North American Bear Co. $17 each) Charming 7" bear and rabbit with articulated arms and legs. Wonderfully whimsical outfits ($10 & up). Young kids may need help with clothing. 6 & up. (800) 682-3427.

SAMANTHA

(Pleasant Doll Co. $74) An 18" Victorian schoolgirl comes with her own storybook. Charming outfits and furniture are available extras. The catalog is a doll lover's dream! The doll is not badly priced compared to others of similar quality. (800) 845-0005.

ELECTRIC TRAIN SETS

Many train buffs will tell you that this is the stage when their romance with trains began.

• •

SHOPPING TIPS:

- Select HO gauge for beginners. Smaller trains and their tracks can be frustrating and tricky to put together. Larger-gauge sets take up a tremendous amount of space, so you generally end up with just a boring circle of track.

- Select a well-known brand such as Lionel or Buchman that can be easily expanded.

- Start with a basic set and enough track to make an interesting roadbed.

- Since trains are plug-in electrical items, they are labeled for 8 & up. Younger children may enjoy them, but they should be used only with adult supervision.

• •

LOAD 'N' HAUL RAILROAD   PLATINUM AWARD

(Lego $114) Build a working cargo train with a mighty engine, three sturdy cars and forklift. Comes with electric power system. This is the first nonbattery, all-electric train kit from Lego. Our testers admired its design and how well it stays on the track at high speed. 8 & up. (203) 763-3211.

RACING CAR AND TRACK SETS

CANNONBALL CLIMB
PLATINUM AWARD

(Darda $45) Our testers were thrilled with the performance of the Darda racing car as it zipped over the tri-

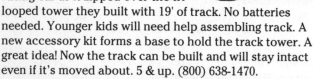

looped tower they built with 19' of track. No batteries needed. Younger kids will need help assembling track. A new accessory kit forms a base to hold the track tower. A great idea! Now the track can be built and will stay intact even if it's moved about. 5 & up. (800) 638-1470.

HOT WHEELS CRISS CROSS   PLATINUM AWARD

(Mattel $34) If you're looking for wows, this newest entry from Hot Wheels is a winner. Cars go superfast on the motorized cloverleaf track. Pure novelty! (800) 524-8697.

RACING SETS

(Tyco $25–$70) When kids outgrow their wooden trains, this is generally what they move on to. The newest electric racing sets come with super sound chips for added excitement. Or look at the Ultra Cliff Hangers that defy gravity. Choose according to budget. 8 & up. (800) 367-8926.

TRUCKS AND CARS

REMOTE CONTROL CARS

(Tyco or Nikko $45 & up) Both of these companies make comparably priced remote control vehicles for this age group. Nikko's zippy little **Sonic Hedgehog ($29) or** Tyco's **Outlaw** ($45) received top ratings. Eights and up will be able to handle the speed and more complex controls of vehicles like Tyco's Turbo Scorcher ($80) or Nikko's Brat ($79). Tyco (800) 367-8926/Nikko (214) 422-0838.

SOUND MACHINE WATER CANNON   PLATINUM AWARD

(Nylint $46) The ultimate fire engine with electronic sounds reproduced from a real fire truck including air brakes, warning signals and sirens. Has flashing lights and a 35" boom that pivots. A memorable gift for inside play. 5 & up. (800) 397-8697.

MIXED EMOTIONS: VOICE COMMAND POLICE WRECKER

(Buddy L $49) Imagine a truck that turns on its lights, blows its horn and starts its engine on voice command. We had mixed emotions because it's not 100% foolproof. This flashy tow truck can be activated (most of the time) by talking to it—except when it doesn't seem to listen. Nevertheless, for sheer cutting-edge novelty this is a winner. (800) 442-7440.

Construction Toys

As their dexterity develops
kids can handle smaller
pieces and more complex
building sets. Providing a
variety of building sets is better than an investment in just one
type because building with Legos and Erector Sets
involves different, but equally valuable, skills.

OPEN-ENDED CONSTRUCTION SETS
BRIO-MEC

(Brio $30 & up) This wooden building system allows kids
to create working vehicles and other mechanical creations with nuts and bolts as fasteners. Involves dexterity and thinking skills. Comes with step-by-step patterns
to follow or can be used for original ideas. 5 & up. (800)
558-6863.

LINCOLN LOGS　　BLUE CHIP

(Playskool $9 & up) You probably had a set of these
building logs. This classic toy can be used with building
blocks to create small houses for action figures. The
updated version is lighter in color and sold with plastic
roofs and accessories; our testers had mixed feelings
about these prefab additions. 6 & up. (800) 752-9755.

TINKERTOYS

(Playskool $5–$30) A classic toy that has been updated
with bigger and brighter plastic pieces. While you may
have regrets about another toy gone plastic, the larger
pieces are fun and easier to work with and produce bigger constructions. Marked 3 & up but really more for
fives and up, who (with help) can figure out how to build
a working windmill, among other things. (800) 752-9755.

Plastic Building Bricks

School-age children are ready for the smaller Lego-
sized pieces that allow for more detailed designs
and structures.

LEGO BASIC BUILDING SETS

(Lego $21.99 & up) One of several open-ended basic sets that comes with a good mix of bricks, wheels, doors and mini-figures. Kids can follow outlines on the box or create their own designs, so there's no right or wrong way as with the more thematic sets, which are for more advanced builders. Ages 5–7. (203) 763-3211.

PLAYTABLES   PLATINUM AWARD

(Table Tops $79 & up) Available with Lego-sized grid. See Preschool section for details.

POLLY PICK UP   PLATINUM AWARD

(Lego $22) Imagine turning "pick up your blocks" into part of the fun! This updated 131-piece Lego brick set comes in a container that has a built in "vac" for picking up bricks as it's rolled across the floor. Works with a turning paddle, not batteries. A very neat toy! (203) 763-4011.

THEME AND PATTERN CONSTRUCTION SETS

BIG TOP CIRCUS SET   PLATINUM AWARD

(Playmobil $17 & up) Depending on your budget, you can buy smaller sets (our favorite is the disappearing assistant in the box) or you can buy everything under the Big Top with the deluxe set that  includes the ringmaster, magic act and acrobats! You and your kids will enjoy hours of putting it all together. Once built it will be enjoyed for dramatic play. (908) 274-0101.

ERECTOR SETS   BLUE CHIP

(Meccano $15 & up) Our testers tried the new plastic version but found the threads inside the screws wear out and the projects are too complex for young kids. The classic metal sets are still excellent and challenging building sets for older kids. A mid-priced set such as Set 2 ($40) with 274 pieces and a motor can build 27 models and will have long-term interest. 8 & up.

ICE PLANET 2002

(Lego $43.99) For the space-minded builder here's a wonderful set with 412 pieces to assemble spaceships and rockets. A long-term building project for the experienced builder. 8–12. (203) 763-4011.

K'NEX

(Connector Set Toy Co. $9.95 & up) Color-coded rods and connectors can be used to build windmills, helicopters, dragsters and space shuttles. This set requires some real strength in the hands and patience, too. The latest entry to the construction toy market is like Tinkertoys for older kids. 8 & up. (800) KID-KNEX.

SNAP MODELS

(Ertl $10 & up) For beginners these are an ideal choice. They need no glue, but do require dexterity and the ability to follow directions. Long-term interest in model building as a hobby often begins at this stage. 7 & up. Toy and hobby stores.

TECHNIC STARTER SET ⭐ PLATINUM AWARD

(Lego $14 & up) Here's the next step up for Lego builders. This is a far more complex and demanding system that introduces kids to how gears, axles, wheels and pulleys work. A Lego **Technic Power Pack** ($35) can be added to motorize models. **Technic Pneumatic Set** ($34), a '94 Platinum Award winner, comes with a special pump that uses air pressure to operate a forklift. 9–14. (203) 763-4011.

GAMES

CLASSIC AND NEW GAMES

Now's the time when kids begin to really enjoy playing games with rules, both with friends and family. Of course, winning is still more fun than losing, and playing by the rules isn't always easy. That's the bad news. The good news is that many of the best board games are both entertaining and educational. Many games can improve math, spelling, memory and reading skills in a more enjoyable way than the old flash card/extra workbook routine. Game playing also builds important cooperative social skills.

For fives and sixes, now's the time for classic Blue Chip games like:

Parcheesi	Dominoes	Chutes and Ladders
Checkers	Lotto	
Uno	Pick-up-Sticks	Pop-o-Matic
Chinese Checkers		

For sevens, eights and up, try classics such as:

Othello	Yahtzee	Monopoly Jr.
Sorry	Pictionary Jr.	Clue
Chess	Scrabble	Twister
Upwords	Bingo	Connect 4
Boggle	Life	

THE COMPLETE GAME DESIGN KIT

(Creative Education of Canada $12) Players create their own games with this attractive set that comes with two game boards, 58 stickers, markers, game pieces and a spinner. There is enough of a framework so that kids will not be overwhelmed while adding their own input to the games they create. (800) 982-2642.

GAME OF THE STATES

(Milton Bradley $9) Provides an introduction to the names of the states, their capitals and products. Fills the bill for younger kids who love watching *Where in the World Is Carmen San Diego?* but are not yet ready for the computer game or more complex geography games. 7 & up. (413) 525-6411.

GUESS WHO?

(Milton Bradley $15) Here's a game that calls for some deductive reasoning and memory. Each player picks one of 24 faces on their matching playing boards and has to guess who their opponent has chosen. Players quiz each other about the unique attributes of the funny faces. 6 & up. (413) 525-6411.

MADELINE GAME

(Ravensburger $17) Storybook fans of Madeline will love this memory game as they turn the playing pieces searching for Madeline's lost puppies. No reading necessary. Comes with directions for competitive or cooperative play. 5 & up. (201) 831-1400.

MUSIC MAESTRO II

(Aristoplay $25) Update of wonderful game with audio cassettes that acquaint players with 48 musical instruments. Five games at varying levels of difficulty with game board and cards. 5–10. (800) 634-7738.

WHAT'S MY NAME?

(Ravensburger $14.95) Child rolls "secret" dice to select a familiar object on the playing board, which he must then describe to others without saying its name. An excellent game that develops observation and language skills along with the ability to use the simple "graph" playing board. 6–10. (201) 831-1400.

USA MAP PUZZLES

(Judy $22.95) This wooden puzzle is a good choice for second- and third-graders. Puzzle pieces of USA have names of states and capitals. Lift the pieces to see cities, rivers and principal products. #KC80816. (800) 533-2166.

MEMORY AND WORD GAMES

HUGGERMUGGER JR.

(Golden $12.99) This is both a mystery word and trivia contest. Players race to answer some of the 1,600 questions to uncover the letters of the mystery word. Questions involve rhyming words, things that go together, missing words in well-known sayings and more. A good party game for 9 & up. (800) 558-5972.

SCATTAGORIES JR.

(Milton Bradley $13) Roll the big letter die and find answers that start with the letter you threw for such categories as animals, clothes, boy's names, places, things you do in winter, things at the circus, etc. Players race against a clock to fill in six categories. For 2–4 players. 8–11. (413) 525-6411.

SENTENCE CUBES

(Golden $12) A fun way to build reading skills with 21 word cubes to toss and arrange in silly or serious sentences. For beginners put the timer away and don't expect long, long sentences. Labeled for 8 & up but late first- and second-graders love using this game solo or as a cooperative team game. (800) 558-5972.

MATH AND NUMBER GAMES AND EQUIPMENT

BATTLESHIP   BLUE CHIP

(Milton Bradley $13) Players learn to read a graph by placing their miniature fleet of ships in a grid and calling numbers and letters to locate "enemy" ships. Winner is first to find her opponent's ships. Our testers preferred the nonelectronic version of this game without the repetitive and intrusive sound effects of ships blowing up. 7 & up. (413) 525-6411.

DINO MATH TRACKS

(Learning Resources $19.95) Dinosaur fans will happily play the three distinct games designed around these favorite extinct creatures that reinforce addition, subtraction, multiplication and place-value concepts. For 2–4 players. Ideal for 7–10. (800) 222-3909.

FUN THINKERS DECODER AND TILES

(Educational Insights $8.95 each) These self-correcting, nonelectronic "games" come in varying levels of difficulty in math and reading. A frame with tiles fits over quiz books. Kids arrange the tiles to answer and then flip the frame. If all is correct, a colored pattern is revealed. (800) 933-3277.

GIANT DICE

(Lakeshore $6.95) Tossing these 5" square dice turns math practice into a game. Order dice with dots for fives

& sixes. Buy dice with numerals for older kids. #LC711 or #LC712. (800) 421-5354.

● ●

ACTIVITY TIP:
Use dice for a quick two-player math game, keeping score with buttons or raisins. Odds or Evens: player 1 = odd, player 2 = even. Take turns tossing. If player 1 tosses odd number, she gets a point. If player 2 tosses even number, he gets a point. Winner is first to score ten points.

● ●

MONEY STAMPERS
(Educational Insights $7) Unlike most toy money, this set of rubber stamps can be used to make realistic pictures of coins. Fun to use for pretend games but can also be used for original games. Try a game of "make a buck": Players use stampers to stamp out a dollar in different ways. An "edutainment" hit with 6s & up. (800) 933-3277.

PRESTO CHANGO GAME
(Educational Insights $24.95) Learning how to make change is much more fun with a fast-paced game of buying and selling. Unlike typical games, this one deals in coins as well as dollars. You may want to play with real coins instead of the plastic play money. 6 & up. (800) 933-3277.

TIC-TOCK ANSWER CLOCK AND CLOCK-O-DIAL
(Tomy $11 & Educational Insights $14.95) Two excellent toys for kids learning to tell time. The Tomy clock is an owl with a large clock face on its chest. Kids move the big hand and check the time with a digital read-out. 5–7. (714) 256-4990. **Clock-o-Dial** features a playful crocodile with a playing board and more advanced self-correcting time drills. 7 & 8. (800) 933-3277.

> **BOOK TIP:** *My First Book About Time* (DK $14.95) Fives will fiddle with the clock, but this is really a book for first- to third-graders who are learning to tell time. 5–8.

PUZZLES AND BRAINTEASERS

Putting jigsaw puzzles and brain teasers together calls for visual perception, eye/hand coordination, patience and problem-solving skills. During their early school years kids should build from 25-piece puzzles to 50 and 100-plus pieces.

A-Z PANELS

(Lauri Capitals & Lowercase each $6.95) Fitting the rubbery letters in and out of the puzzle frame not only helps kids learn to know and name the letters, but handling the 3-D letters also gives kids a feel for their shapes. (207) 639-2000.

BACKSPIN

(Binary Arts $12) A hand-held disc with six color-coded slots. Marbles must be moved to match slots both on front and back. A torment! 8 & up. (800) 468-1864.

BLOCKS AND MARBLES

(Blocks & Marbles $26.50) Chunky wooden blocks and ramps can be arranged in multiple ways to create a runway maze for marbles. This handsome wooden toy is like a 3-D puzzle that challenges creative problem-solving skills in a playful, open-ended way. Comes in natural or multicolor sets of 21 or 45 pieces. (800) 446-7843.

CASTLE PUZZLE

(Ravensburger $15) Our testers really liked the open-endedness of this double puzzle. One scene shows just the castle, the other has the same castle with people. Pieces from each board are interchangable. (201) 831-1400.

DELUXE MAGNETIC PICTURE BOARD

(Battat $26) Colored magnetic chips are neatly sealed inside a see-through frame. Kids move chips with a magnetic wand to fill in patterns that slip into the frame. A wipe-off pattern card and crayons can be used to create pictures. A good choice for developing sequencing and visual skills. 5–8. (518) 562-2200.

DINOSAUR PUZZLE

(Frank Schaffer $12.95) A giant-sized floor puzzle with 50 extra-large pieces creates a 3' Tyrannosaurus! Also recommended: **Endangered Species** (49 pieces become a 5' long mural.) 5 & up. (800) 421-5565.

EMPEROR'S NEW CLOTHES HIDDEN PICTURES PUZZLE

(Ravensburger $8) There's more here than meets the eye at first glance. After you put together this 80-piece puzzle, there are hidden pictures to discover, like Waldo. 6 & up. (201) 831-1400.

FINE ARTS PUZZLES

(Intempo $7.50) Reproductions of famous paintings by artists such as Renoir and Van Gogh are challenging as well as beautiful. You'll find these 150-piece puzzles chiefly in museum shops. 8 & up. (800) 326-TOYS.

KIDS PERCEPTION PUZZLE

(Lauri $6.50) Eighteen kids in different poses fit into this challenging puzzle that pushes kids to look at small differences just as they must when they read words that look almost alike, such as "cap," "cop" and "cup." Others in this series include puzzles full of fish, vehicles, bears and butterflies. 4–7. (800) 451-0520.

PARQUETRY BLOCKS

(Learning Resources $25) Thirty-two geometric-shaped tiles are arranged on top of colorful patterns. More advanced players can use tiles without the pattern.

Helps develop visual skills in matching and following the sequence of patterns—skills that are needed in putting letters together to make words. 5–8. (800) 222-3909.

3 D JIGSAW PUZZLE

(Binary Arts $35) Like art books with transparent layers, these 3-D puzzles are three layers deep. Brilliant scenes are printed on clear plastic and then stacked on top of each other. Themes include the Jungle, Reef, Dinosaurs and more. 540 pieces for 8–108. Great! (800) 468-1864.

TRIAZZLE

(DaMert $12) A triangular puzzle with insect/fish/flower motifs that look deceivingly simple. The object is to match heads and wings of the three insects on each triangular shape. Eights often out perform adults. Addictive! (800) 359-6144.

VEXAHEDRON

(Tensegrity $15) A beautiful puzzle to handle. Take the eight magnetized wooden blocks apart and spend hours trying to put them back together again. A challenge to eyes, hands, patience and problem solving. A terrific travel/desk toy. (800) 227-2316.

IT's MAGIC!

Some kids like to impress friends and family with magic tricks. Learning to do them takes time, practice and real reading skills. Reluctant readers may become avid readers of books that involve doing things such as magic or science experiments that are like magic.

ABRACADABRA

(T. C. Timbers $10) This is a marvelous magic trick that kids can use to read people's minds! A player picks one of 15 pictures from a master board. Next the player is asked to look at four smaller boards. The magician tells the name of the picture the player chose! A little math, a little magic, a lot of fun! 6 & up. (800) 359-6144.

HOCUS POCUS AND OTHER SECRETS

(Back to Basics $46) Here's the secret to dozens of magic tricks, along with props and a 60-minute video that teaches young magicians how to perform tricks and illusions. An elaborate set for serious beginners. 8 & up. #184. (800) 356-5360.

ELECTRONIC LEARNING TOOLS

Kids tend to love the novelty of electronic teaching machines, which don't actually teach new skills, but do reinforce and provide the kind of practice some kids need.

GEOSAFARI AND GEOSAFARI JR.

(Educational Insights $99.95) This electronic quiz game, designed originally for eights and up, is also now made to give first- through third-graders practice with phonics, maps and science. The game machine comes with ten two-sided game cards and is well supported with extra lesson packs ($15 each) in subjects for both young and older kids. Game cards for the original GeoSafari are totally compatible with Jr. version. (800) 933-3277.

WORLD WIZARD

(V Tech $50) Comes with 20 activity cards (10 double-sided), including geography, explorers, famous people, myths and animals. Our testers thought the sound effects were a plus. However, GeoSafari has more software cards for mixed ages and on more subjects. We expect World Wizard will be playing catch-up. 8 & up. (800) 521-2010.

MATH SAFARI

(Educational Insights $99.95) This brand-new math machine looks a lot like GeoSafari, but it has more bells and whistles and is dedicated to math games. It looked like a winner, but we were unable to test this with kids before press time. 5 & up. (800) 933-3277.

SUPER SPEAK AND MATH   BLUE CHIP

(Texas Instruments $55) Updated electronic math machine with story problems, games and computation drills. Varying levels of ability make this a tool for several years' worth of action. Extra software available. For a smaller math machine, see the new Mickey Math Adventures ($22) or a Mickey calculator. 6 & up, up, up. (800) 842-2737.

SUPER SPEAK 'N' SPELL   BLUE CHIP

(Texas Instruments $55) This classic makes spelling into a game. Actually there are several games, including Fill in the Missing Letter, Fix Up the Mixed-up Letters. All games can be played at four different levels of difficulty. Player can keep score. Additional cartridges are available. 6 & up. (800) 842-2737.

VIDEO PAINTER

(V Tech $99) Plug the Video Painter into your TV and kids can draw their own or use 50 premade pictures with 12 colors and many backgrounds from which to choose. They can animate and save their creations on the VCR. Marked 5 & up, but will be more enjoyable for older kids. Won't replace crayons or paint, but the whole family will want to play with this! Easier to use than Sony's My First Animator, which is also double the price. (800) 521-2010.

MARIO PAINT FROM NINTENDO—SEE COMPUTER SOFTWARE/CD–ROM SECTION.

ACTIVITY KITS AND ART SUPPLIES

For school-age kids art class is seldom long enough. Besides, such classes are usually teacher-directed with little chance for kids to explore their own ideas. Giving kids the tools and space for art projects at home is more than pure entertainment. Art helps develop

their ability to communicate ideas and feelings
visually, to refine eye/hand skills and learn how to
stick with a task.

• • • • • • • • • • • • •
Basic Gear Checklist

★ ★ ★

✔ Crayons, colored pencils and pastels
✔ Watercolor and acrylic paints
✔ Watercolor markers of varying thicknesses and
   colors
✔ Origami paper folding
✔ Lanyard kits
✔ Sewing
✔ Needlepoint
✔ Rug hooking
✔ Cutting/pasting
✔ Woodworking
✔ Fabric paints
✔ Loom (weaving, beads, pot holders)
✔ Flower press
✔ Air-hardening clay

NOTABLE TOOLS

COOL CUTS SAFETY SCISSORS
(Alex $4) Paper crafters are going to love these two scis-
sors! Like pinking shears, one cuts zigzags, the other
wavy scallops. Come packed as a pair. (201) 569-5757.

GLITTER CRAYONS
(Crayola $2.49) These hefty crayons produce sparkling
glitter results without the need for glue. (800) CRAYOLA.

MY WORLD COLORS CRAYONS AND MARKERS
(Crayola $2 & up) Finally, these sets include colors that
reflect our many skin, eye and hair tones. As kids
become more exacting they also strive for more realism,
and these crayons and skin-tone markers are right on target! (800) CRAYOLA.

• •

SHOPPING TIP:
Pack your own art exploration kit with assorted supplies—glitter pens, oil and chalk pastels, fabric-painting crayons, watercolors, puff paints and markers. Pack in a carrying case to keep it organized.

• •

ACTIVITY AND CRAFT KITS

BENDITS
(Battat $35) This construction set comes with 76 pieces, the majority of which are straw-shaped, that can be twisted and bent into an endless variety of Calderesque creations. Be forewarned: There are lots of little pieces. Provide a storage container or this toy will dribble away. 5 & up. (518) 562-2200.

DOODLE DOME PLATINUM AWARD
(Tyco $20) An interesting new "drawing" machine in the shape of a magic ball. You can draw up, down and diagonally and, best of all, pick up the stylus from one part of the ball to another without making a line. 5 & up. (800) 367-8926.

ESKIMO ART
(Patail $20) Introduce kids to the art of another culture with molds for making a hunter in a kayak, a whale and a mythological ten-legged bear. Kit includes everything needed to create authentic-looking "scrimshaw," and comes with clear instructions and facts about these pieces. A new **Matreshka Russian Nesting Doll Set** is challenging. 9 & up. (714) 367-0530.

★ **COMPARISON SHOPPER—JEWELRY KITS**
A variety of excellent jewelry kits arrived late this season. These are our testers' top picks: **Jazzy Jewelry Glitter Gems** (Crayola $12.95). Precut shapes are ready to be spread with glitter and gems for quickly made pins, necklaces and earrings. (800) CRAYOLA. **Fashion Magic Deluxe** (Tyco $20) has hair accessories and other jew-

elry to decorate with pearlized and metallic finishes. (800) 367-8926. **Fashion Accessory Kit** (Alex $25). Includes headbands, ribbons, shoe laces, beads, glitter, earrings and tons of doodads all packaged in a neat storage case. (201) 569-5757.

MAKE-A-MASK KIT

(Educational Insights $10.95) Just in time for Halloween, a craft kit with plastic reusable face form, plaster gauze, paint and excellent step-by-step guide, written by the L. A. Mask Theater, for making original masks to wear or display. #1800 (800) 933-3277.

MY PAPER CRAFT CASE

(Alex $25) Who wouldn't love a handsome carrying case chockful of every kind of paper imaginable? Comes with glue tube, glitter pen, scissors and an activity pamphlet for making fans, hats, finger puppets and flowers. A dream gift for fives and up. Other wonderful kits from this maker include collage, clothes decorating, jewelry. Highly recommended. (201) 569-5757.

POTTERY WHEEL

(Natural Science $30) For more advanced potters this pottery wheel kit gives kids a chance to try their hand at throwing a pot and finishing it with decorative flourishes. A tool for developing fine motor skills along with creativity. Has a foot pedal and comes with two pounds of clay, tools, glaze. 8 & up. Back to Basics (800) 356-5360.

TIE DYE KIT

(Creativity for Kids $10) Instead of mixing pots of dye, the color comes embedded in strings that are tied to fabric. The process itself can be done in the microwave or on stove top. Either will need an adult assist. This is just a way to sample the craft—sort of. 8 & up. (216) 589-4800.

★ COMPARISON SHOPPER—WEAVING LOOMS

Brio's loom ($60) comes out of the box threaded and
ready to work! Our testers felt the instructions were
spotty for a true novice but gave the product overall
high ratings for design. (800) 558-6863. The Harrisville
Easy Weaver ($69.95) also comes threaded but does not
fold up like Brio's. Our testers found the instructions easier to follow and also liked the refill kits ($14.95) because
they slip right onto the loom! If you've never been a
weaver, this may be a better bet. 7 & up. (800) 338-9415.

WIZBITS

(Wizbits $22 & up) Day-glow colors and
funky patterns brighten the big sturdy cardboard shapes that fit together to form zany
abstract creatures or structures. Pieces fit
together with notches and imagination. No
glue or little pieces to deal with around the
house. 4–8. (914) 365-1500.

ART WITH A SCIENTIFIC EDGE

BEESWAX CANDLEMAKING KIT

(Creative Education of Canada $11)
No heat is needed to shape 12 to 24
candles from this kit that includes six
sheets of beeswax, wick, glitter and clear instructions for
making candles that can be used for special occasions or
gift giving. 5 & up. (800) 982-2642.

BIRDHOUSE AND FEEDER KITS

(Woodkrafter $6 & up) These wooden kits can be com-
pleted with ease and displayed with pride. Newest models designed to snap together without need for tools or
nails. More traditional models fit together with pegs and
glue. Found in toy and craft shops. 6 & up.

MY MAGNET FRIENDS

(Crayola $9.99) Designed for less mess, this premixed
modeling compound gets molded, then painted as magnets. A craft kit that doesn't take forever and produces
decorative magnets. Other related kits using the same

modeling compound include bugs, dinosaurs and jewelry. 5 & up. (800) CRAYOLA.

PAPER MAKER–RECYCLING KITS

(Galt $48/Chasley $24.95) Our testers liked both of these kits, which really give kids a hands-on recyling experience. The Galt set is more expensive because it comes with another frame for making envelopes. Labeled 8 & up but sixes and sevens will enjoy this with adult assistance. (800) 448-4258/Chasley(800) 888-2898.

SPAGHETTI MACHINE 👑 PLATINUM AWARD

(Natural Science $19.99) Here's a great way to show kids the process behind making a food we usually take out of a box. A brand-new pasta machine that makes two sizes of spaghetti and four pasta shapes. Cooking calls for a little math and reading. Best of all, there's an edible ending! (800) 997-4674.

POUR AND PAINT

(Palmer $9 & up) This easy-to-mix plaster kit comes with five molds, mix, paint and backings for pins and magnets. Dries in 45 minutes. Some adult assistance may be needed. Two new and larger kits come with supplies and molds for 20 items. 7 & up. (800) 521-1383.

> **BOOK TIP:** *Great Newspaper Crafts* (by F. Virginia Walter, Sterling $9.95) Good news—or we should say good ways to recycle the news (paper) to make pinatas, paint brushes, paper beads, maracas and more than 80 projects.

STAMP-A-MANIA TOP-RATED SETS

ALPHABEASTS AND NUMBIRDS

(All Night Media $20) Each beast is in the shape of the letter that begins its name. For example, two alligators create the letter A. Numerals are formed with birds in this 42-piece set. Really neat! (415) 459-3013.

HIEROGLYPHICS STAMP KIT

(Penguin $20) Older students who are studying ancient Eygpt will be enthralled with this set of hieroglyphs that they can use for making messages or decorative art. Museum & book shops. 8 & up.

STAMP-A-STORY ADVENTURES

(All Night Media $19.50 each) The Stamp-A-Story sets are wonderful for creating cartoon strips and illustrating child-made storybooks. Our testers loved the rain forest, fairy tale and underwater adventure themes. The newest is a space theme. (415) 459-3013.

ROLLERSTAMPS

(Rubber Stampede $3–$5) Ducks, teddies, chicks all go merrily rolling along. Great for counting games and making giftwrap. (800) 632-8386.

VICTORIAN PAPER DOLL BEARS

(Rubber Stampede $20) This 15 stamp set includes a wardrobe of Victorian clothes to dress as a boy or girl teddy bear. Fun to cut out, color and dress. (800) 632-8386.

MUSICAL INSTRUMENTS AND TOYS

CHIME ALONG

(Woodstock Instruments $30 & up) Unlike most musical toys, the sound of this metal-chime xylophone won't drive you crazy. Its tone is lovely. Can be played by number/color or musical notation. Can be enjoyed by a preschooler, but becomes a true musical instrument in the hands of older children. 4 & up. (800) 422-4463.

MUSIC MAKER HARP   BLUE CHIP

(Peeleman-McLaughlin $50) No electronic sounds here. This is a cross between a zither and an autoharp, but much easier to learn to play. Slip one of 12 follow-the-dot song sheets under the strings and pluck. Has a soft and lovely tone that won't be intrusive and annoying. Includes folk, Beatles and classic music sheets. 6 & up. (800) 779-2205.

PIANO KEYBOARD

(Casio $40–$150) Without a huge investment, an electronic keyboard gives kids a taste of what learning to play the piano is like. Keyboards from 32 to 49 keys are for young kids. For eights and up consider four- to five-octave keyboards ($149 & up). O.K., it's not a Steinway, but for tight space and budget it's a place to start. Electronics stores. 6 & up.

Miracle Piano—See Computer Software/CD–ROM section.

STRIKE UP THE BAND

(Creativity for Kids $18.95) All the ingredients needed for making a bell tambourine, xylophone, drum, jug rattle, box guitar and more are in this box of goodies with clear directions. Kids will need some adult assistance. 5 & up. (216) 589-4800.

BIG-MUSCLE SPORTING EQUIPMENT

Young school kids are often more eager than able to play many games with rules. Often the real equipment is too heavy for them to use. Balls that are softer don't hurt as much and promote kids' confidence. The same is true of scaled-down bats, rackets and other equipment.

BALL GAMES EQUIPMENT

PITCH HITTER BASEBALL
(Today's Kids $20) Just in time for
spring training, this toy is perfect
for solo batting practice. Easy-to-
operate foot pedal pops the ball
out of the cone. Delayed action
with ticking sound allows the bat-
ter to get ready to hit a home run!
5 & up. (800) 258-8697.

SAFE-T-BALL
(Western Pacific Sports $5) A 9" leather baseball that
looks like, feels like and plays like a real baseball, but it's
much safer because it's lighter! Approved by Little
League. Available in sporting goods stores. (801) 225-
2795.

SOUND SWING BAT II
(Aviva $12) Designed to help beginners refine their bat-
ting skill. Young batters will enjoy practicing their swing
with this colorful marbleized foam bat and ball. The bat
makes the cracking sound of a home run when properly
swung, reinforcing good form and wrist action. 5 & up.
(800) 524-TOYS.

• •

SHOPPING TIP—BASKETBALL SETS:
Several companies make adjustable basketball
hoops for young players. Some with cardboard
posts and electronic scorekeepers are fun but for
indoor use only. Best choices are from Little Tikes,
Ohio Arts and Aviva. For older players go to a
sporting goods store for a real backboard.

• •

PRO NERF SOCCER BALL
(Nerf $12) Black color with hot-neon accents makes this
easy to spot. Like all Nerf balls, this is lighter than a real
soccer ball and safer for beginners. (800) 752-9755.

VOLLEYBALL

(Aviva $14) The neon pink and green fabric cover on this inflatable volleyball provides a sting-free surface that builds painless confidence for young players. Just the right size and weight to be user-friendly and yet have the feel of real equipment. 6 & up. (800) 524-TOYS.

RACKETS, PADDLES AND STICKS

AIR PRO HOCKEY   PLATINUM AWARD

(Mattel $40) An amazing two-player hockey set with powered puck that glides like it's on ice! Works indoors or out on flat, hard surface. Comes with two hockey sticks, goals and a foam-bumpered puck that works like a hovercraft. Requires 4 AA batteries for an hour of play, or use rechargeable batteries. 6 & up. (800) 524-8697.

KOOSH PADDLES

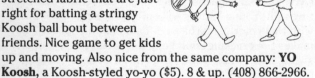

(OddzOn $16) Two paddles with brightly colored stretched fabric that are just right for batting a stringy Koosh ball bout between friends. Nice game to get kids up and moving. Also nice from the same company: **YO Koosh,** a Koosh-styled yo-yo ($5). 8 & up. (408) 866-2966.

TENNIS SET

(Aviva $17) Wimbledon, anyone? If you're not ready to make a big investment, this junior-sized racquet is a good choice. Comes with an oversized ball and a detachable whistle that sounds off when the racket is swung hard. 7 & up. (800) 524-TOYS.

●●

SHOPPING TIP:

To supplement practicing volleys against the garage door, an inexpensive "driveway" net will get good use. The nets are usually flimsy and won't last more than a season, so don't spend a lot.

●●

WHEEL TOYS

Shopping Checklist:

✔ Fives will continue to enjoy many of the wheel toys in the Preschool section. Although many will start pushing for a two-wheeler, they will be safer on a trike.

✔ By six or seven, most kids are ready and eager for a two-wheeler with training wheels. Steer clear of bikes with gears or hand brakes. Learning to balance is a big enough deal.

✔ Tempting as it may be to surprise your child, your best bet is to take your child to the store.

✔ Buy a bike that fits rather than one to "grow into."

✔ When kids straddle a bike they should be able to put a foot on the ground for balance.

✔ Budget and size will dictate the choices. Hedstrom ($100 & up), Schwinn ($130 & up) and Huffy ($100 & up) offer solidly built 16" bikes with adjustable training wheels and an assortment of accessories.

✔ Helmets do help! According to the Consumer Product Safety Commission, one in seven children suffers head injuries in bike-related accidents. While studies show that wearing helmets reduces the risk of injury by 85%, the sad fact is that only 5% of bike-riding kids actually wear helmets.

SCOOTER

(Radio Flyer $50) This classic scooter will give miles of pleasure as kids learn to push and coast and balance on one leg. (800) 621-7613.

KETTLECAR GRAND PRIX RACER

(Kettler $118) This classic racing car has stout wheels, pedal action, a steering wheel and a sporty look. It can be adjusted for kids as their legs grow longer, so it's a toy with a few good years in it. 5–8. (804) 752-9755.

Retro Toys and Games

Yo-yos, jacks and hopscotch are still enjoyed by kids in this age group. Here we've given you some variations on classic toys as well as the rules to games you probably played in the backyard.

BUBBLE WANDS:

Blowing bubbles has come a long way from the small plastic containers of pink liquid with a small, sticky wand. Today there are wonderful large wands (Nubo $5 and up) and novelty bubble blowers in the shape of tennis rackets and bats (Toostie Toys $5 & up).

• •

ACTIVITY TIP:

For super-large bubbles mix 1 cup of Dawn liquid detergent with 3 tablespoons of Karo Syrup in 2 1/2 quarts of cold water. Stir gently. Leftovers (if you have any) need to be refrigerated. Ideal for large groups.

• •

SOCK SCOTCH

(My Dreams $30) For indoors or out (where chalk is a no-no) kids will have a hopping good time in their socks with this 3' × 8' bright-red hopscotch mat. Made of heavy-grade slip-proof fabric, the mat comes with two bean bags and instructions. 5–8. (801) 944-0312.

BOOK TIP: *Hopscotch Around the World* (by Mary D. Lankford, Morrow $15).

ROD HOCKEY: WAYNE GRETSKY'S NHL ALL STAR HOCKEY PLATINUM AWARD

(SLM $99) This handsome tabletop rod-hockey set comes with all-star teams but can be customized with favorite NHL teams or players with kids' own names! 7 & up. (800) 442-7440.

TOPS:

Doodletops (Doodletop Co. $3) are tops with a real twist. Pen fits into top for dashing desktop doodles!

TOPTICAL

(Learning Materials Workshop $11.80) A big wooden spinning top that comes with a rainbow of color discs that slip on the spindle for open-ended experiments in color mixing. (802) 862-8399.

• •

ACTIVITY TIPS:

Here are two great games for the backyard.

"Green Light, Go!" "It" stands at one end of playing area and others stand at starting line. It turns his back and says, "Red light, green light, 1, 2, 3!" Players run toward It. As It says "3" he faces players. Anyone It sees moving is sent back to the line. Object: To be the first to tap It and become the new It.

Shadow Tag A sunny-day game. "It" tries to step on the shadow of other players. Player is out when It steps on his shadow. Last shadow stepped on becomes It.

• •

SCIENCE TOYS AND EQUIPMENT

Science is still best understood with hands-on materials. Favorite equipment: magnifiers, magnets, gyroscopes, kalidoscopes, prisms and a compass.

BACKYARD BUG KIT

(Nature Co. $17.95) Everything you need for close-up bug investigations: a 5" mesh bug house, a 4 ¹/₂" hand-held magnifier, a 3" plastic magnifying box and a booklet. 5 & up. (800) 227-1114.

BUG STAMP KIT

(Rubber Stampede $7.95) Monarch butterflies, dragonflies, spiders, bees and more! Eleven bug stampers and washable stamp pad for making story/counting books. 5 & up. (800) 632-8389.

BUTTERFLY GARDEN KITS

(Constructive Playthings $19.95) Front-row seats to the metamorphosis of a caterpillar. Kit has a 12" square cardboard butterfly habitat with round viewing windows, feeding kit, guide and coupon for five live caterpillars. #ILP-1000. (800) 832-0572.

DINOSAUR HUNTER'S KIT

(Running Press $16.95) Paleontologists-in-training will love this kit, which includes a replica Apatosaurus fossil buried in stone, a dinosaur-hunter's handbook and the necessary tools for excavating the fossil. 6–7 with adult. Solo 8 & up. See also Geode Kit and Gem Hunter's Kit. Available in book stores.

FUN WITH MAGNETS DISCOVERY KIT

(Toys to Grow On $19.95) Comes with magnetic wand, ten magnet balls, block magnet, four shaped magnets, horseshoe magnets, nuts and washers and box with a magnetic bottom. Extra wand $2. # 929. (800) 542-8338.

OH GROW UP

(Creativity for Kids $12.99) Everthing for growing a variety of windowsill experiments. Kit includes bean, grass and corn seeds, peatpots, sponge, planting tubes, a plant maze box, plaster, magnifier and clear directions for hands-on learning. Adult assistance will be needed for children under 6. (216) 589-4800.

SOLARGRAPHICS

($9.95) Kit with 40 sheets of light-sensitive paper. Kids can make a "photo" by simply putting object on paper in the sun and then rinsing paper in water. Presto! A negative image of the object appears. (800) 933-3277.

NEW WAYS OF LOOKING—OBSERVATION TOOLS

GIANT PERISCOPE

(Constructive Playthings $9.25) With this 22" tall periscope kids can look around corners and over fences. Fun for pretend spy games and for getting some new perspectives about the world. Unbreakable mirrors for safety. #HAD-6095. (800) 832-0572.

KALEIDOSCOPES

(Galt $8) This ready-made kaleidoscope allows fives & sixes to get a different view by changing the contents of the end piece. (800) 899-4258. Older kids will love **I Made My . . . Kaleidoscope** (Homecrafters $15). They construct the inside workings of this kaleidoscope. Three unbreakable Mylar mirrors fit into the see-through plastic tube. The end piece can be loaded with ever-changing contents for new sights. A great parent/child project for 5–7 or solo for 8 & up. (800) 972-5235.

MICROSCOPES

GEOSCOPE

(TBS Products $34.95) A sturdy hand-held plastic microscope perfect for studying pond water and other watery environments. #SUS-444 Constructive Playthings. (800) 832-0572.

BEGINNERS MICROSCOPES

(Tasco $18 & up) This company is a great source for classic and innovative desk-top models. 6 & up. (305) 591-3670.

MOVIE MOTION ZOETROPE

(DaMert $10) Like the old-fashioned movie machines you see in science museums, the cylinder spins and animation film strips start moving. Comes with 12 premade film strips and a dozen blanks for creating cartoons. 7 & up. (800) 231-3722.

POLIOPTICON OPTICS

($49.95) Kids can make ten different optical instruments, including telescope, microscope and kaleidoscope, with clear step-by-step instructions. 6 & up. #D38.411 Edmund Scientific. (609) 573-6250.

BEST TRAVEL TOYS AND GAMES

- **Audio tapes and players**. For great choices see Audio section.
- **Hip Pak** (Ritvik $5) A neat way for travelers to take their building bricks along. One hundred micro-sized blocks store in zipped hip pack. (800) 465-MEGA.
- **Lanyard Kit** (Alex $8) This classic craft is quiet, time-consuming and not messy. 7 & up. (201) 569-5757.
- **3-D Slide Puzzles** (DaMert $6) These little hand-held puzzles are real brain-teasers. Our testers loved the dinosaur. Frog, turtle, and sea star also available. 8 & up. (800) 231-3722.
- **Travel Etch-a-Sketch** (Ohio Art $7) With no loose parts, this mini-version of a classic comes in its own red travel tote. 5 & up.
- **Traveling box**. Create your own with a metal cookie tin that can be used with magnetic letters and hold favorite art supplies!

BEST BIRTHDAY GIFTS FOR EVERY BUDGET

Best Gifts $100 & more	Train(Lego) or Dollhouse (Playmobil)
Best Gifts $75	Erector Set (Meccano) or Samantha Doll (Pleasant Co.)
Best Gifts $50	Music Maker Harp (Peeleman) or tape player
Best Gifts $30	Puppets or computer software
Best Gifts $25	Stamp-a-Story Kit (All Night Media) or Koosh Paddles (OddzOn)
Best Gifts $15	Storybook or board game or magazine subscription
Best Gifts $10	Abracadabra Magic (T. C. Timber) or video or art supplies
Best Gifts $5	Paperback book or Graffic Traffic (Matchbox) or Doodle Tops (Doodle Top)

2 ★ BOOKS

Reading to children is more than a great way to entertain them. Studies show that young children who are read to every day learn to read earlier and with greater ease. But quite aside from the academic benefits, sharing books with children is one of the pleasurable ways of being together. With books we can share the thrill of adventure, the excitement of suspense, and the warm satisfaction of happily ever afters. Through books we can help children find answers to their questions about real things and how they work. Books give grown-ups and children a ticket that transports them from everyday events to a world of faraway, long ago and once upon a time.

Books are arranged by age groups. "Coping with life" and holiday book sections include books for mixed ages. You'll also find recommended reference books, encyclopedias and magazines for mixed ages at the end of the section.

An "also" after a review indicates other recommended titles by that author.

BABIES AND YOUNG TODDLERS

At this stage books are not merely for looking at. Babies and toddler tend to taste, toss and tear their books. Even sturdy cardboard books may not survive this search-and-destroy stage. Cloth and vinyl make good chewable choices. The mechanics of turning pages, pointing to pictures and even listening make books among baby's favorite playthings and a key to language development. Choose books with  clear pictures of familiar things to know, name and talk about. Single images on a page are easier to "read." Little stories that center on the child's world are most appropriate for young toddlers.

Ten Blue-Chip Books Every Baby and Young Toddler Should Know

★ ★ ★

- *Baby Animal Friends,* by Phoebe Dunn
- *Baby's Bedtime Book,* by Kay Chorao
- *Baby's First Words,* by Lars Wik
- *I See,* by Rachel Isadora
- *Mother Goose*
- *Spot's Toys,* by Eric Hill
- *This Is Me,* by Lenore Blegvad
- *Tom and Pippo* series, by Helen Oxenbury
- *What Do Babies Do?* by Debby Slier
- *What Is It?* by Tana Hoban

CLOTH, VINYL & BOARD BOOKS FOR INFANTS & TODDLERS

There are loads of wonderful sturdy books for the very young. Here are some favorites.

BABY ANIMAL FRIENDS   BLUE CHIP
(by Phoebe Dunn, Random $2.95) Clear photos of real animals with children, two subjects babies love to watch. Fits in a fat little fist. Also *Farm Animals* and *Zoo Animals.*

BABY INSIDE

(by Neil Ricklen, Simon & Schuster $4.95) Delightful photos of busy tots doing all the things they love to do. Photos are labeled with a single word, but each is ripe for conversation. Also *Baby Outside, Mommy and Me, Daddy and Me*.

BABY'S FIRST WORDS   BLUE CHIP

(photos by Lars Wik, Random $2.95) A little book that fits easily in tiny hands with photos of familiar things. There's something about this particular book, maybe the banana, that makes it a favorite.

HEN ON THE FARM

(by Lucy Cousins, Candlewick $4.95) Using bright, cheerful single images on a page, Cousins has created a series of beautiful cloth books. Also *Flower in the Garden*.

I SEE AND I TOUCH   BLUE CHIP

(by Rachel Isadora, Greenwillow $6.95 each) Two classic baby books trace baby's day and the things he sees and touches.

LET'S EAT/VAMOS A COMER   🏅 PLATINUM AWARD

(illus. by Hideo Shirotani, Simon & Schuster $2.95) For bilingual babies, familiar food and utensils are labeled on each page in English and Spanish. Also *What Color?*

LET'S LOOK AT MY WORLD
🏅 PLATINUM AWARD

(by Dick Witt, Scholastic $5.95) Black-and-white art with patterns, faces and colored borders. Could be used standing on changing board and turned to different pages from day to day or for lap looking time.

> **SAFETY TIP:** Small cardboard books with wheels are not for kids under three because the wheels can be a choking hazard!

MY TOYS

(by Sian Tucker, Little Simon $2.95) Tucker's vivid palette and graphic style is especially pleasing to the eye. Also *Numbers; At Home;* and *My Clothes*.

PAT-A-CAKE, PAT-A-CAKE

(illus. by Moira Kemp, Dutton $2.50) One of a charming set of finger-play rhymes. Perfect for lap games. Actions to go with words are shown. Also *I'm a Little Teapot*.

SPOT'S TOYS

(by Eric Hill, Putnam $3.95) A famous pooch you'll be getting to know in many toddler books is introduced in this washable vinyl book with all his toys.

> **TOY TIP:** Spot Puppet (Eden $18) With Velcro paws and a bright ball, this puppet is ready to play. (212) 947-4400.

THIS IS ME   BLUE CHIP

(by Lenore Blegvad/illus. by Erik Blegvad, Random House $2.95) A little book with a simple verse that begins, "These are my eyes, this is my nose, these are my fingers."

THIS LITTLE BABY GOES OUT

(by Lynn Breeze, Little Brown $5.95) Told in rhyming couplets, this big board book captures an outing to the park and back. Also *Playtime; Bedtime;* and *Morning*.

TOM AND PIPPO ON THE BEACH

(by Helen Oxenbury, Candlewick $5.95) Daddy says Tom needs to wear a sun hat on the beach, but Tom thinks his monkey Pippo needs it more. When Daddy makes a paper hat for Pippo, Tom prefers it to the cloth one. 2 & up.

WHAT DO BABIES DO?

(photos compiled by Debby Slier, Random House $3.95)
A collection of photos of babies doing such typical things
as eating, sleeping, and playing. On sturdy cardboard.

WHAT IS IT?

(by Tana Hoban, Greenwillow $4.95) Striking photos of
objects baby will recognize, by a master photographer.
Also *Red, Blue, Yellow Shoe* and *Black on White*.

RESOURCES FOR PARENTS

MOTHER GOOSE

There are many beautiful collections of Mother Goose
Rhymes. Take the time to
look for an illustrator that's
your personal favorite. You'll
use this as a resource for
poems to recite aloud long
before you sit and read it to
your child. Here are a few
favorites to consider: *Mother*

Goose (illus. by Michael Foreman, Harcourt Brace
$19.95); *Mother Goose* (illus. by Tomie de Paola, Putnam
$18.95); *Mother Goose* (illus. by Arnold Lobel, Random
House $15); *The Little Books of Nursery Animals* (illus. by
Diane Goode, Dutton $11.99).

PAT-A-CAKE AND OTHER PLAY RHYMES

(compiled by Joanna Cole and Stephanie Calmenson.
Morrow $14) A great resource full of 30 hand-clapping
and knee-bouncing rhymes to say and play almost any
time of day. Rhymes are illustrated with step-by-step
"how-to" directions.

FINGER RHYMES

(illus. by Marc Brown, Dutton $12.95) Fourteen finger-
play rhymes are illustrated in small frames beside the
verse. Includes rhymes like "Thumbkin," "Eensy Weensie
Spider" and others. 2 & up.

BABY'S BEDTIME BOOK

(by Kay Chorao, Dutton $13.95) Beautifully illustrated collection of slumber songs from all over the world. Also *Baby's Lap Book*.

OLDER TODDLERS

By age two toddlers are ready for new kinds of books. Just as they can understand almost anything you say, they can also follow books with small  stories. They like playful language with rhythm, rhyme and repetitive lines they can chime in on. They enjoy stories about children like themselves. Toddlers also love books about real things like colors, caterpillars and cars. Choose books you really like because toddlers like to hear their favorites again and again!

• • • • • • • • • • • • • •

Ten Blue-Chip Books Every Toddler Should Know

★ ★ ★

- *Good Night Moon,* by M. W. Brown
- *Jamberry,* by Bruce Degen
- *Wheels on the Bus,* adapted by Paul Zelinsky
- *Polar Bear, Polar Bear, What Do You Hear?* by Bill Martin, Jr.
- *Sheep in a Shop,* by Nancy Shaw
- *Where's Spot?* by Eric Hill
- *First Words for Babies and Toddlers,* by Jane Salt
- *You Go Away,* by Lois Axeman
- *When You Were a Baby,* by Ann Jonas
- *A Very Hungry Caterpillar,* by Eric Carle

BOOKS WITH REPETITIVE LINES— RHYTHM AND RHYME

ARE THERE SEALS IN THE SANDBOX?

(by Ethel and Len Kessler, Simon & Schuster $4.95) Toddlers enjoy the zany upside-down humor and power of shouting "Oh no!" to the unlikely places seals appear. 1 1/2 & up.

HICKORY DICKORY DOCK

(illus. by Carol Jones, Houghton Mifflin $10.95) A handful of the best-known nursery rhymes, such as "Little Bo-peep," "Hey Diddle Diddle" and others, are wonderfully illustrated. Every other page has a peekaboo hole that frames the characters. 1 1/2 & up.

JAMBERRY   BLUE CHIP

(by Bruce Degen, HarperCollins paper $3.95) A totally delicious nonsense rhyme about every kind of berry in the world. The playful lilt of the rhyme and rhythm will be enjoyed and chanted by preschoolers as well. 2 & up.

MOO, BAA, LA LA LA

(by Sandra Boynton, Simon & Schuster $3.95) Boynton's wacky verses and visual humor make for a silly lap book. 1 & up.

MOONBEAR'S CANOE

(by Frank Asch, Simon & Schuster $3.95) With a repetitive refrain that toddlers will soon know by heart, Moonbear keeps adding friends to his canoe until at last they all end up swimming together. One of a charming series about Moonbear. 2 & up.

MOTHER HUBBARD'S CUPBOARD   '94   PLATINUM AWARD

(illus. by Laura Rader, Tambourine $12.95) A wonderfully clever take on familiar nursery rhymes with split pages that reveal both action and verse. 1 & up.

SHEEP IN A SHOP   PLATINUM AWARD

(by Nancy Shaw/illus. by Margot Apple, Houghton Mifflin $12.95) Five woolly sheep set out on a zany shopping trip. After stirring up a storm in a store they end up getting fleeced to pay the bill. Tots love the bouncy rhyme and birthday cake ending! 2 & up.

First Little Mysteries

LITTLE BUDDY GOES SHOPPING
⭐'94 **PLATINUM AWARD**

(by Patrick Yee, Viking $10.95) A juanty bunny goes shopping in this lift-and-look flap book. "Do you sell carrots?" he asks each shopkeeper. Young readers will soon "read" the windows of the shop and predict what's inside. 2 & up.

MISTER MOMBOO'S HAT

(by Ralph Lemmis/illus. by Jeni Bassett, Cobblehill $11.95) Mister Momboo's hat flies off his head and has some unusual experiences. The traveling hat's adventures are recounted in rhyme. 2 & up.

POLAR BEAR, POLAR BEAR, WHAT DO YOU HEAR?
PLATINUM AWARD

(by Bill Martin, Jr./illus. by Eric Carle, Henry Holt $13.95) Eric Carle's bold and brilliant beasts and Martin's simple but rhythmic rhyme make perfect harmony! Young listeners love chiming in on the telling. Also see *Brown Bear, Brown Bear, What Do You See?* 2 & up.

WHAT CAN RABBIT SEE? AND WHAT CAN RABBIT HEAR?

(by Lucy Cousins, Tamborine $12. 95 each) Two charming lift-the-flap books featuring Rabbit using his senses to find creatures hiding in the grass, a stable, a tree. There's always enough of the hidden creature peeping out to give kids a hint. 2 & up.

WHERE'S MY BABY?   BLUE CHIP

(by H. A. Rey, Houghton Mifflin $2.95) Where is cow's baby? Open the flap and you'll find the calf. One of a small set of fold-out books by the author of *Curious George*. We wish they were on sturdier stock, but these are classics. 2 & up.

WHERE'S SPOT?

(by Eric Hill, Putnam $11.95) Spot the pup is missing! Where can he be? Lift the flaps and see! Not much story here, but the suspense is toddler-sized. Be prepared: Little hands may not be able to lift without a rip. Series is uneven—some are better than others.

SLICE-OF-LIFE BOOKS

Day-to-day events with family and friends make just the right-sized story for toddlers.

ANNABEL PLATINUM AWARD

(by Janice Boland/illus. by Megan Halsey, Dial $12.99) Annabel does not want to be little. She wants to do important things like the other creatures. She discovers that being herself is what others like about her the best. 2 & up.

BENNY BAKES A CAKE

(by Eve Rice, Greenwillow $14) Benny and his mom make a cake that his big dog Ralph devours. But Dad saves the day. A reissue of a simple story with a happy ending about a topic toddlers adore. 2 & up.

GOLDEN BEAR PLATINUM AWARD

(by Ruth Young/illus. by Rachel Isadora, Viking $14) A rhythmic verse captures the special bond between a small African-American child and his teddy bear as they play together through the day. 2 & up.

NICKY AND GRANDPA

(by Cathryn Falwell, Clarion $5.95) A charming romp featuring Nicky and his Grandpa. One of an excellent series about Nicky and the people in his life, including Daddy and his brother Alex. 1 & 2.

COPING WITH LIFE'S LITTLE UPS AND DOWNS

GOING TO THE DOCTOR

(by Fred Rogers/photos by Jim Judkis, Putnam paper $5.95) For toddlers this is often an unhappy event. Reading and talking about it with the reassuring Mr. Rogers may help older toddlers get a handle on what to expect and lessen the fears. Maybe.

JESSE BEAR, WHAT WILL YOU WEAR?
(by Nancy White Carlstrom/illus. by Bruce Degen, Macmillan $13.95) Here's a story with a sense of humor about getting dressed, which isn't always easy or funny.

WHEN YOU WERE A BABY   BLUE CHIP
(by Ann Jonas, Greenwillow $6.95) Toddlers sometimes need assurance that they are growing up and able to do things that babies can't do. An especially good choice for dealing with the arrival of a baby when kids have ambivalence about growing up.

YOU GO AWAY   BLUE CHIP
(by Dorothy Corey/illus. by Lois Axeman, Whitman $10.95) With the repeated refrains of "You go away" and "You come back," this reassuring book tells little ones that although parents sometimes go out for a bit, we do come back. 1–3.

POTTY CORNER (RESULTS NOT GUARANTEED!)

GOING TO THE POTTY
(by Fred Rogers/photos by Jim Judkis, Putnam $5.95) In his usual reassuring way, Mister Rogers talks with children about using the potty. This photo essay reinforces the idea that using a potty is another step toward growing up. 2 & up.

KOKO BEAR'S NEW POTTY
(by Vicki Lansky, Bantam $3.95) Koko is a little bear who is learning how to become more independent by using the potty. Each page also includes a few of Lansky's tips for parents on their role. 2 & up.

YOUR NEW POTTY

(by Joanna Cole/photos by Margaret Miller, Morrow paper $4.95) Steffie and Ben make the switch from diapers to potty. Excellent parents' section. 2 & up.

SWEET DREAMS—BEDTIME BOOKS

ASLEEP, ASLEEP
PLATINUM AWARD

(by Mirra Ginsburg/illus. by Nancy Tafuri, Greenwillow $14) A hypnotic, repetitive pattern and rhyme make this a perfect bedtime poem that's like a lullaby to soothe little ones off to sleep. 2 & up.

GOOD NIGHT MOON   BLUE CHIP

(by M. W. Brown/illus. by C. Hurd, HarperCollins $6.95) Happy news! This bedtime classic is available in a sturdy board book that toddlers can enjoy without ripping. 18 mos. & up. Also packaged with bunny in blue-striped pajamas. ($19.95).

TIME FOR BED ⭐ PLATINUM AWARD

(by Mem Fox/illus. by Jane Dyer, Harcourt Brace $13.95) There's a quiet charm, simplicity and rhythm as each of the big creatures tells its little one that it is time for bed. You won't mind reading this one again and again. 2 & up.

EARLY CONCEPT BOOKS—
COLOR, COUNTING AND MORE

CAN YOU GUESS?

(by Margaret Miller, Greenwillow $14) Young listeners get right into the silly questions and find great satisfaction in knowing the answers to what you do and do not put into a mailbox, on your head, or in the sink. A terrific sequel to *Where Does It Go?* 2 & up.

FIRST WORDS FOR BABIES AND TODDLERS

(by Jane Salt/illus. by Gerald Hawlsley, Random House $9.95) Like an encyclopedia for toddlers! More than 200 familiar objects sorted by likenesses are shown separately and also embedded in scenes. On sturdy pages, this thick oblong book is fun for "I spy" games and for talking together. 1 & up.

I LOVE MY MOMMY BECAUSE AND I LOVE MY DADDY BECAUSE   PLATINUM AWARD

(by Laurel Porter-Gaylord/illus. by Ashley Wolff, Dutton $5.95) Two concept books about many different kinds of parent and baby pairs. With just one line of text per page, the books manage to convey the link we and the animals share in caring for our young.

MY FIRST LOOK AT COLORS

(by Jane Yorke, Random House $7) Each two-page spread has objects of a single color, all easy to identify and splendidly photographed. From the excellent *My First Look At* series, all with luscious full-color photos to count, sort and talk about. On kid-proof slick stock sturdy enough for toddlers. 2 & up.

ONE RED ROOSTER

(by Kathleen Carroll/illus. by Suzette Barbier, Houghton Mifflin $13.95) Big toddlers who love to count and make animal sounds will enjoy doing both with the bouncy rhythms and vibrant illustrations in this simple 1 to 10 counting book. 2–5.

ONE, TWO, ONE PAIR!

(by Bruce McMillan, Scholastic $12.95) With crisp photos and a repetitive pattern, McMillan builds a basic math concept of what we mean by a pair. All the familiar items such as socks, shoes, etc., are capped off with a surprise pair—of twins! 2–5.

ONE YELLOW LION
PLATINUM AWARD

(by Matthew Van Fleet, Dial $7.95) A color and counting concept book with surprises behind each fold-out page that reveal colorful zany critters to count. Builds to a five-page mural with all the featured creatures. On sturdy stock. 2 & up.

PRETEND YOU'RE A CAT
(by Jean Marzollo/illus. by Jerry Pinkney, Dial $13) In bouncy verse kids are asked to sound and act like a variety of animals. A delightful invitation to role-playing and understanding the differences between animals. 2 & up.

A VERY HUNGRY CATERPILLAR BLUE CHIP
(by Eric Carle, Philomel $15.95) Toddlers love the repetition of the text, the subject of eating and poking their little fingers into all the little holes the hungry caterpillar has eaten through. A science book that will also be enjoyed by preschoolers. 2 & up.

TRANSPORTATION

CARS AND TRUCKS AND THINGS THAT GO
(by Richard Scarry, Golden $12.50) Busy transportation scenes with tons of details and humor that older toddlers and preschoolers adore.

THE LITTLE CAR
(by Sian Tucker, Little Simon $2.95) Bright Matisse-like palette has great visual appeal in this cardboard book about a little car that takes a small trip. Others in series feature The Little Boat, Plane or Train. 1 & up.

PEOPLE, PEOPLE EVERYWHERE!
(by Nancy Van Laan/illus. by Nadine B. Westcott, Knopf $13) A snappy read-aloud tour from city to country and people everywhere. 2–5.

WHEELS ON THE BUS

(illus. by Paul Zelinsky, Dutton $14.95) The wheels on the page actually do go round and round—and that's just the beginning of the fun! Pull tabs to make the doors "open and shut," the driver motion "move on back." This book gets so much use it can't stand up to the wear and tear—but it is a favorite! Old twos love it, but it may last longer with threes and fours. Lots of luck!

WHERE'S DADDY'S CAR?

(by Harriet Ziefert/illus. by Andrea Baruffi, HarperCollins paper $5.95) Lift the flaps and find Daddy's car at the gas station, on the bridge, at the garage and home again. Also *Where's Mommy's Truck?* Mommy, a carpenter, drives a truck to work and knows how to change a tire. 2 & up.

ZIP, WHIZ, ZOOM!
PLATINUM AWARD

(by Stephanie Calmenson/illus. by Dorothy Stott, Little Brown $13.95) Everyone in this huge family is going somewhere in a different mode of transportation and everyone has a gift. Moves right in on toddlers' love of things that go and birthdays—in this case, Grandma's! 2 & up.

PRESCHOOL BOOKS FOR THREES AND FOURS

Preschoolers delight in books of all kinds. They enjoy longer stories about real kids like themselves and animal stories that are really about "kids in fur" with whom they can identify. Folktales and fantasy are fine as long as they're not too scary. They like the rhythm and rhyme of verse as well as prose that touches their hearts and funny bones. Eager to learn, they like playful counting and alphabet books. Kids are also interested in true facts about real things that match their curiosity about the world.

● ● ● ● ● ● ● ● ● ● ● ● ●
*Ten Blue-Chip Books
Every Preschooler Should Know*

★ ★ ★

- *Runaway Bunny,* by M. W. Brown
- *Tale of Peter Rabbit,* by Beatrix Potter
- *Little Engine That Could,* by Watty Piper
- *Curious George,* by H. A. Rey
- *Caps for Sale,* by Esphyr Slobodkina
- *Millions of Cats,* by Wanda Gag
- *Ask Mr. Bear,* by Marjorie Flack
- *A Snowy Day,* by Ezra Jack Keats
- *Nutshell Library,* by Maurice Sendak
- *Make Way for Ducklings,* by Robert McCloskey

GREAT READ-ALOUDS

ASK MR. BEAR BLUE CHIP

(by Marjorie Flack, Aladdin paper
$3.95) Danny is looking for a perfect
gift for his mother's birthday. He asks
each animal he meets along the way.
Hen offers him eggs, Goose offers feathers, Lamb
offers wool, but Mother has all of these. Finally, a brown
bear tells Danny exactly what he can give his mother—a
great big bear hug! Repetitive refrain makes this a sure
read-aloud hit.

CAPS FOR SALE BLUE CHIP

(by Esphyr Slobodkina, HarperTrophy paper $3.95) What
happens when an old peddler falls asleep and a treeful of
monkeys take his stack of hats? With its repetitive refrain
and humor, this has been a favorite read-aloud for generations.

CURIOUS GEORGE BLUE CHIP

(by H. A. Rey, Houghton Mifflin $14.95) One of many sat-
isfying tales of an adventuresome monkey and the man
in the big yellow hat. You probably grew up with this storybook character who remains a favorite. 3–7.

THE DRESS I'LL WEAR TO THE PARTY   PLATINUM AWARD

(by Shirley Neitzel/illus. by Nancy Winslow Parker, Greenwilllow $14) A cumulative tale done in the style of "The House That Jack Built," but here a small girl is dressing in her mother's things—until Mother discovers. 4–7.

FROGGY GETS DRESSED

(by Jonathan London/illus. by Frank Remkiewick, Viking $13) Kids will giggle over the all-too-familiar bother of bundling up to go out in the snow, and they'll love chiming on the repetitive "zoop! zup! zap!" sound effects as Froggy keeps dressing and undressing and forgetting little things like his pants. 3–6.

IF YOU GIVE A MOUSE A COOKIE   BLUE CHIP

(by Laura J. Numeroff/illus. by Felicia Bond, Harper-Collins $12.95) What happens if you give a mouse a cookie? The next thing you know he'll want a glass of milk. Kids love the delicious cause-and-effect way the story builds.

THE LITTLE ENGINE THAT COULD   BLUE CHIP

(by Watty Piper/illus. by George and Doris Hauman, Platt & Munk paper $4.95) What better way to give kids the words for building perserverance and confidence? I think it can, I think it can, I think it can! 3–6.

NOAH'S ARK

(retold & illus. by Lucy Cousins, Candlewick $14.95) With her own exuberant style, Cousins has created a visual delight that makes this version of Noah's Ark especially appealing to young audiences. 3 & up.

THE NUTSHELL LIBRARY   BLUE CHIP

(by Maurice Sendak, HarperCollins $11.89) Each of the four little books in this collection is a gem in its own right. Fours adore the defiant Pierre who declares he doesn't care . . . until a lion teaches him to do so. Then there's the most delicious compendium of months to sip and chant in *Chicken Soup and Rice*. *One Was Johnny* is a counting book and *Alligators All Around* an amusing alphabet.

PIGS APLENTY, PIGS GALORE

(by David McPhail, Dutton $13.99) This is the kind of slapstick humor and rhythmic verse that kids relish. Imagine pigs arriving by boat and plane, by parachutes, a bus and train for a feast of pizza that makes a house look like a sty! A quick, light good-night bonbon. 2-6.

SHEEP OUT TO EAT   PLATINUM AWARD

(by Nancy Shaw/illus. by Margot Apple, Houghton Mifflin $13.95) Get ready, you'll be reading this one "Again!" and "Again!" Five bumbling sheep go out to eat and turn a tea shop upside down. A deliciously crafted blend of rhythmic text and witty illustrations. Also *Sheep in a Jeep.* 2 & up.

STOP THIEF! PLATINUM AWARD

(by Robert Kalan/illus. by Yossi Abolafia, Greenwillow $14) A grey squirrel finds a nut, but a red squirrel claims it's his because it fell from his tree. So it goes as one creature after another claims it until it goes full circle. 3–6.

WHEN THE ROOSTER CROWED

(by Patricia Lillie/illus. by Nancy Winslow Parker, Greenwillow $13.95) Lots of kids will identify with a farmer who doesn't want to get up when rooster crows or horses neigh. But the farmer's wife and a cast of barnyard creatures make sleep impossible.

WHERE'S MY TEDDY?

(by Jez Alborough, Candlewick $14.95) What a mix-up! A big bear and a small boy have lost their teddy bears and find the wrong ones. All's well that ends well in this funny fantasy. 4 & up.

ALL IN THE FAMILY

DADDIES
(by Adele A. Greenspun, Philomel $15.95) Inspired by the love of her own father, this beautiful photo essay is accompanied by a lyrical homage to daddies. 3–6.

MAMA, DO YOU LOVE ME?
(by Barbara Joosse/illus. by Barbara Lavallee, Chronicle $12.95) An ode to unconditional love. With a series of "what if?" questions a child tests the limits and finds reassuring answers. Set in the Arctic, Lavallee's illustrations convey a picture of another culture along with the universal theme of love between parent and child. 3 & up.

RED DANCING SHOES
(by Denise L. Patrick/illus. by James E. Ransome, Tamborine $14) Happiness is a pair of shiny red shoes—until someone steps in a puddle. Anyone who has ever loved the unwrinkled sheen of new shoes will understand the highs and lows of this story. 4–7.

THE TALE OF PETER RABBIT   BLUE CHIP
(by Beatrix Potter, F. Warne paper $5.95) A timeless tale of a mischievous bunny who goes where he is not supposed to and suffers the consequences of his actions. Don't miss some of the other gems in the Potter collection, such as *Jemima Puddleduck* and *The Tale of Benjamin Bunny*.

THUNDER CAKE
(by Patricia Polacco, Philomel $14.95) When the lightning and thunder frighten a little girl under the bed, Grandma helps her overcome her fear by baking a Thunder Cake. Polacco's folk art is topped off with a recipe you can stir up for a finale. 4–6.

TRADE-IN MOTHER

(by Marisabina Russo, Greenwillow $14) Max's mother just won't do things his way. Max is so angry he says that he's going to trade her in! There's plenty of tongue-in-cheek humor and a happy ending when Mother assures Max she would never trade him in—no matter what! 3–7.

WHEN I AM OLD WITH YOU

(by Angela Johnson/illus. by David Soman, Orchard $14.95) A tender, lyrical love poem in prose between a little girl and her granddaddy. "When I am old with you" . . . she tells him of all the things they will do together. 4–7.

WHEN I WAS LITTLE ★ PLATINUM AWARD

(by Jamie Lee Curtis/illus. by Laura Cornell, Harper-Collins $14) Subtitled "A Four-Year-Old's Memoir of Her Youth," this spirited narrative captures the can-do attitude of a little girl who has a very positive sense of how big she has grown. 3–5.

SEPARATION

OWEN

(by Kevin Henkes, Greenwillow $14) When it's time for young Owen to go off to preschool, finding a way to leave his security blanket behind becomes a cause célèbre in the family. Mama finds a way to cut through the problem and comes up with a perfect solution. 3–6.

THE RUNAWAY BUNNY BLUE CHIP

(by Margaret Wise Brown/illus. by Clement Hurd, Harper-Collins $12) A little bunny declares his independence and his mother assures him that wherever he goes she'll be there for him.

WHERE'S OUR MAMA?
PLATINUM AWARD

(by Diane Goode, Dutton $13.95) Two French children get separated from their Mama in a train station. The gendarme asks, "What does your Mama look like?" Like most children, they say

Mama is the most beautiful woman in the world. So begins a comic search to match the children's superlatives. Magnifique! 3–7.

YOU'RE MY NIKKI
(by Phylis Rose Eisenberg/illus. by Jill Kastner, Dial $14) As Mama prepares to start a new job, Nikki worries that Mama may forget her and her favorite things. A warm and reassuring read-aloud, especially for moms and kids who are getting ready or just making the transition to working outside the home. 3–5.

BEDTIME

GOING TO SLEEP ON THE FARM   PLATINUM AWARD
(by Wendy C. Lewison/illus. by Juan Wijngaard, Dial $13) A little boy asks his dad how each of the animals goes to sleep. An almost hypnotic, quiet book for bedtime. 2–5.

THE STORY BOOK PRINCE
(by Joanne Oppenheim/illus. by Rosanne Litzinger, Harcourt Brace $12.95) In a faraway kingdom, a long time ago, when bedtime came the Prince said, "No!" So begins a series of comic attempts to lull the boy to sleep. 3–6.

TEN, NINE, EIGHT
(by Molly Bang, Greenwillow $15) A delightful counting-backward book in bouncy rhyme as a girl goes to sleep counting the things in her room.

FRIENDSHIP

THE LION AND THE LITTLE RED BIRD   PLATINUM AWARD
(by Elisa Kleven, Dutton $14) Every day the tuft on Lion's tail is a different color, which puzzles the little red bird. Although they do not speak the same language, the friendship between them leads to a rescue and an answer. 3–6.

PETER'S SONG PLATINUM AWARD

(by Carol Saul/illus. by Diane deGroat, Simon & Schuster $14) Peter Pig can't find anyone to listen to his song, until at last a frog not only listens but sings along. Preschoolers will empathize with Peter and this gentle tale about friendship. 3–5.

FIRST FOLKTALES

THE LITTLE RED HEN PLATINUM AWARD

(retold and illus. by Byron Barton, HarperCollins $12.95) Always a favorite for young naysayers, this version of the story of the Little Red Hen includes three chicks who do get to feast with Mama in the end. Barton's bold graphics and colors are also a feast for the eyes! 2 & up.

MILLIONS OF CATS BLUE CHIP

(by Wanda Gag, Coward $9.95) What poor child has not heard or joined in and chanted the refrain "Hundreds of cats, thousands of cats, millions and billions and trillions of cats"? This rather longish tale about an old man who brings home too many cats has pleased children for more than 60 years and it's still a gem! 4 & up.

ONCE UPON A TIME PLATINUM AWARD

(by Peter Prater, Candlewick $14.95) Nothing ever happens according to one small boy who is oblivious as the Three Bears, Red Riding Hood, Humpty Dumpty and Jack's Giant all pass through his neck of the woods. For kids who are up on their fairy tales. 4–8.

READ ME A STORY: A CHILD'S BOOK OF FAVORITE TALES

(by Sophie Windham, Scholastic $16.95) Fifteen classic tales include "Henny-Penny," "The Elves and the Shoemaker" and more. Young listeners will love them, and beginning readers will enjoy the familiar tales set in bold type. Also see Tomie dePaola's beautiful *Favorite Nursery Tales* (Putnam $18.95). 3 & up.

GOLDILOCKS AND THE THREE BEARS ★ PLATINUM AWARD

(by Jonathan Langley, HarperCollins $11) Guess who's cooking the porridge in this house? Papa's in the kitchen. Mama has power tools. A *Three Bears* for the '90s! Terrific! 3 & up.

CONCEPT BOOKS—NUMBERS, LETTERS, WORDS AND MORE

THE ACCIDENTAL ZUCCHINI

(by Max Grover, Harcourt Brace $13.95) From apple autos to a zigzag zoo, here's a jolly alphabet with bold, bright and amusing illustrations that will tickle the funny bone of a preschooler. 3–5.

ALISON'S ZINNIA

(by Anita Lobel, Greenwillow $15) A must-see, beautiful alphabet book. You and your child will "ooh" and "ah" and learn the names of the flowers. 4 & up.

COUNTING ZOO

(by Lynette Ruschak/illus. by May Rousseau, Aladdin $13.95) An exuberant pop-up counting book with oversized numbers that leap off the page and a review of 1 to 10 hidden behind lift-and-pop windows for a flourish at the end. 3–7.

HOW MANY?

(by Debbie MacKinnon/illus. by Anthea Sieveking, Dial $10.99) Brilliant photos of children holding or using the objects to be counted on one page; on facing page the same items are shown in isolation for ease and clarity of counting from 1 to 10. Also *What Shape?* 2–5.

MOUSE PAINT

(by Ellen Stoll Walsh, Harcourt Brace $11.95) When three white mice get into some paint the results stir up a demonstration of mixing colors. 3 & up.

RED LIGHT, GREEN LIGHT

(by M. W. Brown/illus. by Leonard Weisgard, Scholastic $14.95) From morning to night the truck, car, jeep, horse, boy, dog and cat go moving along. "Red light they can't go. Green light they can go." A welcome reissue of a classic. 3–6.

TEN LITTLE RABBITS

(by Virginia Grossman/illus. by Sylvia Long, Chronicle $12.95) Here's a most unusual counting book that borrows its decorative motifs from Native American customs, costumes and art. Using a simple rhyming verse, this is a beauty for any season. 3–7.

THE QUIET NOISY BOOK   BLUE CHIP

(by M. W. Brown/illus. by Leonard Weisgard, Harper-Collins $15) Muffin the dog is awakened by a very quiet sound—what can it be? Kids love answering the questions in this classic guessing game. A reissued edition with newly formatted art gives this sensory concept book a fresh, zingy look! Also *The Noisy Book*. 3–6.

WHY COUNT SHEEP?

(by Karen Wallace/illus. by Patrice Aggs, Hyperion $13.95) More of a concept book than a bedtime counting tale, this entertaining volume asks what do people count. An open-ended book with tons of delightful details to count and sort. 3–6.

DINOSAURS FOR YOUNG SCIENTISTS

BONES, BONES, DINOSAUR BONES

(by Byron Barton, HarperCollins $9.95) Preschool dinoholics will love this very simple pictorial explanation of what paleontologists do, from digs to museums. For a bit more info see *Dinosaurs* (by Gail

Gibbons, Holiday House paper $5.95), which has facts without overload. 4 & up.

DINOSAUR ENCORE

(by Patricia Mullins, HarperCollins $15) Using torn-tissue collage, Mullins gives young dinoholics a feast for the eye, with several fold-out pages and simple facts that compare certain features of dinosaurs to creatures that live today. 3–7.

ANIMALS

GROWING UP

(by Sarah Waters/illus. by Teresa O Brien, Reader's Digest $12) Want to see how a tadpole changes to a toad, or a caterpillar to a butterfly? Pull the tab and—abra-cadabra!—these and other transformations happen instantly. Accompanied by a simple but clear text, these pictures are worth a million words. 4–7.

IS THIS A HOUSE FOR HERMIT CRAB?

(by Megan McDonald/illus. by S. D. Schindler, Orchard $14.95) Hermit Crab has outgrown his old shell and looks along the shore for a bigger one. One is too deep, another too heavy, still another too full of holes. Crab finds the perfect home just in the nick of time. 4–7.

MAKE WAY FOR DUCKLINGS   BLUE CHIP

(by Robert McCloskey, Viking $12.95) This Caldecott Medal classic about a duck family and their struggle to reach their home in the park (with a bit of help from a policeman) is now immortalized with statues in the Boston Public Garden. 3 & up.

SALAMANDER ROOM

(by Anne Mazer/illus. by Steve Johnson, Knopf $13.95) When Brian brings a salamander home from the woods his mom asks where it will sleep. Imaginative Brian, who has an answer to everything, turns his room into a sala-mander paradise. 4 & up.

THE SEASHORE BOOK

(by Charlotte Zolotow/illus. by Wendell Minor, Harper-Collins $15) Here's a splendidly illustrated pretend visit to the beach. The illustrations capture the heat of the sand, the spray of waves, wings of birds and rhythm of a day at the seashore. 4 & up.

THE VERY QUIET CRICKET

(By Eric Carle, Philomel $17.95) A tiny cricket making his silent way through the bug world is greeted by buzzing, clicking and whining insects. When at last he meets a female cricket the silence is broken. 4 & up.

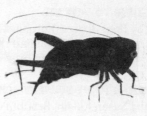

TIME AND THE SEASONS

OH SNOW

(by Monica Mayper/illus. by June Otani, HarperCollins $14.95) Mayper's lilting verse and Otani's snowy illustrations capture a young child's view and first delight in the white hush of fresh snow and how it feels to "stamp giants' tracks where no one's been" or to make angel wings. 3–6.

SNOWSONG WHISTLING

(by Karen Lotz/illus. by Elisa Kleven, Dutton $14.99) Rhythmic, action-packed rhymes and colorful collages herald the change of seasons and dance through the pages of this ode to winter that will bring the snowsong whistling. 3–7.

A SNOWY DAY   BLUE CHIP

(by Ezra Jack Keats, Viking $14) Peter's snowball may melt away, but the strength of this beautiful book continues to captivate small children. Also in Spanish. 3 & up.

WEATHER: A FIRST DISCOVERY BOOK

(by Gallimard Jeunesse and Pascale de Bourgoing/illus. by Sophie Kniffka, Scholastic $10.95) This innovative young science book has transparent overlays so that kids change the weather as they turn the pages. The text is brief and clear, and won't go over the heads of young listeners. Others in series: *Egg; Flower; Apple;* and more. 3 & up.

STARTING PRESCHOOL

GOING TO DAYCARE
(by Fred Rogers, Putnam $12.95) Kids who know and trust Mr. Rogers will find this photo essay about going to daycare a reassuring preview of things to come.

GOING TO MY NURSERY SCHOOL
(by Susan Kuklin, Bradbury Press $13.95) A photo story of four-year-old boy's experiences as he begins nursery school, accompanied by his dad. His story will give kids a sense of what to expect.

PEOPLE AND PLACES AND THINGS IN THE BIG WORLD

AN AUTO MECHANIC
(by Douglas Florian, Greenwillow $14) One of the fascinating places kids are curious about is the garage where the family car gets taken away and "worked on." But what do they do? Clear, colorful illustrations and very simple text tells just enough for young listeners. Also *A Carpenter.* 3–7.

CIRCUS

(by Lois Ehlert, HarperCollins $15) Welcome to the greatest circus on earth, featuring the amazing musclemen, the Pretzel Brothers, Lena and Lila the leaping lizards and the daring Flying Zucchinis, among others. A visual delight. 3–6.

DIGGERS AND DUMP TRUCKS

(by Angela Royston/illus. by Tim Ridley, Aladdin $6.95) Preschoolers are going to love the wonderful photos of the big construction trucks. Simple but clear information and close-up details. Printed on sturdy stock, this is part of a handsome new series called *Eye Openers.* Other titles include *Cars, Jungle Animals,* and *Pets.* 3–7.

FREIGHT TRAIN

(by Donald Crews, Greenwillow $16) An utterly spartan text runs through this Caldecott Honor book that young train buffs can also learn their colors by. 2–5.

HARRY AT THE AIRPORT

(by Derek Radford, Aladdin $10.95) Harry, a small hippo, is the star of this lively book that takes kids behind the scenes at the airport, answering questions they have, such as where the luggage goes (we hope), how the food gets on and who's in the control tower. An all-hippo cast gives loads of info with a dab of good humor. 4–8.

I WANT TO BE AN ASTRONAUT

(by Byron Barton, HarperCollins $12.89) Blast off on the space shuttle as a member of the crew! With his usual bold graphics and minimal text, Barton conveys enough information to satisfy space-minded kids. The cutaway of the shuttle is great. 3–6.

PLANE SONG ⭐ PLATINUM AWARD

(by Diane Siebert/illus. by Vincent Nasta, HarperCollins $15) Fasten your seatbelt and get ready to take off on a lyrical flight. From jumbo jets to sky writers and crop dusters, this is Siebert's hymn to planes and flight that will expand a child's view. 4–8.

TOOLS

(by Ann Morris/photos by Ken Heyman, Lothrop $14) In a series of photos of people at work all over the world, Heyman shows the many things we do with tools and the universality of that need. They've done the same concept in *Bread, Bread, Bread* and *Hats, Hats, Hats*. 4–8.

TRUCKS

(by Byron Barton, HarperCollins $12.89) Kids who can't get enough truck watching will love this catalog of trucks done in bold stokes and informative language that doesn't overload young listeners. 2–6.

WHOSE SHOES ARE THESE?

(by Ron Roy/photos by Rosmarie Hausherr, Clarion $13.95) Who wears tall boots, thick-soled white shoes and sneakers with knobs on the bottom? This doesn't just tell who but why shoes are designed for the jobs people do. 4–7.

SONGS IN BOOK FORM

ARROZ CON LECHE

(selected & illus. by Lulu Delacre, Scholastic paper $3.95) An excellent collection of 12 Latin American songs, games and rhymes, with music and lyrics in both Spanish and English and illustrations that capture the flavor.

MARY HAD A LITTLE LAMB
(by Sarah J. Hale/photos by Bruce McMillan, Scholastic $13.95) Photos give this classic rhyme a whole new feeling. Mary is an African-American girl who, by the way, wears glasses. The words we usually sing have more repetition than the text. Just add your own triple "school one day" lines. 3–6.

OLD MACDONALD
(adapted by Nancy Heller, Orchard $13.95) Die-cut pages make this version of a favorite song great fun to look at as well as sing. Heller's bold drawings are on sturdy pages for solo turns at "e- i- e- i- o-ing."

OVER IN THE MEADOW
(text adapted by Stacie Strong/illus. by Michael Foreman, Simon & Schuster $13) This beautifully illustrated pop-up book based on the popular children's counting song is truly a special treat. The six crows flapping in the nest are a must-see! Twos will enjoy with supervision.

EARLY-SCHOOL-AGE CHILDREN

During the early school years, as kids become readers and not just listeners, keeping them "in books" is a challenge. Reading is something they should do for pleasure, not because it's "good for them." By bring-

ing home a rich variety of books—fact and fantasy, science and history, humor and adventure, read-alouds and read-alones, you will be building that link to a lifetime of the pleasures found in books.

●●●●●●●●●●●●●●●●●●●●●●●●●●●

Ten Blue-Chip Books Early-School-Age Kids Should Know

★ ★ ★

- *Alexander and the Terrible, Horrible, No Good, Very Bad Day,* by Judith Viorst
- *Amos and Boris,* by William Steig
- *Charlotte's Web,* by E. B. White
- *The Empty Pot,* by Demi
- *Jolly Postman,* by Janet and Allan Ahlberg
- *Magic Schoolbus* series, by Joanna Cole
- *Ramona* series, by Beverly Cleary
- *Sylvester and the Magic Pebble,* by William Steig
- *The True Story of the Three Little Pigs,* by Jon Scieszka
- *Where the Wild Things Are,* by Maurice Sendak

GREAT READ-ALOUDS

FAMILIES THEN AND NOW

Kids love stories about families like their own as well as those that are totally different. We ve chosen family stories about kids today and those who lived in the past. The historic settings offer kids a glimpse into another time and place. Past or present, the heart of a good story speaks to kids about the human experiences of being part of a family.

ALEXANDER AND THE TERRIBLE, HORRIBLE, NO GOOD, VERY BAD DAY   BLUE CHIP

(by Judith Viorst/illus. by Ray Cruz, Atheneum $13.95) Is there anyone who hasn't had one of those terrible, horrible, no good days when nothing seems to go right? A blend of comic relief and self-recognition that is a comfort to young listeners. 5 & up.

ALL THOSE SECRETS OF THE WORLD   PLATINUM AWARD

(by Jane Yolen/illus. by Leslie Baker, Little Brown $14.95) Children who have been through the ache of being sepa-

rated from a parent will find a part of themselves in this moving picturebook. Set in World War II, Janie learns one of the secrets of the world about distance and size and that they may not be what they seem. 5 & up.

CHARLOTTE'S WEB (SEE PAGE 201)

CHICKEN SUNDAY
(by Patricia Polacco, Philomel $14.95) Miss Eula longs for a new Easter bonnet that her grandsons and their friend try to earn for her—but not without trouble a-plenty. Through their own work and a bit of help from the adults in their lives, the kids achieve their goal. Set in the '40s, this is a story of family and friendship. 5–9.

GOING WEST
(by Jean Van Leeuwen/illus. by Thomas Allen, Dial $15) A very quiet but moving account of one family's journey west by covered wagon. Told through the eyes of a seven-year-old girl, this will fascinate young history buffs. 6–9.

GREAT GRANDFATHER'S HOUSE
(by Rumer Godden/ illus. by Valerie Littlewood, Greenwillow $18) Keiko's parents must go away on business. Against her wishes, she is to stay with her great-grandparents. Her small cousin Yoji, whom she does not know, is also there. Things get off to a rough start, but Keiko comes to care for the new people in her life. 6–9.

HUE BOY
(by Rita P. Mitchell/illus. by Caroline Binch, Dial $13.99) Everyone has advice for making Hue Boy grow. But in time he learns that walking tall and happiness have nothing to do with your height. 5–9.

J.B.'S HARMONICA
(by John Sebastian/illus. by Garth Williams, Harcourt Brace $13.95) J.B. is a young bear who plays a harmonica very well until people make a fuss, comparing him to his dad, a famous harmonica player. J.B. learns that he

doesn't need to be just like Dad. He can make his own kind of music. Williams' furry bears are totally appealing characters. 4–8.

KLARA'S NEW WORLD

(by Jeanette Winter, Knopf $15) Here is the story of a Swedish girl and her family's move to America. Winter's striking illustrations and story give a sense of the sadness of leaving loved ones behind and of hopefulness for the future. 5–8.

THE LILY CUPBOARD

(by Shulamith L. Oppenheim/illus. by Ronald Himler, HarperCollins $15) Set in the days of World Warr II, a small girl who is Jewish is sent to live with a family that is not. A story that celebrates the courage of a child and friends who risked their lives to save her. 6–8.

THE LOTUS SEED

(by Sherry Garland/illus. by Tatsuro Kiuchi, Harcourt Brace $14.95) In a hasty departure from war-torn Vietnam, a young woman carries only a single Lotus seed. Years later the seed is taken and planted by her grandson. When spring comes the flower of hope blooms and produces seeds for the future. 5–9.

MY GREAT-AUNT ARIZONA

(by Gloria Houston/illus. by Susan Condie Lamb, Harper-Collins $15) Arizona was born in a log cabin, wore high-button shoes and dreamed of traveling. Houston's tribute to her great-aunt takes us back to a one-room schoolhouse. Arizona's longing for faraway places becomes a metaphor for the way in which memorable teachers travel with us always. 5 & up.

RAMONA THE PEST   BLUE CHIP

(by Beverly Cleary/illus. by Allen Tiegreen, Morrow $13.95) Spunky Ramona almost becomes a kindergarten dropout when the teacher fails to appreciate her original approach to writing. This and the other endearing books in the Ramona series are ideal read-alouds for 6–7s that kids enjoy rereading on their own as their skills grow.

ROSES SING ON NEW SNOW   PLATINUM AWARD

(by Paul Yee/illus. by Harvey Chan, Macmillan $13.95)
Set in San Francisco at the turn of the century, the story
of a Chinese girl who does all the cooking in her father's
restaurant while her lazy brothers take all the credit—
until they tell one lie too many. A totally delicious tale. 6
& up.

SCOOTER

(by Vera B. Williams, Greenwillow $15) Elana Rose
Rosen, whose folks are divorced, has just moved to the
city with her mom. Like Williams picturebooks, this long
chapter book manages to be both moving and amusing.
Elana is a memorable character. 8 & up.

SONG AND DANCE MAN   BLUE CHIP

(by Karen Ackerman/illus. by Stephen Gammell, Knopf
paper $4.99) Grandpa was a song-and-dance man. Make
that "is"—when he opens his trunk and does a command
performance in the attic for his grandchildren. Caldecott
Award winner. 5–8.

> **TOY TIP:** Art from award winners *Song and Dance
> Man* and *Tar Beach* is available in handsome
> puzzle form. (JTG $6 each). (800) 222-2584.

TAR BEACH   PLATINUM AWARD

(by Faith Ringgold,
Crown $14.95) In
this flying fantasy,
Cassie Lightfoot
takes off from the
rooftop "tar beach"
of her home in
Harlem, claiming
whatever she sees
as her own. Cassie
wears the lights of the George Washington Bridge like a
diamond necklace. Illustrations began as a "story quilt"
that hangs in the Guggenheim. 5–9.

TELL ME A STORY, MAMA

(by Angela Johnson/illus. by David Soman, Orchard $13.95) Children love to hear long-ago stories about when parents were small. Old stories are often learned by heart. In this tale, a little girl asks for such a story and then proceeds to tell it herself. After sharing this, try spinning some family history of your own. 5–9.

THIS QUIET LADY   PLATINUM AWARD

(by Charlotte Zolotow/illus. by Anita Lobel, Greenwillow $14) A little girl discovers pictures of her mother's growing up. Lobel's gloriously romantic portraits capture the circle of life. A beauty! 4–8.

FANTASIES OLD AND NEW

ABUELA   PLATINUM AWARD

(by Arthur Dorros/illus. by Elisa Klevens, Dutton $14) When Rosalba takes off like a bird, her abuela (grandma, in Spanish) leaps into the sky, and together they soar above Manhattan, over trains, parks and skyscrapers and, most memorably, around the Statue of Liberty. Laced with Spanish phrases that are always clarified in English. A joyful fantasy that's a feast for the eyes and a lift for the spirits! 4–8.

AMOS AND BORIS   BLUE CHIP

(by William Steig, Farrar Straus $17) Few storybooks capture so well the meaning of friendship as this classic tale of a small mouse and a giant whale and how they help each other—one with his brain, the other with brawn. 5–8.

BENTLY AND EGG   PLATINUM AWARD

(by William Joyce, HarperCollins $15) Bently, a frog, agrees to care for the unhatched egg of his duck friend Kack Kack. Little did Bently know how difficult that might be. Like a comic "Perils of Pauline," Bently learns the joy and the heartache of taking charge and being responsible. 5–8.

ELMER BLUNT'S OPEN HOUSE   PLATINUM AWARD

(by Matt Novak, Orchard $14.95) Harried Elmer Blunt runs off to work, leaving his front door open. In come a pack of curious woodland creatures who turn things upside down à la Goldilocks until they hear a robber enter the house. Told in cartoon-strip style, this comic caper will please beginning readers especially. 5 & up.

THE ESCAPE OF MARVIN THE APE

(by Caralyn and Mark Buehner, Dial $14) It was feeding time when Marvin, an amiable ape, escaped from the zoo and took off on a tour of Manhattan, where he seemed to fit right in. Kids will enjoy the tour as well as spotting the ostrich and cat hidden on every page. 4–8.

GARTH PIG STEALS THE SHOW   PLATINUM AWARD

(by Mary Rayner, Dutton $13.99) Once again Garth Pig and his family forestall being "wolfed" down by the mysterious hairy musician who tries to join their family band. Rayner's illustrations will bring squeals of delight! 5 & up.

GRUSHA

(by Barbara B. Falk, HarperCollins $15) Grusha, a soulful-looking bear, is captured and taken to the circus. He learns well and becomes a star. His trainer, Peter, is kind and gentle, but as time  passes Grusha longs for freedom. As an act of friendship, Peter gives Grusha the gift he longs for most. Memorable illustrations. 5 & up.

HOW I CAPTURED A DINOSAUR

(by Henry Schwartz/illus. by Amy Schwartz, Orchard $12.95) Talk about bringing home a souvenir from a trip—Liz, an eight-year-old dinoholic, goes on vacation with her parents and finds a giant blue Albertosaurus, a perfect pet for Los Angeles. 5–8.

I AM REALLY A PRINCESS ⭐ PLATINUM AWARD

(by Carol Diggory Shields/illus. by Paul Meisel, Dutton $13.99) Just wait until her true parents, the king and queen, rescue the narrator from these foolish folks who expect her to pick up her things, share a room, set the table and other such nonsense! Meisel's spirited illustrations add much to the joyous fantasy of being a displaced royal. 4–8.

JAMES IN THE HOUSE OF AUNT PRUDENCE

(by Timothy Bush, Crown $13) From the moment he enters Great Aunt Prudence's house with bear rugs and claw-footed pedestals, James's active imagination takes over in a wild fantasy romp. 5–8.

JUNE 29, 1999   PLATINUM AWARD

(by David Wiesner, Clarion $15.95) Stunning illustrations of giant flying veggies fill the pages of this science-fiction picture book. It all begins when Holly Evans of Ho-Ho-Kus, New Jersey, launches seedlings for her school science project. Also see Wiesner's Wordless gem, *Tuesday*. 7 & up.

MARTHA SPEAKS
PLATINUM AWARD

(by Susan Meddaugh, Houghton Mifflin $13.95) A funny caper about a dog who starts talking after eating alphabet soup. In fact, Martha talks so much she gets scolded and clams up until  one night her gift of gab saves more than the day. 4–8.

MAXI, THE STAR

(by Debra and Sal Barracca/illus. by Alan Ayers, Dial $13.99) New York's own Maxi the Taxi Dog heads to Hollywood to make a TV commercial. In this romp, Maxi travels cross-country, enjoys the glitzy lifestyle of the rich and famous, but like all true New Yorkers is happiest to get back to his home sweet home! 5 & up.

THE MINPINS   PLATINUM AWARD

(by Roald Dahl/illus. by Patrick Benson, Viking $17) "Little Billy was awfully tired of being good" . . . that's how this fantasy adventure begins as Billy enters a forbidden forest. Though the beginning is preachy, it takes off when Billy meets the Minpins, the little people who live in the trees. A read-aloud chapter book for 5 & up.

NO PROBLEM

(by Eileen Browne/illus. by David Parkins, Candlewick $14.99) Mouse gets a huge gift, a pile of parts that he boasts will be "no problem" to put together. But Mouse and his friends have problems until one actually reads the directions! There's a jaunty rhythm to this tale along with a cut-out model that can be put together—if you follow the directions. 5–8.

THE SWEETEST FIG   PLATINUM AWARD

(by Chris Van Allsburg, Houghton Mifflin $17.95) Monsieur Bibot, a cruel and greedy dentist, cares more for his fee than his patients' comfort. A poor old woman pays him with three magic figs that make dreams come true and therein lies the Kafkaesque tale. 7 & up.

SYLVESTER AND THE MAGIC PEBBLE   BLUE CHIP

(by William Steig, Farrar Straus $12.95) Young Sylvester finds a magic pebble that grants him one wish too many. It is his devoted parents who free Sylvester from the magic. A not-to-be-missed Caldecott Award–winning classic that speaks about love and interdependence. 6 & up.

TIME TRAIN   PLATINUM AWARD

(by Paul Fleischman/illus. by Claire Ewart, HarperCollins $14.95) On a remarkable class trip to Dinosaur National Monument, the train whisks the kids back to prehistoric times. Ewart's stunning illustrations will transport young time travelers on a rollicking fantasy adventure. 5–9.

WHERE THE WILD THINGS ARE   BLUE CHIP

(by Maurice Sendak, HarperCollins $15) When Max is punished by being sent to his room without dinner, he embarks on one of the most remarkable fantasy romps in children's literature. Some fours may enjoy this, but it's a better choice for slightly older kids who understand the difference between real and make believe. 5 & up.

LEGENDS, BIBLE STORIES AND FOLKTALES

BAMBOO HATS AND A RICE CAKE

(by Ann Tompert/illus. Demi, Crown $13) A poor couple must sell a precious kimono in order to have rice cakes. The poor old man ends up with nothing but a stack of straw hats that he places on six statues of Jizo. The statues magically bring the couple a giant rice cake. The text of this folktale includes characters from the Japanese alphabet that can be read like a rebus. 5–9.

BORREGUITA AND THE COYOTE   PLATINUM AWARD

(by Verna Aardema/illus. by Petra Mathers, Knopf $15) You've heard of trickster rabbits like Br'er Rabbit and trickster spiders like Anansi, but here's a little lamb who manages to trick a hungry coyote. A Mexican folktale told with few words (some *en español*). Mathers's witty illustrations capture the storyteller's humorous tone. 5–8.

THE CHASE

(by Beatrice Tanaka/illus. by Michel Gay, Crown $14) Based on a Native American tale in which one false assumption sets all the animals running for fear. A funny story with a gentle lesson about making snap judgments or assuming the worst. 5–8.

THE EMPTY POT   BLUE CHIP

(by Demi, Henry Holt $15.95) The emperor is ready to find his successor. All the children in the kingdom are challenged to "grow" a special plant. Only one child returns with an empty pot. A tale about honesty and the courage it takes. 5–9.

THE FORTUNE-TELLERS

(by Lloyd Alexander/illus. by Trina Schart Hyman, Dutton $15) A case of mistaken identity becomes a stroke of good fortune for a poor young carpenter who trades his hammer for a crystal ball. A witty tale from a master storyteller. 5–8.

JOSEPH AND HIS MAGNIFICENT COAT

(by Marcia Williams, Candlewick Press $13.95) What a refreshingly lively retelling of this favorite Bible story! Done in cartoon-strip style, with bubbles and playful decorative details for young readers to return to again and again. 5 & up.

THE KING'S EQUAL   PLATINUM AWARD

(by Katherine Paterson/illus. by Vladimir Vagin, Harper-Collins $17) A modern twist on an age-old theme. A selfish prince cannot become king until he marries a woman who equals him in beauty, intelligence and wealth. A chapter book for 7 & up.

THE KOREAN CINDERELLA   PLATINUM AWARD

(by Shirley Climo/illus. by Ruth Heller, HarperCollins $15) Almost every culture has its own version of the tale of Cinderella and this Korean story of Pear Blossom is beautifully told with stunning illustrations. Older kids will like comparing how this telling differs from the tale they know. 5 & up.

MOON ROPE

(by Lois Ehlert, Harcourt Brace $14.95) Inspired by ancient Peruvian art, Ehlert's bold and stunning graphics illuminate a folktale from Peru about a fox and a mole who try to get to the moon. 4–8.

RAVEN

(by Gerald McDermott, Harcourt Brace $14.95) Who tricked the Sky Chief and brought light to the people? A trickster bird known as Raven. Based on a Native American tale from the Pacific Northwest, this is a visual treat. 5–9.

A RIDE ON THE RED MARE'S BACK   PLATINUM AWARD

(by Ursula K. LeGuin/illus. by Julie Downing, Orchard $15.95) A girl's brother is stolen by trolls. With nothing but her knitting needles, some bread and her small painted horse she goes off to rescue him. Magically her toy mare springs to life—just for one night, but long enough to help the brave girl. A memorable story. 5–8.

SIR WHONG AND THE GOLDEN PIG

(retold by Oki S. Han, Dial $13.99) A stranger borrows a huge sum of money from the generous Whong, leaving a golden pig behind as security. The pig turns out to be less than golden, but the wise Whong tricks the thief into returning. Based on an old Korean folktale. 5–9.

THE STINKY CHEESE MAN

(by Jon Scieszka and Lane Smith, Viking $16) Zany versions of ten folktales that will tickle kids. The title story is a comic send-up of "The Gingerbread Boy" redubbed "The Stinky Cheese Man." He smells so foul nobody wants to catch him! 6 & up.

TALE OF THE MANDARIN DUCK

(by Katherine Paterson/illus. by Leo and Diane Dillon, Lodestar $14.95) A wild duck is captured by a wealthy lord. The unhappy duck longs for his mate and is allowed to escape by Shozo, one of the lord's servants. In return the duck helps Shozo and his own true love. The magnificent illustrations look like classic Japanese prints. 5–9.

THE TALKING EGGS   BLUE CHIP

(by Robert SanSouci/illus. by Jerry Pinkney, Dial $15) A young girl gives a drink to a strange old woman who turns out to be a good witch. For her kindness she is given a gift of talking eggs that magically give her riches and make her unkind sister jealous. In this Cajun folktale, once more generosity triumphs over greed. 5–9.

THE THREE LITTLE WOLVES AND THE BIG BAD PIG
✸ PLATINUM AWARD

(by Eugene Trivizas/illus. by Helen Oxenbury, McElderry $15.95) Talk about role reversals—here's a comic send-up of the story of the Three Pigs—in this instance we have three little wolves who are constantly pursued by a Big Bad Pig whom they eventually turn into a friend. 5–8.

THREE PIGS—THREE WAYS

THE THREE PIGS AND THE FOX

(by William Hooks/illus. by S. D. Schindler, Macmillan $13.95) As Mama sends each of her little pigs off into the world, she warns them to watch out for the mean old fox, to build a strong house and to come home to see Mama every Sunday! A funny Appalachian version of a classic, told by a master storyteller. 5–8.

THE TRUE STORY OF THE THREE LITTLE PIGS

(by Jon Scieszka/illus. by Lane Smith, Viking $13.95) At last, according to the author, a fellow by the name of A. Wolf, we are privy to what *really* happened when a poor wolf wanted to borrow a cup of sugar from a certain pig. A great way to help kids begin to think about how point of view can change a story. 5–8.

WHO'S AT THE DOOR?

(by Jonathan Allen, Tamborine $11.95) Just when you thought no one could come up with yet another version of "The Three Pigs," here comes a wolf in all kinds of get-ups who can't fool this wise trio. This flap book with pages that open is sure to amuse kids 4–8.

THE TROJAN HORSE
PLATINUM AWARD

(retold & illus. by Warwick Hut-ton, Macmillan $14.95) When the Greek army turns away from Troy, leaving only a huge wooden horse outside the city, the Tro-jans celebrate and sow the seeds of their own defeat. Retold for young listeners and readers, this myth is suspenseful, with memorable watercolors. 7 & up.

THE WOODCUTTER'S COAT

(by Ferida Wolff/illus. by Anne Wilsdorf, Little Brown $15.95) A woodcutter buys a warm coat that gets stolen by a thief and then bought, sold and traded many times over. There is a predictable but satisfying roundness to this tale. 5–8.

ALPHABET BOOKS

THE ABC MYSTERY

(by Doug Cushman, HarperCollins $15) A is the art that was stolen and B is the butler who has disappeared in this lively little alphabetical mystery with a new clue at every turn. 4–8.

A IS FOR ANIMALS   PLATINUM AWARD

(by David Pelham, Simon & Schuster $15.95) Wait till you see the 26 pop-up animals hiding behind 26 "doors," each labeled with an upper- and lower-case letter. This alphabet with amazing paper engineering makes a perfect gift. 4 & up.

A LITTLE ALPHABET

(by Trina Schart Hyman, Morrow $5.95) In this charming little book each letter of the alphabet frames five or more miniature items that begin with the featured letter and sound. 4 & up.

THE ALPHABET PARADE

(by Seymour Chwast, Harcourt Brace $13.95) In this playful, wordless alphabet there are marchers, spectators and objects on each page that start with the same letter or sound. More than 300 items to be found. Need help? There's a list at the back. 4–8.

ALEF-BET

(by Michelle Edwards, Lothrop $15) With zippy illustrations of a lively family doing everyday things, this unusual Hebrew alphabet gives the phonetic way to say each letter. The featured word is given in Hebrew and English. The zany family includes a child with spina bifida who uses a wheelchair. 5 & up.

JAMBO MEANS HELLO   BLUE CHIP

(by Muriel Feelings/illus. by Tom Feelings, Dial $15) With 24 words, one for each letter in the Swahili alphabet, a picture of life in an East African village. A prize-winning way to introduce another culture. 5–9.

OLIVER'S ALPHABET

(by Lisa Bruce/illus. by Debi Gliori, Bradbury $13.95) There are eight big scenes with a full alphabet of objects from A to Z to be found in each. Great for beginning readers to hunt through. 5–8.

MATH BOOKS

ANNO'S COUNTING BOOK   BLUE CHIP

(by Mitsumasa Anno, HarperCollins $16) More than a simple counting book, this wordless wonder deals with the sequence of the months and seasons and how a country setting changes over time. Fine details to ponder. 5–9.

I SPY TWO EYES—NUMBERS IN ART
★ PLATINUM AWARD

(by Lucy Micklethwait, Greenwillow $19) A playful way to introduce children to great paintings from the 15th century to the present. The reader must spot the correct number of items identified from 1–20 as they explore exquisitely reproduced art by Botticelli, Léger, Picasso, Van Gogh and other masters. A game that can be played in museums too. A handsome sequel to *I Spy: An Alphabet in Art*. 4–8.

MY FIRST NUMBER BOOK

(by Marie Heust, DK $12.95) Eye-appealing photos explore many math concepts, from simple counting to weight, patterns, order, time, adding, subtracting and more. Big ideas here for 5–8.

OUT FOR THE COUNT
(by Kathryn Cave/illus. by Chris Riddell, Simon & Schuster $14) A clever counting book for first- and second-graders who are dealing with 10s and 1s. Animals are embedded in full-color illustrations and shown grouped by 10s and 1s in black-and-white silhouettes. 6–8.

THE 12 CIRCUS RINGS
(by Seymour Chwast, Harcourt Brace $14.95) This is more than a variation on the Twelve Days of Christmas. There are 12 circus rings, each more crowded and complex than the last, with collections of clowns, acrobats, animals and others to count, add, subtract, multiply and search for other number patterns. 5–9.

TWO BY TWO
(by Barbara Reid, Scholastic $14.95) Using her unique style of sculpting stunning illustrations with colorful clay, Reid has created a Noah's Ark that is an unusual counting book and a visual delight! The text's playful verse based on the old song *Who Built the Ark?* 5 & up.

MANNERS

NO BAD BEARS
(by Michele D. Clise, Viking $14) Move over, Miss Manners! Ophelia, an elegant Victorian bear, and her friends give kids good-humored but clear guidelines for being well mannered and polite. Charming photos of stuffed bears take the edge off of what could be a preachy do and don't book. 5–8.

PERFECT PIGS
(by Marc Brown and Stephen Krensky, Little Brown $14.95) What better cast could one have than a pack of perfect pigs to introduce kids to good manners on the phone, during games, at mealtime and wherever perfect pigs may go. The cartoon style lightens the messages with good humor. 5–8.

WHAT DO YOU SAY, DEAR?   BLUE CHIP

(by Sesyle Joslin/illus. by Maurice Sendak, HarperCollins $14) In this classic book of manners, a child is caught in a series of outrageous and absurd situations. After that familiar question "What do you say?" the polite answer is served up with wit. 4 & up.

TALES OUT OF SCHOOL

AMAZING GRACE

(by Mary Hoffman/illus. by Caroline Binch, Dial $14) When her teacher announces the class play will be *Peter Pan,* Grace wants to be the star. A classmate insists Grace can't get the part because she's a girl and she's black. Thanks to her Gram and Mom, Grace goes for it! 5–8.

ANNABELLE SWIFT, KINDERGARTENER

(by Amy Schwartz, Orchard $14.95) With more help than she needs from her third-grade sister Lucy, Annabelle gets off to a bumpy start in kindergarten. A humorous and gentle story about sisterly love and confidence. 4–6.

FROG MEDICINE   PLATINUM AWARD

(by Mark Teague, Scholastic $13.95) Poor Elmo puts off writing his book report on frogs. He procrastinates so long he starts turning into a frog! A wise and rather large frog doctor assures Elmo that he doesn't need medicine—just to do his homework. A gentle lesson delivered with wit and amusing illustrations. 6–9.

GOING TO MY GYMNASTICS CLASS

(by Susan Kuklin, Bradbury $13.95) Beginning gymnasts or those who anticipate starting will enjoy this narrative told by a young boy who obviously loves working on the rings, balance beam and trampoline. Nice use of both boys and girls, so book is not gender-specific. 4–6.

JOIN THE BAND!

(by Marjorie Pillar, HarperCollins $15) An upbeat photo essay about the work and fun of joining the school band and what it's like to play in the big spring concert. 6–9.

LITTLE HIPPO GETS GLASSES

(by Maryann Macdonald/illus. by Anna King, Dial $11) Although he can't see the blackboard, Little Hippo doesn't want to be the first in his class to wear glasses. He's sure his friend Sophie will laugh at him. Hippo's glasses end up helping both. 5–7.

MARTIN AND THE TOOTH FAIRY

(by Bernice Chardiet and Grace Maccorne/illus. by G. B. Karas, Scholastic $11.95) When Martin gets more quarters than his friends from the tooth fairy, a new business is born! Martin decides to buy his friends' teeth and collect a profit from the fairy. A truly funny story for second-graders or as a read-aloud. 5–8.

More about School—Easy-to-read Chapter Books:

- *The Beast in Ms. Rooney's Room* (by Patricia R. Giff, Dell paper $2.99)
- *Ramona the Pest* (by Beverly Cleary, Dell paper $3.95)
- *Mary Marony Hides Out* (by Suzy Kline, Putnam $13.95)

INFORMATION, PLEASE: SCIENCE, HISTORY & MORE

School-age kids have an appetite for information about the real world. They want to know where things come from, how they are made and how they work. They're curious about plants and animals and how they grow. Though they live very much in the present, they are curious about the past and how things were. Such information used to be found

only in encyclopedias or dull textbooks. Today
there are gloriously beautiful and lively nonfiction
books for young readers.

ANIMALS

ALL PIGS ARE BEAUTIFUL

(by Dick King-Smith/illus. by
Anita Jeram, Candlewick
$14.95) A delightful blend of
humor, facts and story told by
a knowledgeable pig lover and
illustrated with wit. 5–8.

THE ANIMAL KINGDOM

(by Jenny Wood/illus. by Andrew Bale, Macmillan $14.95)
Divided by habitat, clear and simple descriptions of animals that live in the Arctic, deserts, swamps, mountains,
grasslands, forests, jungles and Antarctica. Although the
creatures are not always drawn to scale, the paintings
are handsome in texture and detail. 5 & up.

BIG CATS

(by Seymour Simon, HarperCollins $17) From the four
that roar to the three that don't, Simon's book intro-
duces children to the powerful beauty of big cats. An
oversized picture book with lush color photos and clear,
informative text. 5–8.

AN ELEPHANT NEVER FORGETS ITS SNORKEL

(by Lisa Evans/illus. by Diane DeGroat, Crown $10) This
unusual book combines fact with humor as it looks at 18
ways animals and humans accomplish similar tasks. For
example, to breathe underwater we use snorkels, but an
elephant uses its trunk. 5–8.

EYEWITNESS JUNIOR SERIES

(Knopf $6.95) These won't replace the encyclopedia, but
they are more engaging and designed for younger readers. Subjects on an ever-growing list include birds, frogs,
snakes and spiders. 6 & up.

HAVE YOU SEEN BIRDS?

(by Joanne Oppenheim/illus. by Barbara Reid, Scholastic $8.95) Beautiful clay illustrations capture many of the birds of the world. A young science concept book that introduces children to a variety of birds in different habitats in playful verse. 4–8.

HIDDEN ANIMALS

(by Sarah Waters/illus. by Teresa O'Brien, Reader's Digest $12) How do animals protect themselves and hide from their enemies? Pull the tabs and see a chameleon change color, an eel revealed in a reef and more. Simple but clear text introduces kids to the concept of how animals are protected with natural camouflage. 5–7

NEVER GRAB A DEER BY THE EAR

(by Colleen S. Bare, Cobblehill $13)Deer live almost everywhere, and this lively text with full-color photos answers questions children may have about these wild creatures that may wonder through their backyards. Bold type and moderately easy text. 5–9

A SEA FULL OF SHARKS

(by Betsy Maestro/illus. by Giulio Maestro, Scholastic $12.95) Sharks are a favorite and fascinating subject for kids. This handsome book gives clear info about the many kinds of sharks and their habits and behavior— without drowning kids in facts. Also *Sharks in Action* (by T. O. Gay, Aladdin $7.95) 6 & up.

WHAT NEAT FEET!

(by Hana Machotka, Morrow $13.95) Handsome photos zoom in on the distinctively different feet of a swan, seal, rabbit, goat, cat, camel and elephant. Text examines how each is designed for a particular environment. An excellent concept book with clear text that won't overwhelm young listeners or readers. Also *Breathtaking Noses*. 4–8.

WHERE'S THAT INSECT?

(by Barbara Brenner and Bernice Chardiet/illus. by Carol Schwartz, Scholastic $10.95) One of a new *Hide and Seek Science* series that combines information with a game of looking for a particular insect that's embedded in a larger picture of many bugs. Unlike many hunt-and-find game books, this one builds kids' knowledge. 5–8

REPRODUCTION

EGG!

(by A. J. Wood/illus. by Stella Stilwell, Little Brown $12.95) A dozen different eggs are opened on fold-out pages to reveal 12 very different creatures that hatch from eggs. Multiple pictures in small frames add still more information to the engaging text. An excellent science/concept book for 5–8.

FROGS—SEE HOW THEY GROW

(by Mary Ling/photos by Kim Taylor, Dorling Kindersley $7.95) One of a new series, with beautiful close-up photos and text about the life cycle of a frog in easy-to-read language. Other books in the series examine ducks, kittens, rabbits and puppies. 5–8. Also see Videos.

HOW YOU WERE BORN

(by Joanna Cole/photos by Margaret Miller, Morrow $14.95) In clear, straightforward prose, Cole explains how babies are born. Photos include several of baby in the uterus and being born. In addition to the text for children there is an excellent section for adults on dealing with children's questions and concerns. Also *My Puppy Is Born*. 4–9.

ECOLOGY

More than a few of the current crop of pro-planet books are pretty but preachy. Pure as the messages may be, kids are rarely won over by lectures. We prefer books that celebrate nature and encourage kids to respect and explore the environment.

ANIMALS IN DANGER

(by William McCay/illus. by Keith Moseley, Aladdin $12.95) Amazing paper engineering went into this striking pop-up book with brief but interesting information about eight endangered animals. 7 & up.

BROTHER EAGLE, SISTER SKY   PLATINUM AWARD

(painting by Susan Jeffers, Dial $16) Concerns about the environment are not new to this generation. As long ago as the 1850s Chief Seattle, a Native American leader, spoke about his people's land and its creatures. His poetic words inspired some of Jeffers's most exquisite paintings. This moving book says more than most and it says it eloquently! 6 & up.

DINOSAURS TO THE RESCUE!

(by Laurie K. Brown and Marc Brown, Little Brown $14.95) Those zany dinosaurs dish out a lot of sound advice on recycling and using less of the things kids can do something about. Brown's cartoon style will amuse young environmentalists. 5–8

THE PUFFINS ARE BACK

(by Gail Gibbons, HarperCollins $14) A fascinating account of the puffins' annual return from the sea to the land, and their mating season. Gibbons recounts how scientists successfully brought baby birds from Newfoundland to Maine to reestablish a breeding ground that was vanishing. Also *Recycle.* 7 & up.

Resources:
50 Simple Things Kids Can Do to Save the Earth (by the EarthWorks Group $6.95)
Going Green: A Kid's Handbook to Saving the Planet (by John Elkington et al., Pufflin $8.95.

Both are chockful of information about everyday things kids can do to improve the environment. 8 & up.

LOOKING SKYWARD: STARS AND SPACE

THE BIG DIPPER

(by Franklyn Branley/illus. by Molly Coxe, HarperCollins $4.50) An easy-to-read book about the easiest-to-find constellation, the Big Dipper. A good intro to the stars. Also *The Sun, Our Nearest Star* and others by this scientist who writes with great clarity for young readers in the *Let's Read and Find Out* series. 6 & up.

THE MAGIC SCHOOL BUS LOST IN THE SOLAR SYSTEM
PLATINUM AWARD

(by Joanna Cole/illus. by Bruce Degen, Scholastic $13.95) On their field trip to the planetarium, Ms. Frizzle's class finds the museum closed. Does that faze the Friz? Not with a Magic Bus that carries them off on a zany, fact-filled tour of the solar system. One of a series that proves science and humor can mix. 6–9.

VENUS

(by Seymour Simon, Morrow $15) One of Simon's many books about the planets and solar system. Breathtaking photos accompany his clear, informative text. Also *The Sun, Stars, Our Solar System*. 7 & up.

DINOSAURS

CHILDREN'S GUIDE TO DINOSAURS AND OTHER PREHISTORIC ANIMALS

(by Dr. Philip Whitfield, Macmillan $16.95) A resource for older children that is organized chronologically by geological periods. Panoramic landscapes, maps, time charts are all followed by profiles of more than 125 animals. 7–12.

DINOSAUR BABIES AND PLAYFUL PANDAS

(National Geographic, $21.95 for both) Exquisite paper engineering has produced Mama pandas that lift, feed and play games with their babies and dinosaurs with eggs you can see and hear cracking! Pull tabs make one baby scratch and another swim and turn. Written in clear, informative language. (800) 638-4077. 5–8.

GREAT DINOSAUR ATLAS

(by William Lindsay/illus. by Giuliano Formari, Simon & Schuster, $14.95) An oversized dream book for dino-haulics. Solid information, stunning illustrations and maps. 5 & up.

MY VISIT TO THE DINOSAURS

(by Aliki, HarperCollins $14) An easy-to-read introduction to dinosaurs that sorts a few examples by meat eaters and plant eaters. Part of the *Let's Read and Find Out* series for which Aliki has also done *Digging Up Dinosaurs*. Now comes packaged with a game deck of dinosaur cards. 5–10.

NATURE

GROW IT!

(by Erika Markmann/illus. by Gisela Konemund, Random House $6.95) Great activities that can be done in the backyard or on the windowsill. Experiments in pruning, growing new plants from old, making perfume and more. 6 & up.

MY FIRST GARDEN BOOK

(by Angela Wilkes, Knopf $13) A stunning guide to gardening, with photos and clear, step-by-step directions for sprouting seeds and growing bulbs, herbs, vegetables and tabletop/windowsill gardens. Also *My First Nature Book*. 6–10.

KID'S GARDENING BOOK

(by Kevin and Kim Raftery/illus. by Jim M'Guinness, Klutz Press $12.95) Packaged with a hand trowel, packets of seeds and all the directions needed for young gardeners to get started with developing a green thumb. 6–12. See Videos section for: *Look What I Grew!* and *My First Nature Video.*

SCIENCE ACTIVITY AND EXPERIMENT BOOKS

EXPLORABOOK
(by John Cassidy, Klutz $17.95) Created by the staff of the Exploratorium, a science museum in San Francisco, this book of experiments comes with all sorts of bells and whistles. Along with tons of fascinating ideas, there's a magnetic wand, a mirror, a moire spinner, a Fresnel lens and more. A terrific birthday gift for 8–12.

MY FIRST SCIENCE BOOK
(by Angela Wilkes, Knopf $13) Early-school-years kids will be able to follow most of the experiments in this big handsome book. Activities shown in full-color photos include such fun as making a fingerprint kit, kitchen chemistry, magnetic fishing, color spin tops and a watery volcano. Also *My First Batteries and Magnets* (DK). 7–12.

THE SCIENCE BOOK OF WATER
(by Neil Ardley, Harcourt Brace $9.95) One of an excellent and handsome series of activity books with photos and simple experiments that demonstrate the properties of water with materials readily found in most homes. Also *Color, Light* and *Air.* 6 & up.

PEOPLE, PLACES, THINGS AND HOW THEY WORK

AMAZING BUILDINGS
(by Philip Wilkinson/illus. by Paolo Donati, Dorling Kindersley $16.95) For armchair travelers, here are twenty cutaway views of such wonders as the Paris Opera, the Statue of Liberty and the Imperial Palace. This oversized book is full of visual delights and information for travelers of the future. 8 & up.

ANCIENT EGYPT
(by Judith Crosher, Viking $14.99) From the pyramids to the little details of everyday life, this handsome oversized book is a great resource for class reports and

curiosity. Includes four lift-up pages that show exterior
and interior of major sites. One of an excellent series.
Other cultures include Aztecs, ancient Greece, and
Rome. 8–12.

AUNT HARRIET'S UNDERGROUND RAILROAD

(by Faith Ringgold, Crown $15) An imaginative time-travel
account of a young girl and her brother who fly off to
meet Harriet Tubman and the Underground Railroad.
7 & up.

THE BIONIC BUNNY SHOW

(by Marc Brown and Lau-
rene K. Brown, Little
Brown $14.95) There are a
lot of books around that
try to show kids how
things work. This one takes
kids behind the scenes of a TV show, helping them think
about what's real vs. make-believe and doing it with
humor. An informative and entertaining gem. 6–9.

IF YOUR NAME WAS CHANGED AT ELLIS ISLAND

(by Ellen Levine/illus. by Wayne Parmenter, Scholastic
$15.95) Ellis Island opened in 1892, and more than 12 mil-
lion people passed through it. Now that it's been
reopened as a museum, millions of people stand in the
great hall again and think back to the past. With a ques-
tion-and-answer format, this is an ideal choice before or
after such a visit. 5–12.

INCREDIBLE CROSS-SECTIONS   PLATINUM AWARD

(by Stephen Biesty, Knopf $20) This is the ultimate "look
inside" book in an oversized format that takes you inside
a jumbo jet, the Empire State Building, a castle, an ocean
liner, a subway and more. 8–80.

LEARNING TO SWIM IN SWAZILAND

(by Nila K. Leigh, Scholastic $15.95) When her parents took eight-year-old Nila to live in Swaziland, she began a series of letters to her schoolmates in New York. The result is a travel book filled with the vitality of a child's point of view. Using photos and drawings, this is a model for kids writing about places less exotic than Swaziland. 5–8.

MISTAKES THAT WORKED

(by Charlotte F. Jones/illus. by John O Brien, Doubleday $15) What do Slinky, Ivory Soap, potato chips and paper towels have in common? They and dozens of other things we eat, wear and use were invented by accident! Each of the 40 discoveries is explained in a brief, lively account. 9 and up.

MY NEW YORK ✯'94 PLATINUM AWARD

(by Kathy Jakobsen, Little Brown $15.95) In a "pictorial" letter to a friend who is moving from the Midwest to New York, the young narrator gives the reader a whirlwind tour of the city. Jakobsen's folk art is full of vitality and small details, including a hint for the narrator who appears somewhere—à la Waldo—in every scene. 5–9.

PLANES OF THE ACES ✯'94 PLATINUM AWARD

(concept & paper engineering by Keith Moseley/text by Joan Bowden, Doubleday $14.95) Each spread in this incredible book features a plane that made flying history from 1917 to the present. The concise text gives young readers interesting anecdotes about each plane. 7 & up.

THE STORY OF THE WHITE HOUSE

(by Kate Waters, Scholastic $12.95) Here's an excellent tour and brief history of the White House. Illustrated with recent and archival photos and drawings, along with interesting facts about its famous occupants. For those who have visited or hope to one day, this will be a memorable book. 5–8.

STRINGBEAN'S TRIP TO THE SHINING SEA

(by Vera B. Williams/illus. by Vera and Jennifer Williams, Greenwillow $14) From a cross-country trip, a zippy collection of postcards, all signed by a boy called String-bean, make a delightful record. A nice mix of humor, adventure and painless geography. 6–9.

SPORTS

To get reluctant readers to pick up a book, try a topic they have a lively interest in. Reading about sports is a key for some kids.

THE FIELD BEYOND THE OUTFIELD

(by Mark Teague, Scholastic $13.95) Ludlow Grebe, a boy with an active imagination, gets signed on to play base-ball (by his parents). Stuck in the outfield, Ludlow becomes a hero—a star! A zany, kid-sized Field of Dreams for Little Leaguers. 6–9.

MAJOR LEAGUE BATBOY

(by Chuck Solomon, Crown $11.95) With full-color pho-tos and clear, crisp text, a trip behind the scenes of a major-league baseball team. Following a day in the life of the Phillies, we tour the clubhouse, locker room, equip-ment room and dugout practice sessions. 7 & up.

TAKE ME OUT TO THE BALLGAME

(illus. by Maryann Kovalski, Scholastic $14.95) Using the old song, Kovalski has spun a lively visual story of a zany Granny who takes her grandkids out to the old ball game—and she gets into it, too! The images of Granny and the kids on the video scoreboard are topped only by Granny being carried off the field in triumph by the team. 5–8.

A VERY YOUNG SKATER

(by Jill Krementz, Knopf $14) One of a series of photo essays about kids who dedicate a good part of their lives to mastering a demanding skill. Also *A Very Young Dancer* and *Gymnast*. 7 & up.

EASY-TO-READ BOOKS

Most books in this section are from series designed especially for young readers and are available in paperback. These are new titles, but don't forget some you probably started with, not so long ago.

• •

Ten Blue-Chip Books Every Beginning Reader Should Know

★ ★ ★

- *Amelia Bedelia,* by Peggy Parish
- *Are You My Mother?* by P. D. Eastman
- *Frog and Toad,* by Arnold Lobel
- *Go, Dog, Go,* by P. D. Eastman
- *Green Eggs and Ham,* by Dr. Seuss
- *Henry and Mudge* series, by Cynthia Rylant
- *Little Bear,* by Else H. Minarik
- *My Father's Dragon,* by Ruth S. Gannet
- *Polk Street* series, by Patricia R. Giff
- *Stories Julian Tells,* by Ann Cameron

To help your beginner:
- Choose books that are not a struggle. Easy does it!
- If every other word is too hard, you've got the wrong book for now.
- If your child gets stuck on a word, say the word. Some words can't be sounded out.
- A book mark under the line they are reading can help them keep their place.

JUST BEGINNING BOOKS

THE BIG, RED BLANKET
(by Harriet Ziefert/illus. by David Jacobson, Harper-Collins paper $3.95) Kara asks her family to play with her and finally finds a playful way to get everyone involved. The repetitive pattern makes for easy, predictable reading. This has only 46 words.

DINOSAUR BABIES
(by Lucille Penner/illus. by Peter Barrett, Random House paper $2.95) A subject that's always a hit with first- and second-graders in a manageable book for beginners. From the *Step into Reading* series, with tons of fact and fiction for novice to more experienced readers.

LITTLE CHICK'S FRIEND DUCKLING
(by Mary DeBall Kwitz/illus. by Bruce Degan, Harper-Collins paper $3.50) Broody Hen is about to hatch new chicks, and Little Chick is afraid she and his friend Duckling are going to like the new chicks best. Sibling rivalry in the barnyard!

MINE'S THE BEST
(by Crosby Bonsall, HarperCollins paper $3.50) A playful, humorous argument between friends makes this repetitive easy-to-read a lively choice for new readers.

MY TOOTH IS LOOSE
(by Martin Silverman/illus. by Amy Aitken, Viking $8.95) An ultra-easy-to-read tale about a loose tooth and friends with cures.

MODERATELY EASY BOOKS

CHANG'S PAPER PONY
(by Eleanor Coerr/illus. by Deborah K. Ray, Harper-Collins paper $3.50) A Chinese boy who has come to America with his grandfather

gets gold fever, and he wishes for a pony of his own. One of many excellent *I Can Read* "history" books.

DESPERATE FOR A DOG

(by Rose Impey and Jolyne Knox, Dutton $3.50) Two sisters do everything they can to sell their parents on a dog. When a neighbor goes to the hospital the girls get their wish. From the Speedsters series, which combines prose with action-packed drawings and cartoon bubbles to take the story forward. Also *Harvey and Rosie . . . and Ralph.*

EEK! STORIES TO MAKE YOU SHRIEK

(by Jane O'Connor/illus. by Brian Karas, Grosset & Dunlap paper $3.50) Three fairly spooky stories about a strange doll, someone in a monster suit and a shaggy dog that disappears–almost.

HENRY AND MUDGE

(by Cynthia Rylant/illus. by Sucie Stevenson, Aladdin $3.95) One of a dozen adventures shared by a boy and his best friend, a lovable puppy who grows and grows into a 180-pound, three-foot pal.

OLD ENOUGH FOR MAGIC

(by Anola Pickett/illus. by Ned Delaney, HarperCollins paper $3.50) Peter's big sister sneaks into his room to use his new magic kit and turns herself into a frog. It's Peter who finds the magic to save her. A funny story!

OLD TURTLE'S 90 KNOCK-KNOCKS, JOKES AND RIDDLES

(by Leonard Kessler, Greenwillow $13.95) Exactly on target for first- and second-graders, who love reading and guessing and retelling knock-knocks, jokes and riddles. Readers will relish the simple word play and humor in this collection.

SIX SICK SHEEP: 101 TONGUE TWISTERS

(collected by Joanna Cole and Stephanie Calmenson/ illus. by Alan Tiegreen, Morrow $15) Can you say "lemon liniment" three times fast? How about "Greek grapes"?

More than 100 tongue twisters, games and poems to tickle young readers. 6 & up.

SPACEY RIDDLES

(by Katy Hall and Lisa Eisenberg/illus. by Simms Taback, Dial $11) Here are 41 riddles about astronauts, Martians and other spacey subjects. One to a page and easy to read, with amusing illustrations. One of a series of riddle books. 6–8.

THE WHITE STALLION   BLUE CHIP

(by Elizabeth Shub/illus. by Rachel Isadora, Bantam paper $2.99) On their journey westward the heat is fierce. Pa ties his daughter, Gretchen, to their old mare, Anna. No one guessed that the wagon would break down or that the mare would stray off with the sleeping girl on her back. Miles later, a wild white stallion saves Gretchen. 7 & up.

TRANSITION CHAPTER BOOKS FOR ADVANCED BEGINNERS

ALEX FITZGERALD, TV STAR

(by Kathleen Krull, Little Brown $10.95) Alex plays so well at a class show that she gets a spot on a music video. Star-struck, she learns the hard way about what really counts.

THE DRINKING GOURD

(by F. N. Monjo/illus. by Fred Brenner, HarperCollins paper $3.50) An adventure story about the Underground Railroad that combines history and suspense. Young Tommy and his father help a family make their escape to Canada. Newly reissued with handsome full-color illustrations.

FOURTH-GRADE RATS

(by Jerry Spinelli, Scholastic $13.95) Suds wishes he was still a third-grade angel so he wouldn't have to be a fourth-grade rat. A funny, touching chapter book about peer pressure and growing up. 7–9.

THE LUCKY BASEBALL BAT

(by Matt Christopher, Little Brown $11.95) A young player who needs confidence is given a gift of a bat that he's told is lucky. Christopher has done a series of easy-to-read baseball stories that is bound to motivate sports-minded kids to read.

OLYMPIC OTIS

(by Gibbs Davis, Bantam paper $2.99) One of a sports-centered series that will appeal to both boys and girls. In this one, Otis, who was left back in third grade, feels like a failure till he learns an important lesson while helping a girl train for the Special Olympics.

RATS ON THE RANGE

(by James Marshall, Dial $12.99) A rib-tickling collection of funny stories about a bossy mouse, a tomcat she tames and a pig who learns table manners. A great read-alone or read-aloud. 6–9.

STORIES JULIAN TELLS

(by Ann Cameron/illus. by Ann Strugnell, Knopf paper $2.95) A beginner's chapter book about two brothers and the small but amusing events of their life. Despite the usual squabbles between brothers, a strong bond between Julian and his little brother, Huey, comes shining through this and the sequel *More Stories Julian Tells*. 8 & up.

A TURKEY DRIVE AND OTHER TALES

(by Barbara Ann Porte/illus. by Yossi Abolafia, Greenwillow $14) A collection of amusing stories, each told by a different member of the family, all inspired by pictures drawn by their artist mother. The third book featuring Abigail, Sam, their taxicab driver father and artist mother. If your reader likes this one, try *Taxicab Tales*. 7 & up.

READ-ALOUD CHAPTER BOOKS

Long before school-age kids can tackle big chapter books on their own, they enjoy the more fully drawn characters, richer language and multi-layered plots found in story-books. These first novels, with more words than pic-

tures, push children to imagine with the mind's eye—something they will need to do as they grow into reading. In time these books may be re-read independently. For now, the best way to motivate the next level of readership is to continue reading good books to your child.

- *Charlotte's Web,* by E. B. White
- *The Black Stallion,* by Walter Farley
- *The Littles,* by John Peterson
- *Mary Poppins,* by P. L. Travers
- *The House at Pooh Corner,* by A. A. Milne
- *Ramona* series, by Beverly Cleary
- *The Borrowers,* by Mary Norton
- *Stuart Little,* by E. B. White
- *James and the Giant Peach,* by Roald Dahl
- *My Father's Dragon,* by Ruth S. Gannett
- *Little House* series, by Laura Wilder
- *Wizard of Oz* series, by L. Frank Baum
- *Charlie and the Chocolate Factory,* by Roald Dahl
- *Catwings,* by Ursula LeGuin
- *Sarah Plain and Tall,* by Patricia MacLachlan
- *The Real Thief,* by William Steig

RECENT ANTHOLOGIES: POEMS & STORIES

These are ideal for read-aloud storytimes or for solo reading by older kids.

AMERICAN TALL TALES

(by Mary Pope Osborne/illus. by Michael McCurdy, Knopf $18) Nine of our best-loved American tall tales,

including tales about Paul Bunyan, Mose, and Sally Ann
Thunder among others. Well told with historical head-
notes. McCurdy's woodcuts are bold and lively as the
stories themselves. 6 & up.

THE BIG BOOK FOR OUR PLANET

(Edited by Ann Durell, et al., Dutton $17.99) More than
forty distinguished authors and illustrators have con-
tributed stories, poems, essays and art for this handsome book that reinforces our need to live in harmony
with our planet. 6 & up.

BROWN ANGELS

(by Walter D. Myers, HarperCollins $16) Great beauty
abounds in this collection of turn of the century pho-
tographs of African-American children. They are the
music and his poems are the loving lyrics that blend to
make an exquisite book for families to share. 6 & up.

FROM SEA TO SHINING SEA ✸'94 PLATINUM AWARD

(compiled by Amy L. Cohn, Scholastic $29.95) A splendif-
erous collection of more than 140 American folktales,
songs, poems and essays. Art by a Who's Who of award-
winning artists. Each chapter centers on a period or
theme from our history. 7 & up.

I SEE THE MOON, AND THE MOON SEES ME

(collected and illus. by Helen Craig, HarperCollins $16)
More than 50 best-loved nursery rhymes, with wonder-
fully lively illustrations by the creator of the well-known
Angelina Ballerina books. 3–7.

MAGICAL TALES FROM MANY LANDS

(retold by Margaret Mayo/illus. by Jane Ray, Dutton
$19.95) Wonderfully crafted stories from India, Africa,
Peru, Australia, China, Japan and other lands are illustrated with great style. Ideal for reading aloud or solo
reading. 8 & up.

RANDOM HOUSE BOOK OF FAIRY TALES

(retold by Amy Ehrlich/illus. by Diane Goode, Random
House $17) A treasure! Tales from Grimm, Andersen and

Perrault, with charming illustrations. Includes "Sleeping Beauty," "Rapunzel," "Hansel and Gretel" and many more. 5 & up.

SING A SONG OF POPCORN

(compiled by Beatrice Schenk de Regniers, Scholastic $18.95) A popping good collection of well-known poems to share. The whole family will enjoy the delightful illustrations done by Caldecott-winning artists. All ages.

OF SWANS, SUGARPLUMS AND SATIN SLIPPERS: BALLET STORIES FOR CHILDREN

(by Violette Verdy/illus. by Marcia Brown, Scholastic $15.95) Here are princes, sorcerers, and even birds of fire! Brown's gossamer watercolors capture the romance of six ballet tales, including "Swan Lake," "The Nutcracker" and "Sleeping Beauty." 6 & up.

RESOURCE/ACTIVITY BOOKS

THE MAGIC HANDBOOK

(by Malcolm Bird and Alan Dart, Chronicle $12.95) Dozens of easy-to-follow magic tricks with step-by-step illustrations for doing magic tricks. Sixes and sevens will need help but eights and up will want to keep the source of their magic tricks a secret.

MY FIRST BAKING BOOK

(by Helen Drew, Knopf $12) Recipes for treats are made easy with step-by-step photos and captions (and adult assistance). The whole family could enjoy learning to make (and eat) puff pastries, cookies, scones, dinosaur cake and more. An excellent way to reinforce math and reading with delicious pay-off! Also *My First Party Book*.

THE RAMONA QUIMBY DIARY

(by Beverly Cleary/illus. by Alan Tiegreen, Morrow $10.95) Here is a diary for beginners with spaces to fill in feelings, experiences, likes and dislikes. There's plenty of room for regular entries, but this is user-friendly for the novice journal keeper. 7–9.

HOW TO MAKE SUPER POP-UPS
(by Joan Irvine/illus. by Linda Hendry, Morrow $14)
Irvine walks readers through the fun of making pop-up
cards, books, boxes and other creations, using materials
easily found at home. A great sequel to the simpler *How
to Make Pop-ups.* 8 & up.

COPING WITH LIFE'S UPS AND DOWNS: BOOKS FOR MIXED AGES

Many of the books in this section are what we call
bridge books—they span two age groups. Some are
on the young side, others are for older kids and
many will do for both. This section includes books
that address problems that families often need to
cope with.

A New Baby

A BABY SISTER FOR FRANCES   BLUE CHIP
(by Russell Hoban/illus. by Lillian Hoban, HarperCollins
$14)When her baby sister arrives, Frances has a hard
time sharing her parents' attention. Like all the Frances
stories, this one reflects children's feelings. A bit wordy
for young preschoolers. 4–7.

DARCY AND GRAN DON'T LIKE BABIES
PLATINUM AWARD
(by Jane Cutler/illus. Susannah Ryan, Scholastic $14.95)
Thank goodness that Gran understands how Darcy feels
about the new baby. Instead of correcting all of Darcy's
negative views, Gran mirrors them along with a growing
acceptance. 3–7.

THE NEW BABY AT YOUR HOUSE   BLUE CHIP
(by Joanna Cole/photos by Hella Hammid, Morrow paper
$5.95) Unlike a lot of cutesy books that play up the
rivalry aspect of a new baby, this book explores many
aspects of having a sibling. In addition to the solid information for kids, there is an excellent section for parents
that alone is worth the price of the book! 3–6

A NEW BABY AT KOKO BEAR'S HOUSE

(by Vicki Lansky, Book Peddlers $4.95) Koko's story walks young listeners through the big moments of becoming a sibling, from anticipation to Mama's departure and homecoming—and all the mixed feelings. Lansky also gives practical tips to parents. 3–5.

ON MOTHER'S LAP　　BLUE CHIP

(by Ann H. Scott/illus. by Glo Coalson, Clarion $14.95) A reassuring, gentle tale about a little boy who learns there's always room for him and his little sister on Mother's lap. A newly re-illustrated classic. 2 & up.

SHE COME BRINGING ME THAT LITTLE BABY GIRL

(by Eloise Greenfield/illus. by John Steptoe, HarperCollins $14) Kevin wanted a brother, not a sister. To make matters worse, she gets all the attention and presents. Mama helps him understand that being a big brother might not be all that bad. 4–8.

SIBLINGS

DANCE, TANYA

(by Patricia L. Gauch/illus. by Satomi Ichikawa, Philomel $13.95) Little Tanya longs to dance like her big sister, but Mother says she's too young for lessons. On the night of her sister's dance recital when all the relatives come to see Elise, they get an encore performance by you know who. A warm story that rings true. 3–5.

MAX AND RUBY'S FIRST GREEK MYTH

(by Rosemary Wells, Dial $10.99) Ruby tells her snoopy little brother, Max, a cautionary tale—her own version of Pandora's Box. As always, Wells serves up a honey of a story! 4–8.

NOW EVERYBODY REALLY HATES ME

(by Jane R. Martin and Patricia Marx/illus. by Roz Chast, HarperCollins $14) Celebrating one sibling's birthday often brings out the worst in older and younger sibs.

Patty Jean gets sent to her room to stew in this tongue-in-cheek comic tale. 4–8.

SILLY BILLY!

(by Pat Hutchins, Greenwillow $14) Hazel is enjoying playing with her family until baby Billy wants a turn and Grandma says, "Let Billy have a turn. He's only little." Again and again, Billy gets his way and spoils whatever his big sister is doing. Illustrated with those very green, droll monsters from *The Very Worst Monster*. 4–6.

ADOPTION

ADOPTION IS FOR ALWAYS

(by Linda W. Girard/illus. by Judith Friedman, Whitman $11.95) Celia had been told many times that she was adopted, but she "hadn't really heard what they said." Then a day comes and Celia understands, but she also has anger and questions about why her birth mother gave her up. Could it happen again? A reassuring book. 5–8.

A FOREVER FAMILY

(by Roslyn Banish with Jennifer Jordan-Wong, Harper-Collins $14) Eight-year-old Jennifer tells what it's like to finally be adopted, after being a foster child in several homes. Easy-to-read text makes this right for young readers as well as listeners. 5–8.

A MOTHER FOR CHOCO

(by Keiko Kasza, Putnam $14.95) Choco, a small yellow chick, goes looking for a mother who looks like him. But when he meets Mrs. Bear he tells her all the things a mother would do, and Choco discovers not only a loving mother but a family of a little hippo, gator and pig, all of whom Mrs. Bear has adopted as her own. 4–8.

THROUGH MOON AND STARS AND NIGHT SKIES

(by Ann Turner/illus. by James G. Hale, HarperCollins $13) A child who was adopted from a distant country tells the story of his journey and fears as he traveled to his new home and loving family. Truly a beautifully told story that will be especially meaningful for children who are adopted from overseas. 4–8.

MOVING

GILA MONSTERS MEET YOU AT THE AIRPORT BLUE CHIP

(by Marjorie W. Sharmat/illus. by Byron Barton, Macmillan $14.95) An amusing tale of a small boy with great fears and fantasies about moving from east to west meets a boy who has fears in the opposite direction. 4 & up.

I'M NOT MOVING, MAMA!

(by Nancy White Carlstrom/illus. by Thor Wickstrom, Macmillan $13.95) Again and again Mouse tells Mama why he's not moving. As Mama continues to pack she offers assurance that their new home will be different but fine, as long as they are together. 3–6.

STARS FOR SARAH

(by Ann Turner/illus. by Mary Teichman, HarperCollins $13.95) Awakened and worried about moving to a new house, Sarah's mom answers her many questions about their new house. Acknowledging how some things will change, but not the important things, this is a reassuring and comforting book, with evocative paintings. 4–8.

VIDEO TIP: *Let's Get a Move On!* (Kidvidz $14.95) Four experts on moving—four different kids— tell about their feelings and the experience of moving. Includes military family and single-parent household. 5–10. (617) 965-3345.

DIVORCE AND SEPARATION

CHARLIE ANDERSON
(by Barbara Abercrombie/illus. by Mark Graham, McElderry $13.95) Charlie is no ordinary cat. He seems to lead two lives, disappearing and reappearing. Indeed his mysterious double life turns out to be not unlike that of the children in the story, who split their time between parents in a shared-custody arrangement. 5–8.

DINOSAURS DIVORCE
(by Marc and Laurene Brown/illus. by Marc Brown, Little Brown $14.95) Using humor and a cartoon cast of dinosaurs, Brown manages to convey plenty of solid information to young readers who are in anything but a funny situation. 5–8.

NO ONE IS GOING TO NASHVILLE
(by Mavis Jukes/illus. Lloyd Bloom, Knopf paper $3) Many kids spend time with stepparents, and this is a warm story of one such family. Sonia's stepmother is anything but the mean old stereotype. What Sonia wants most is to keep a stray dog that her father says she can't have. A moving story with people you care about. 8 & up.

THE STORY OF MAY
(by Mordicai Gerstein, HarperCollins $16) May lives with her mother, April, but longs to meet her father, who lives at the opposite end of the year. In this lyrical allegory, May travels from month to month meeting her relatives, who help her find her father. Not for everyone, but it is powerful! Gerstein's month people are splendid. 6–9.

STAYING HEALTHY

GOING TO THE DOCTOR AND GOING TO THE DENTIST
(by Fred Rogers, Putnam $12.95 each) With photos of preschoolers doing what must be done, Mister Rogers

give kids a preview of routine trips to the doctor and dentist. 3–7.

LITTLE RABBIT'S LOOSE TOOTH   BLUE CHIP

(by Lucy Bate/illus. by Diane de Groat, Crown $15) There are lots of stories about losing the first tooth, but few more endearing than this gentle tale about that big event. 5–7.

NORMAN FOOLS THE TOOTH FAIRY

(by Carol Carrick/illus. by Lisa McCue, Scholastic $13.95) Norman, a whimsical alligator, is so eager to collect from the fairy he tries to fool the fairy and ends up scaring himself. All's well that ends well. Norman not only loses a tooth and collects, he learns how to take good care of his teeth. 5–7.

ONE DAY, TWO DRAGONS

(by Lynne Bertrand/illus. by Janet Street, Potter $14) Nobody likes getting shots, least of all two dragons who need four shots for measles, mumps, scale rot and morning breath. A trip to the doctor that will give kids a laugh of recognition. 3–6.

RITA GOES TO THE HOSPITAL

(by Martine Davidson/illus. by John Jones, Random House $2.95) One of a series developed by the AMA to prepare kids for medical events that may be worrisome. Rita is having her tonsils out. The illustrations and child's dialogue lack grace, but this answers more questions than most on the subject. 5–7.

DEATH

ANNIE AND THE OLD ONE   BLUE CHIP

(by Miska Miles/illus. by Peter Parnall, Little, Brown $13.95) Annie watches as her grandmother weaves a Navaho rug. Grandmother, the Old One, tries to prepare Annie for the inevitable—that when the weaving is done she will die. So Annie gets up each night to pull out the threads and keep her grandmother alive. A moving story with universal appeal. 6–8.

CHARLOTTE'S WEB   BLUE CHIP

(by E. B. White/illus. by Garth Williams, HarperCollins $12) No story talks so eloquently about the fear of death and the cycle of life than this classic tale. Ideal for reading loud to sixes and eights and revisiting by independent readers.

I'LL SEE YOU IN MY DREAMS ⭐ PLATINUM AWARD

(by Mavis Jukes/illus. by Stacey Schuett, Knopf $15) How do you say good-bye to someone you love who is dying? If she were a skywriter she would put her farewell in the sky. In an age when so many young people are dying of AIDS, this is a particularly meaningful book. 7 & up.

THE SADDEST TIME

(by Norma Simon/illus. by Jacqueline Rogers, Whitman $11.95). Using three distinct situations—a young uncle, a child killed in an accident and an elderly grandmother—Simon explains death as an inevitable end of life but not of remembering. 5–8.

DEATH OF A PET

THE TENTH GOOD THING ABOUT BARNEY

(by Judith Viorst/illus. by Eric Blegvad, Atheneum $12.95) When his cat, Barney, dies, a young boy deals with his loss by remembering the good things about him. This bittersweet storybook says it all. 4–8.

WHEN A PET DIES

(by Fred Rogers, Putnam paper $5.95) Mister Rogers talks in clear language about what happens when a pet dies because it is hurt or ill. 4–8.

HOLIDAY BOOKS

HOLIDAYS AMERICAN STYLE

THE BUCK STOPS HERE: THE PRESIDENTS OF THE UNITED STATES

(by Alice Provensen, HarperCollins $18) Each president is presented in a rhyming couplet and detailed, poster-like montage paintings that are crammed with historic events that happened while he was in office. 6 & up.

ENCOUNTER PLATINUM AWARD

(by Jane Yolen/illus. by David Shannon, Harcourt Brace $14.95) Unlike so many books about Columbus's "discovery," Yolen tells the story through the eyes of a Taino Indian boy and what the arrival of Columbus meant to his people. A moving story with glorious, memorable illustrations. 6 & up.

FOLLOW THE DREAM

(by Peter Sis, Knopf $15) Among the many tellings of the Columbus story, this is one of the most visually stunning. Fashioned from maps and 15th-century sources, a rich and painterly view of the events leading up to the voyage to the New World. 5–8

GEORGE WASHINGTON

(by James Giblin/illus. by Michael Dooling, Scholastic $14.95) A handsome picturebook biography with Rockwell–style oil paintings. Giblin gives young readers a full picture of the man and his role in shaping our country. 5–8.

HONEST ABE ⭐ PLATINUM AWARD

(by Edith Kunhardt/illus. by Malcah Zeldis, Greenwillow $15) Folk art in vivid colors and bold strokes gives a rough-hewn flavor to this memorable biography of Lincoln. Begins with the hardships of his boyhood and includes the highlights of his life. 6–9.

THE STAR-SPANGLED BANNER

(illus. by Peter Spier, Doubleday paper $3.99) From the dawn's early light, Spier recreates the battle at Fort McHenry that inspired Francis Scott Key to write our national anthem. Includes historic notes, flags and reproduction of the original manuscript. 6 & up.

HAPPY BIRTHDAY, MARTIN LUTHER KING

(by Jean Marzollo/illus. by J. Brian Pinkney, Scholastic $14.95) With just a few lines on each page, Marzollo tells young children what Dr. King wanted to change in America and what he accomplished. Pinkney's rich illustrations add much to the elegance of this story crafted for the young. 3–7

HALLOWEEN

FACE PAINTING

(Klutz Press, $16.95) A set of face paints and a brush come with this excellent how-to book of face painting, illustrated with photographs. Also included are costume designs. Sure to come in handy for Halloween and school plays. 6 & up.

MONSTER MOTEL

(by Douglas Florian, Harcourt Brace $13.95) A collection of monster poems that are more funny than scary but right for the season. 4–8.

SPOT GOES TO A PARTY

(by Eric Hill, Putnam $11.95) Halloween and costumes are sometimes a bit scary to toddlers and preschoolers. You can't always tell who is behind that mask. In this lift-and-look book, Spot finds out and has a good time dressing up, too. 2–4.

THE WIDOW'S BROOM   PLATINUM AWARD

(by Chris Van Allsburg, Houghton Mifflin $17.95) "Witches' brooms don't last forever." So begins a mysterious tale of a clever broom that loses its power of flight but not its magic to stir up trouble for the spunky widow who sees things differently from her neighbors. A perfect choice for Halloween. 6 & up.

THANKSGIVING

IF YOU SAILED ON THE MAYFLOWER BLUE CHIP

(by Ann McGovern/illus. by J. B. Handelsman, Scholastic paper $3.95) One of an excellent series, which uses a question-and-answer format. Gives kids small nuggets of information that add up to a big picture of how things were. 6–9.

MOLLY'S PILGRIM

(by Barbara Cohen/illus. by Michael Deraney, Lothrop $14) A young Russian/Jewish immigrant is taunted by her classmates because of her clothes and accent. She brings an unusual pilgrim doll for her third-grade Thanksgiving project. A modern-day story brings rich meaning to the religious freedom we celebrate. A short gem. 6 & up.

KWANZAA

MY FIRST KWANZAA BOOK

(by Deborah M. N. Chocolate/illus. by Cal Massey, Scholastic $10.95) An introduction to the African-American holiday. The seven days of celebration are explained, along with the customs of lighting candles, telling stories and gathering for family feasts of food and joy. 3–7.

CHRISTMAS BOOKS

Of the hundreds of children's books published each year, Christmas books are often among the most beautiful. Such books not only make great gifts, they are especially enjoyed during the pre-holiday nights when anticipation runs high.

THE BEST CHRISTMAS PAGEANT EVER

(by Barbara Robinson/illus. by Judith Brown, Harper-Collins $14) A grand read-aloud chapter book about the unconventional Herdman kids, who get involved in a Christmas pageant and change others as well as themselves. 6–60.

CARL'S CHRISTMAS

(by Alexandra Day, Farrar Straus $5.95) In this almost wordless adventure, Carl, a canine nanny, is left with the baby on Christmas Eve. After an evening of adventure, Carl is rewarded with a visit from Santa. A cardboard version will sustain many readings. 4 & up.

THE CHRISTMAS BEAR

(by Henrietta Strickland/illus. by Paul Strickland, Dutton $15.99) A baby polar bear at the North Pole falls down a hole and into Santa's wondrous workshop. A visual delight! 3–7.

EMMA'S CHRISTMAS

(adapted by Irene Trivas, Orchard $14.95) A prince asks for Emma's hand in marriage, but she is not eager to live in a castle. What can the prince do? He sends an abundance of gifts for each of the Twelve Days of Christmas. A funny version! 4 & up.

I SPY CHRISTMAS

(by Jean Marzollo/photos by Walter Wick, Scholastic $12.95) Kids will pore over the marvelous photos searching for objects named in the playful rhyming riddles. One of a series of game books.

JINGLE BUGS

(by David Carter, Simon & Schuster $16.00) A totally silly pull-tab, pop-up, light-up-and-play-you-a-tune book. A comic novelty gift item that's bound to bring smiles. 3 & up.

THE JOLLY CHRISTMAS POSTMAN   PLATINUM AWARD

(by Janet and Allan Ahlberg, Little Brown $16.95) In a jolly sequel, the postman is delivering Christmas mail to favorite storybook characters. There's a card from Goldilocks and her sister to Baby Bear and his brother. Mr. Wolf sends a miniboardgame to Red Riding Hood. A delight for storybook-wise fours and up.

THE LAST CHRISTMAS PRESENT

(by Matt Novak, Orchard $14.95) In Santa's rush to get on his way, one present is left behind. As in the *Perils of Pauline*, Irwin, the smallest elf, delivers it despite thin ice, avalanches or abominable snowman. An irreverent, comic romp with elves like you've never seen! 5–9.

THE NIGHT BEFORE CHRISTMAS

(by Clement C. Moore) There are many versions of this classic, illustrated by well-known artists. Each year new ones appear. These are a few special ones.

- *The Grandma Moses Night Before Christmas* (Random House $15)
- *The Night Before Christmas* (illus. by James Marshall, Scholastic $13.95)
- *The Night Before Christmas* (illus. by Anita Lobel, Knopf $12)

NIGHT TREE

(by Eve Bunting/illus. by Ted Rand, Harcourt Brace $13.95) "On the night before Christmas we always go to find our tree," the story begins. But this is not a book about cutting down a Christmas tree. This family brings popcorn chains and a feast of fruits so creatures of the forest will have Christmas dinner. Charming! 4–8.

THE NUTCRACKER

(retold by Jenni Fleetwood/illus. by Phillida Gili, HarperCollins $14.95) The ballet based on the story of the Nutcracker is often the first ballet children see, and this pop-up book captures the main scenes with assorted flaps to lift, tabs to pull and pages that spring to life! 4–8.

O CHRISTMAS TREE

(illus. by Michael Hague, Henry Holt $4.95) Hague's illustrated carol gets an "E" for the ecological subplot. When the bears go out to find their tree, they dig one up and replant it in the ground after the holiday. All ages.

THE POLAR EXPRESS   BLUE CHIP

(by Chris Van Allsburg, Houghton Mifflin $17.95) A young boy travels to the North Pole, where Santa offers him any gift. The gift is granted but soon lost. A magical fantasy! Available on audio tape, narrated by William Hurt. 5 & up.

THE REINDEER CHRISTMAS

(by Moe Price/illus. by Atsuko Morozmi, Harcourt Brace $15.95) Time was when Santa delivered his gifts by foot. His elves came up with a magic sleigh. But who would pull it? We know the answer, but the creatures who try and the glorious illustrations make this a gem. 4–8.

SANTA CALLS

(by William Joyce, HarperCollins $18) Art Atchinson Aimesworth is an orphan, crimebuster and reluctant big brother until that fateful Christmas when S.C. sends for him. A fantasy with extravagantly magical illustrations and a tasty story. 6–10.

THE SHOEMAKER AND THE ELVES

(retold and illus. by Ilse Plume, Harcourt Brace $14.95) Four elves help a poor shoemaker regain success and are repaid with gifts. A perfect story about the gift of giving and not just getting. An ideal read-aloud for 3-8.

THANK YOU, SANTA

(by Margaret Wild/illus. by Kerry Argent, Scholastic $12.95) Everyone writes to Santa before Christmas—but what about afterward? Samantha, who is sick in bed, writes Santa a thank-you letter. So begins a year-long series of letters between two pen pals. Set in Australia, here's a look at the seasons at the North Pole and down under. 5–9.

TREE OF CRANES

(by Allen Say, Houghton Mifflin $16.95) A small Japanese boy's mother shares a custom from her American childhood. She gives him the gift of a treeful of origami paper birds, and he in turn gives her a promise. A beautiful blend of two cultures. 4–8.

WE WISH YOU A MERRY CHRISTMAS
(arranged by Dan Fox, Little, Brown $16.95) Here are 25 easy-to-play holiday songs illustrated with works of art from the Metropolitan Museum collection. All ages.

HANUKKAH STORIES AND SONGS

ELIJAH'S ANGEL
(by Michael Rosen/illus. by Aminah Robinson, Harcourt Brace $13.95) Michael's friend, an African-American man, gives him a Hanukkah gift of a carved angel. Michael is afraid to keep a "graven image"—forbidden to Jews— until his family assures him that "it's an angel of friendship." Striking illustrations. 5–8.

IN THE MONTH OF KISLEV
(by Nina Jaffe/illus. by Louise August, Viking $15) Mendel the peddler is so poor that the only way his children get latkes is to stand at the window of the rich man, Feivel, and smell them. Selfish Feivel takes them to the rabbi, claiming they should pay him for the smell of his latkes. The wise rabbi comes up with a perfect solution. 4–8.

JUST ENOUGH IS PLENTY: A HANUKKAH TALE
(by Barbara Diamond Goldin/illus. by Seymour Chwast, Puffin paper $3.95) Malka is worried because her family is poor and Papa has no extra kopeks for treats. But when a poor stranger comes to the door, her parents share what little they have and the stranger in turn provides gifts of his own. 5 & up.

SONGS OF CHANUKAH
(compiled by Jeanne Modesitt/illus. by Robin Spowart, Little Brown $15.95) Traditional and contemporary songs with some background notes. Relatively easy to play.

WE CELEBRATE CHANUKAH

(Pockets of Learning $29.99) A fabric toy/book that comes with Velcro-backed candles, latkes, and a dreidel. 2 & up. Constructive Playthings (800) 832-0572.

EASTER

MARUSHKA'S EGG

(by Elsa O. Rael/illus. by Joanna Wezyk, Four Winds $14.95) When her mother sends Marushka to market to buy a special egg for their Easter bread, she chooses a magic one from an old woman who turns out to be the witch Baba Yaga! Peeking into the egg, she is whisked into the shell and taken away to the evil witch's cottage. 6 & up

RECHENKA'S EGGS

(by Patricia Polacco, Philomel $14.95) When old Babushka rescues a wounded goose the bird accidentally breaks the old woman's beautiful handpainted Ukrainian eggs. But all is not lost! Rechenka, the goose, gives the old woman more than a dozen miraculous gifts. A beauty! 4–8.

PASSOVER

THE MAGICIAN'S VISIT

(retold by Barbara Goldin/illus. by Robert A. Parker, Viking $15) A poor couple have nothing but faith as Passover approaches and they have no money for a seder feast. Enter the Magician! Adapted from a tale by I. L. Peretz. 4–9.

MRS. KATZ AND TUSH

(by Patricia Polacco, Bantam $15) What can an old Jewish widow and a young African-American boy have in common? For starters, there's a tailless cat that she dubs "Tush," and that's not where it ends. An unusual book about friendship. 5–8

MUSIC

Here are several resource books for family sing-along fun.

GONNA SING MY HEAD OFF!
(collected by Kathleen Krull/illus. by Allen Garns, Knopf $20) Arlo Guthrie wrote the intro to this big beauty of a song book. Includes 62 well-known American folksongs. Music for piano and guitar arranged for kids or less-than-expert adults to play.

MY FIRST MUSIC BOOK   PLATINUM AWARD
(by Helen Drew, Dorling Kindersley $12.95) Our testers loved using this book that clearly describes how to make shakers, tambourines, drums, horns and many more instruments from easy-to-locate materials. A visual treat before the music begins! 6 & up.

READER'S DIGEST SONGBOOK
(ed. by William Simon, Reader's Digest $29.95) This big songbook contains folksongs and many favorites from old Disney movies. The arrangements are not super-easy, but the small lyrics book that comes with the big one is handy.

WHAT INSTRUMENT IS THIS?
(by Rosmarie Hausherr, Scholastic $14.95) Using photos of children playing real instruments, the author asks, "What instrument is this?" Turn the page for the name and solid information about the instrument. 6–9.

BILINGUAL BOOKS

Some of these are totally written in two languages. Others are done chiefly in English with a fair sprinkling of words and phrases in another language.

BALLERINA/LA BAILARINA
(by Fred Burstein/illus. by Joan Auclair, Bradbury $14.95) A girl and her father take a lively walk through the city. The story is conveyed almost entirely in pic-

tures accompanied by single words or phrases in English, Spanish and Japanese. 4–8.

BORN IN THE GRAVY

(by Denys Cazet, Orchard $14.95) Margarita tells her papa all about her first day in kindergarten. Papa asks her many questions in Spanish and her answers in English translate his words in context. 5–8.

MARGARET AND MARGARITA ✸ PLATINUM AWARD

(by Lynn Reiser, Greenwillow $14) Two little girls and their mothers go to the park. Margaret speaks no Spanish and Margarita speaks no English, yet they have so much in common that language is not a barrier. A charming story told in both languages that children will understand. 3–7.

MY DAY/MI DÍA

(by Rebecca Emberley, Little, Brown $14.95) Bright paper cutouts of familiar objects are labeled in both English and Spanish. One of a handsome series for young children who are bilingual or learning a second language. Also *Let's Go/Vamos*; *My House/Mi Casa*. 4–8.

THE TAMARINDO PUPPY

(by Charlotte Pomerantz/illus. Byron Barton, Greenwillow $14) Imagine poems written in English and Spanish that need no translating! These playful verses not only sing trippingly on the tongue—they have a special flavor for children who are bilingual (and not) to savor. 4–8.

REFERENCE BOOKS FOR MIXED AGES
DICTIONARIES

Preschool: Very young children don't really need a dictionary, but their love of words and their exploding vocabulary make books with tons of pictures and labels great for looking. Most are arranged in categories rather than alphabetical order. Any of these would be a good choice.

- *Good Morning, Words* (HarperCollins $8.95) 2–5
- *My First 100 Words in Spanish and English* (also French and English) (Simon & Schuster $11) 4–7
- *My First Word Book,* also available in Spanish (Dorling Kindersley $12.95) 4–7
- *Macmillan Picture Wordbook* (Macmillan $8.95) 5–8

Early School Years—First to Third Grades: Beginning readers and writers start to use dictionaries with A to Z listings and pictures to find words they need. Too big a book will be hard to sift through, so less is best!

- *Words for New Readers* (HarperCollins $10.95) 1,500 words with definitions, used in sentences. A mix of cartoons, photos and illustrations. 5–7
- *My First Dictionary* (HarperCollins $12.95) Easy-to-read definitions with pictures and the word used in a sentence. 4,000 words. A good choice for second- and third-graders. 6–9.
- *American Heritage First Dictionary* (Houghton Mifflin $11.95) Definitions are numbered when a word has several meanings. Illustrations and verb tenses. 6–9.
- *Macmillan First Dictionary* (Macmillan $12.95) Illustrated with photos and drawings. Gives plurals of nouns, past tenses of verbs and numbers definitions for words with multiple meanings. 6–9

Later School Years—Fourth Grade and up: These dictionaries are more complex, with syllabication, pronunciation and often word histories. They have fewer illustrations and many more words. Most also include maps and biographical and other historical data. For 9 & up.

- *Macmillan Dictionary for Children* (Macmillan $14.95)
- *Thorndike–Barnhart Children's Dictionary* (HarperCollins $16.95)

ENCYCLOPEDIAS

Before making a big investment in an encyclopedia, go to the public library or your child's school. Look at several sets without pressure from a salesperson. Keep in mind:

- Most kids won't regularly use an encyclopedia before fourth grade, so don't rush.
- Look up the same entry in each set—for example, look at the presentation for "dogs" or "dinosaurs" in each encyclopedia and compare content, style and illustrations.
- Visuals such as photos, charts and drawings will be very important to your child.
- A used edition costs less, but statistics, maps and other information will be dated.

Following are the best choices.

COMPTON'S ENCYCLOPEDIA

(Encyclopedia Britannica $599) This 26-volume set will be used by students from fourth grade through high school. The entries are not super-easy to read, but they are clear and well written and easy to understand. Attractive colorful illustrations and photos. To locate nearest dealer, call (800) 858-4895.

NEW BOOK OF KNOWLEDGE

(Grolier $995) This 21-volume set is written for elementary students. Entries are printed in fairly large type. It is illustrated with colorful pictures and focuses on subjects that interest younger students. Sold through Discovery Toys salespeople; call (800) 426-4777.

WORLD BOOK

(World Book $599) Students from fourth grade through high school will make good use of this 22-volume set for browsing and homework assignments. Clearly written entries are easy to understand; although they are not simplified for beginning readers, they are accessible for young readers. Colorful illustrations and photos. To locate the nearest representative, call (800) 621-8202.

SINGLE-VOLUME RESOURCE BOOKS

ANIMAL ATLAS
(by Barbara Taylor/illus. by Kenneth Lilly, Knopf $20) An oversized book illustrated with maps and full-color paintings of animals arranged by geographic locations. Clear info, such as what animals eat and where and how they build their homes. 7 & up.

EYEWITNESS BOOKS
(Knopf $15) Although the information is often more artful than useful for school reports, these are like stunning coffee-table books that whet kids' appetites for deeper digging. Eyewitness Jr. books are for 5 & up. The big books are great gifts for 8 & up.

RANDOM HOUSE CHILDREN'S ENCYCLOPEDIA
(Random House $60) A huge one-volume encyclopedia that kids love to get lost in. Won't replace World Book or Compton's, but it is great for browsing. 7 & up.

READER'S DIGEST CHILDREN'S WORLD ATLAS
(Reader's Digest $20) With 61 maps plus hundreds of photos and illustrations, this is a resource book that older students will find useful. 8 & up.

RECOMMENDED BOOK CLUBS

If you don't have access to a book store with an extensive selection of children's books, you may find it convenient to join a children's book club. Two recommended clubs that require minimum purchases but allow you to do the selecting are: Children's Book-of-the-Month Club (800) 233-1066. Childern's Quality Paperback Book Club (800) 233-1066.

RECOMMENDED MAGAZINES

PRESCHOOL

- *Highlights for Kids* (11 issues $19.95) Stories, puzzles, science articles, crafts and thinking games. Dept. CA, P.O. Box 269, Columbus, OH 43216-0269. 4 & up.
- *Ladybug* (12 issues $30) Stories, poems and art from well-known children's authors and illustrators. Has a parent's guide with suggestions for extending the theme of each issue. P.O. Box 58343, Boulder, CO 80321-8343. 2–7.
- *Sesame Street Magazine* (10 issues $15) Kids' issue is designed to be cut up for active play with skills like numbers, letters and colors. Comes with a separate parents' guide with informative articles. P.O. Box 55518, Boulder, CO 80322-5518. 2–6.
- *Your Big Backyard* (National Wildlife Federation, 12 issues $12) Big colorful photos and short features plus simple activities. Guide for parents helps introduce preschoolers to nature. (800) 432-6564. 3–5.

EARLY SCHOOL YEARS
Literature and Art

- *Cricket* (12 issues $30) A literary magazine with book excerpts and adaptations from some of our best-known writers and artists. Includes fact and fiction. P.O. Box 51144, Boulder, CO 80321-1144. 6–14.
- *Spark* (9 issues $19.95) A marvelous magazine that features great activities for kids as well as art history, writing ideas and a parents' pull-out section, with activities for preschoolers, too. P.O. Box 5027, Harlan, IA 51593-2527. 5–12.

Writing

- *Boodle: By Kids for Kids* (4 issues $10) Every issue is chockful of original stories, poems and art by children. P.O. Box 1049, Portland, IN 47371. 6–12
- *Stone Soup* (6 issues $23) For aspiring young writers, this magazine publishes original stories, poems and art by children. P.O. Box 83, Santa Cruz, CA 95063. 6–13.

Puzzles

- *Games Junior* (6 issues $12) Like *Games* for adults, this is a zippy magazine with a rich variety of challenging word, picture, logic and number puzzlers. P.O. Box 2082, Harlan, IA 51593. 6–12.
- *Hidden Pictures* (6 issues $14.95) Crosswords, mazes and hidden pictures to ponder from the editors of Highlights. P.O. Box 53781, Boulder, CO 80322. 6–10.

Sports, Scouts and Shopping

- *Boy's Life* (12 issues $15.60) The magazine of the Boy Scouts of America. Articles on scouting and sports, prose fiction and cartoons. 1325 W. Walnut Hill Lane, P.O. Box 152079, Irving, TX 75015-2079. 8 & up.
- *Sports Illustrated for Kids* (12 issues $17.95) Stories about athletes and their experiences as kids and pros. Features for girls as well as boys. A lively spin-off . P.O. Box 83069, Birmingham, AL 35283-0609. 8–13.
- *Zillions—Consumer Reports for Kids* (6 issues $13.95) Preteens test, rate and report on products directed to them. Develops kids' consumer savvy. P.O. Box 54861, Boulder, CO 80322-4861. 8–14.

Science

- *World* (National Geographic Society, 12 issues $12.95) Environmental features, high-quality photos, science activities, stories about kids, plus contests, puzzles and handsome pull-out maps. P.O. Box 2330 Washington, DC 20078-9955. 8 & up.

- *Ranger Rick* (National Wildlife Federation, 12 issues $15) Features on animals and plants, and people who are involved with both. Also games, activities and puzzles. 8925 Leesburg Pike, Vienna,VA 22184-0001. 6 & up.
- *3–2–1 Contact* (Children's Television Workshop, 10 issues $15.97) Features on science and scientists, computers, ecology, animals and other info. Includes games, cartoons, stories, science and math activities. P.O. Box 51177 Boulder, CO 80322. 8 & up.

3 ★ VIDEOS

In just a few short years the world of children's video has grown immensely. There are real choices, wonderful alternatives to the typical "pow, pow, zap" fare served up on commercial TV. In this section you'll find music, stories and informational and how-to videos that involve kids in active doing. These are arranged from choices for the very young to those for older viewers. Some videos bridge a broader age range, from preschool to early school years. If you have a child between four and eight, look at the choices in both Toddlers and Preschoolers and Early School Years.

MUSIC

BABY'S MORNINGTIME
(Lightyear $12.98) Judy Collins sings this collection of "Good morning" songs to accompany poems by Robert Browning, Emily Dickinson and others. Soft-pastel animation is based on the award-winning book by Kay Chorao. Also *Baby's Nursery Rhymes*. 2–5 (25 min). (800) 229-STORY.

MIXED EMOTIONS: BARNEY
(Lyons Group $14.95) We were stunned by the varying responses our testers had to Barney. Parent comments

ranged from, "I can't be in the room with it" and "I go to sleep singing that damn song," to "I like the multi-ethnic cast of kids and the songs." All agreed that Barney conveys really positive messages. Our kid testers particularly enjoyed Barney's birthday video with birthday songs from several cultures. 2–6. (30 min.) (800) 527-4747.

BE OUR GUEST SING-ALONG
(Disney $12.99) Musical clips from such Disney favorites as *Pinocchio, Beauty and the Beast, Mary Poppins* and more. The best of Disney without the scary parts for young kids! Words to the songs bounce along the bottom of the screen so kids who can read (or are learning) can sing along. All ages.

FRIEND LIKE ME
(Disney $12.99) Newest of the sing-along songs, inspired by *Aladdin* with clips of *A Whole New World* and *Friend Like Me* along with songs from *The Jungle Book, Songs of the South,* and other Disney features. 30 mins. Closed captioned.

PETE SEEGER'S FAMILY CONCERT   PLATINUM AWARD
(Sony $14.98) An outdoor concert by one of our best-loved folksingers, who does 12 folksongs everyone should know. No cutesy stuff here, just good foot-tappin', hand-clappin', sing-along music. All ages. (45 min.) (800) 551-7200.

SESAME STREET SING, HOOT AND HOWL
(Random House $9.95) Sesame Street fans are going to love this lively songfest! A zesty mix of live action and puppets. Wait till you hear their take-off of "La Bamba" called "Baa Baa Bamba!" Also *Monster Hits.* 2 & up. (28 min.) (800) 733-3000.

SESAME STREET 25TH BIRTHDAY ✸ PLATINUM AWARD
(Random House $12.95) An hour-long musical celebration of some of the best songs and stars of *Sesame Street.* Closed captioned. Also *Sing Along Earth Songs.* 2 & up. (60 min.) (800) 733-3000.

SHARI LEWIS ACTION SONGS

(A & M Video $9.98) These songs involve more hand and finger play than whole body action—but who's complaining? As always, Shari Lewis is in top form with engaging songs. Lamb Chop and kids sing along in these segments from her PBS show. 3–6. (30 min.) (800) 541-9904.

ELLA JENKINS LIVE AT THE SMITHSONIAN

(Smithsonian/Folkways $14.98) Talk about "interactive"—this is it! Without gimmicks, here's a master teacher involving kids in sing, clap, snap, tap-along fun! Singing traditional and original songs, she leads kids in music and motion that involves active doing instead of just watching. 2–5. (28 min.) (800) 443-4727.

RAFFI IN CONCERT

(A&M Video $19.95) This is like having the best ticket in the concert hall! Unlike a lot of kid video musicals, this one really is music. Includes "This Little Light of Mine," "Tingaloyo," "Rise and Shine" and many more. (50 mins.) Also *A Young Children's Concert with Raffi*. 2 & up. (45 min.) (800) 541-9904.

ROSENSHONTZ–TEDDY BEARS' JAMBOREE

(Lightyear $12) Two terrific performers make happy music for a gathering of kids, their Teddy Bears and parents on the Boston Common. A nice mix of humor, action, wisdom and warmth. 2–6. (30 min.) (800) 229-STORY.

SHARON, LOIS AND BRAM SING A TO Z

(A&M Video $14.95) This is not an ABC tape. It's an entertaining live concert with this well-known trio singing a song for every letter in the alphabet. Some are vintage folksongs or old pops like "Mairzy Doats" and "Five Little Fishies." Also *The Elephant Show*. 3–8. (50 min). (800) 541-9904.

BEETHOVEN LIVES UPSTAIRS   PLATINUM AWARD

(Children's Group $19.98) Here's a pleasing way to introduce the great masters and their music to young audiences. Ten-year-old Christoph is most unhappy when his widowed mother rents rooms to a moody and strange composer. But soon the majesty of Beethoven's music changes the boy's feelings. A beauty to see and hear! 7 & up. (51 min.) (800) 668-0242.

THE NUTCRACKER   BLUE CHIP

(MGM $19.95) Short of orchestra seats that would cost more than twice the price, here's the best way to enjoy the American Ballet Theater production of *The Nutcracker,* starring Baryshnikov and Kirkland. This Christmas fantasy, long a holiday tradition, is often the first ballet children are introduced to. Now it can be enjoyed at any time of year. 4 & up. (78 min.) #NUTO5. (800) 262-8600.

PETER, PAUL AND MOMMY, TOO ⭐ PLATINUM AWARD

(Warner $19.98) From the opening bars of "Puff," the magic is still here! In a live performance, this full-length concert includes some of the trio's classics, such as "Garden Song" (as in "inch by inch, row by row"), "If I Had a Hammer" and a moving rendition of "We Shall Overcome." This is one of the best of '93! All ages. (90 min.) Video/record stores.

THIS PRETTY PLANET: TOM CHAPIN LIVE IN CONCERT

(Sony $14.98) Fans of Chapin are going to adore this concert featuring 13 of his best-loved songs, such as "The Wheel of the Water," "Good Garbage" and others with an ecology theme. The beautiful title song is a duet with Judy Collins. Combines scenes from nature with the live footage of the concert. All ages. (50 min.) (800) 551-7200.

PICTUREBOOK VIDEOS

Many wonderful picturebooks have been brought to life as videos. Still other stories are being written and produced for video and then turned into picturebooks. Either way, video offers another way to connect  kids and books and reading. To save space and avoid repeats, many Blue Chip picturebooks not reviewed in the book section appear here. Try them both ways!

TODDLERS AND PRESCHOOLERS

ARE YOU MY MOTHER?

(Random House $9.95) For decades beginning readers have relished *Are You My Mother?*, *Go, Dog, Go!* and *The Best Nest.* Previewing the book on video may be helpful. We wish the text appeared on the screen, but this is a bridge video that will be enjoyed differently by varying ages from 2 & up. (30 min.) (800) 733-3000.

BABY'S STORYTIME

(Lightyear $12.98) Don't be misled by the title. This is not for babies. Singer and songwriter Arlo Guthrie tells folktales every child should know, such as "Henny Penny" and "Little Red Riding Hood." Animation is based on award-winning art by Kay Chorao. 4–7. (26 min.) (800) 229-STORY.

ELIZABETH AND LARRY/BILL AND PETE

(MCA $12.98) Here are two amusing animated alligator stories. Jean Stapleton narrates *Elizabeth and Larry,* a warm tale of a quirky friendship between an old lady and a gator who arrives by accident in a box of oranges from Florida. *Bill and Pete* is about an alligator and the bird who cleans the gator's teeth and ends up saving his life. 4–8. (25 min.) (800) 727-2233.

EZRA JACK KEATS LIBRARY

(Children's Circle $14.95) Many parents will recognize these now-classic stories—"The Snowy Day," "Peter's Chair," "A Letter to Amy," "Whistle for Willie" and "The Pet Show" as favorites they grew up with, and they can now share them with their kids. These stories retain a child's-eye view of the world, whether Peter is reveling in snow or relating to a sibling. 3 & up. (45 min.) (800) 543-7843.

FIVE LIONNI CLASSICS

(Random House $14.95) Lionni's collage illustrations translate beautifully to the screen. In "Frederick," a mouse poet brightens everyone's day; in "Cornelius," a crocodile has a taste for new experiences; "Fish is Fish," is a story about friendship; "It's Mine" is a tale about sharing; best of all, in "Swimmy," a clever little fish fools a big fish by using his head. Closed captioned. 3 & up. (30 min.) (800) 733-3000.

HAROLD AND THE PURPLE CRAYON AND OTHER HAROLD STORIES
★94 PLATINUM AWARD

(Children's Circle $14.95) Crockett Johnson's imaginative Harold goes walking with his marvelous purple crayon and draws several stories that are possibly even better on video than between the pages of a book! This all-Harold video also includes "Harold's Fairy Tale," "A Picture for Harold's Room" and a special segment that shows how the stories were animated. 4–8. (27 min.) (800) 543-7843.

HORTON HATCHES THE EGG　PLATINUM AWARD

(Random House $9.95) Billy Crystal's performance of this classic Dr. Seuss story is 100% grand. He plays every role with a distinctive voice and wit in a tale that speaks to the virtues of loyalty and sticking with a task. Video also includes *If I Ran the Circus*. For more vintage Seuss, see *Yertle the Turtle*. Closed captioned. 4 & up. (30 min.) (800) 733-3000.

MADELINE'S RESCUE   PLATINUM AWARD

(Golden $12.95) Madeline falls into the river Seine and a big brown dog, Genevieve, rescues her. But keeping a dog is no simple matter. Told by Christopher Plummer, this animated musical version ends happily, with enough "hound to go around." Other stories such as the original *Madeline,* and *Madeline and the Gypsies,* have been done in this wonderful series. 4–8 (25 min.) (800) 236-7123.

MIKE MULLIGAN AND HIS STEAM SHOVEL

(Golden $12.95) An animated musical version of the classic tale of Mike Mulligan, who believed in his old steam shovel, Mary Anne. Narrated by Robert Klein, this 50-year-old story is still a moving and meaningful tale of loyalty and friendship versus greed. 4 & up. (25 min.) (800) 236-7123.

MILLIONS OF CATS AND BLUMPOE THE GRUMPOE MEETS ARNOLD THE CAT 🌟 PLATINUM AWARD

(MCA $12.98) Remember the old man who trys to find his wife one little cat and comes home with "hundreds of cats, thousands of cats, millions and billions and trillions of cats"? Splendidly narrated by James Earl Jones. The less-familiar *Blumpoe the Grumpoe* is an amusing tale of a grumpy man and a shy cat who befriends him in spite of his disposition. 4–8 (25 min.) (800) 727-2233.

MORE STORIES FOR THE VERY YOUNG

(Children's Circle $14.95) The lazy friends in "The Little Red Hen" will have young listeners chiming in with a chorus of "Not I's." In "Max's Christmas," his bossy big sister tries to convince Max to go to bed or Santa won't come. As always, Max does it his way. "Petunia," a silly goose, believes she can become smart simply by holding a book under her wing! In "The Napping House," everyone settles down for a nap until a tiny flea bites one small mouse. 3–7. (36 min.) (800) 543-7843.

OWL MOON AND OTHER STORIES

(Children's Circle $14.95) A memorable video that connects kids to both nature and literature. The title story by Jane Yolen captures the thrill of owling in the winter woods. "Caterpillar and the Polliwog" is an amusing tale about change. Also "Hot Hippo" and the award-winning "Time of Wonder." Don't miss this one! 4–8. (800) 543-7843.

PEEP AND THE BIG WIDE WORLD

(Smarty Pants $14.95) Peter Ustinov narrates the delightful adventures of three birds who set off to find out about the big, wide world. Unlike most cartoons, the pace here is closer to Mr. Rogers and the story lines are not complex. A quiet sort of cartoon about friendship, curiosity and shared adventure. 3 & up. (30 min.) (800) 331-6197.

THE SNOWMAN BLUE CHIP

(Children's Circle $14.95) An enchanting fantasy of a snowman who takes a small boy on a flying adventure. Like the wordless book it's based on, this is a timeless classic. A word of warning: One three-year-old dissolved in tears when the snowman melted. Rewinding the film to "bring the snowman back" was no consolation. A better choice for 4 & up. (26 min.) (800) 543-7843.

THE TALE OF PETER RABBIT AND BENJAMIN BUNNY
94 PLATINUM AWARD

(Goodtimes $19.95) Even purists will be impressed by the artistry that brings Beatrix Potter's well-loved stories and watercolors to life with a technique called rendered art. Opening with a live-action scene portraying Potter at work, the film melts from her little drawings to animation. From a series that promises to become a classic treasure. *The Tale of Samuel Whiskers* is a bit scarier and would be better for older kids. 3 & up. (30 min.)

WHERE'S SPOT 94 PLATINUM AWARD

(Disney $14.99) Not just in books anymore! Spot makes his first appearance in this charming video that translates the lift-the-flap discovery format to an animated video especially for toddlers. Includes five good stories; our favorite is "Spot's Birthday"—always a theme toddlers love. These won't replace the fun of the interactive Spot books, but they make a pleasing connection. 2 & up.

EARLY SCHOOL YEARS

Some of the videos in this section have pieces that may be enjoyed by older preschoolers, but for the most part these are stories for 5 and up.

ABEL'S ISLAND   BLUE CHIP

(Random House $14.95) In a raging storm, Abelard Hassam di Chirico Flint is swept away to a desert island where he must survive by his wits. Tim Curry plays Abel the mouse in William Steig's tale of independence. Share this in book form, too! Closed captioned. 6 & up. (30 min.) (800) 733-3000.

ARTHUR'S EYES

(Family Home Entertainment $12.98) One of the best from Reading Rainbow, this video explores the many ways we "see" things, not just with our eyes. Bill Cosby narrates *Arthur's Eyes*, about an aardvark who hates his glasses but learns it's better to see than to worry about what others think. Also includes a piece on sign language and a poem, "All the Colors of the Race," narrated by Maya Angelou. 4 & up.(30 min.) (800) 288-LIVE.

DOCTOR DE SOTO

(Children's Circle $14.95) When Sly Fox comes to the dentist with a sore tooth and designs on biting the hand that cures him, Doctor De Soto and his good wife find a way to save honor and themselves. Tape includes such favorites as  "Curious George Rides a Bike," "Patrick," who fiddles up a pastoral romp, and "The Hat," about a poor man who finds good luck when he finds a magic black hat. 4–8. (35 min.) (800) 543-7843.

ENCYCLOPEDIA BROWN

(Golden $12.95) Always a favorite of young readers, junior sleuth Encyclopedia Brown solves "The Case of the Amazing Race Car" in this live-action production. Although the series of books by Donald Sobol are semi-easy, this video will serve as an introduction to kids who are just starting to read chapter books. 6–10. (30 min.) (800) 236-7123.

IRA SLEEPS OVER ⭐'94 PLATINUM AWARD

(Family Home Entertainment $12.98) In this musical version of Bernard Waber's picturebook, Ira is going to sleep at a friend's house but can't decide if his friend will laugh at him if he brings his teddy bear, Ta-Ta. Ira's sister is a bit mean-spirited, but this is a reassuring story about being yourself and making your own choices. 5 & up. (27 min.) (800) 288-LIVE.

JAZZ TIME TALE

(Family Home Entertainment $9.98) Set in New York's Harlem in 1919, this is an animated film about Fats Waller's career. His father was a preacher who considered jazz sinful, but Fats thinks otherwise and gets discovered playing the organ at a movie house. Narrated by Ruby Dee. 5–8 (29 min.) (800) 288-LIVE.

LYLE, LYLE, CROCODILE

(Video Treasures $9.95) Imagine moving into a house and finding a crocodile in the bathtub! Left behind by his former owner, Lyle finds a true home with the Primm family. When his old owner returns to claim him, Lyle is grief-stricken and so are the Primms. A lively animated version of Bernard Waber's storybook favorite. 4–8 (25 min.) (800) 745-1145.

THE PIG'S WEDDING

(Children's Circle $14.95) Helme Heine's witty story and illustrations of the comic preparations for the wedding of two loving pigs is the first treat on this excellent video, which also includes animated storybooks of "The Selkie Girl," "The Happy Owls," "A Letter to Amy" and "The Owl and the Pussy-Cat." 4–7. (39 min.) (800) 543-7843.

RAMONA: SQUEAKERFOOT/GOODBYE, HELLO

(Warner $29.95) There are a number of live-action dramatizations from Beverly Cleary's wonderful Ramona books. This two-episode video will serve as an introduction to the books or a pleasing way of seeing them come alive. *Squeakerfoot* is about a pair of very loud shoes. *Goodbye, Hello* is a bittersweet tale about the death of a cat and the news of a baby being on the way. 5 & up. (60 min). #RAMO2. (800) 262-8600.

THE RED SHOES

(Family Home Entertainment $9.98) Lisa and Jennie are best friends until Lisa's family wins the lottery. After they move Lisa seems to forget Jennie. Their friend, Alfonso the shoemaker, makes a pair of red ballet shoes, which Lisa steals. But when she puts them on she can't stop dancing! Those magical shoes teach Lisa a lesson about the value of friendship. Told by Ossie Davis. 6 & up. (30 min.) (800) 288-LIVE.

THE SAND CASTLE

(Smarty Pants $14.95) You won't forget the poetic animation of the title story, in which the Sandman creates magic creatures who build a remarkable castle until it is swept away. Also on this ususual video from Canada are an Aesop fable, "The North Wind and the Sun," an amusing "Alphabet" and an Eskimo legend, "The Owl and the Lemming." 5 & up. Also *The Tender Tale of Cinderella Penguin.* 5 & up (30 min.) (216) 221-5300).

THE SWEATER   BLUE CHIP

(Smarty Pants $14.95) Who says clothes don't make the man—or, in this case, boy? Here's the dilemma: A mixed-up mail order brings a young hockey player the wrong sweater, which makes him an outcast among his teammates. Narrated with the flavorful cadence of a French Canadian accent, this witty video also includes "The Ride" and "Getting Started." 6 & up. (30 min.) (800) 331-6197.

THE TOMI UNGERER LIBRARY

(Children's Circle $14.95) Four quirky tales from a master artist and storyteller. In *The Three Robbers* a little girl changes the ill-gotten gains of three thieves into a way of helping the needy. Tape includes the delightful version of *Moon Man,* who rockets to earth thinking it is better than the moon. Also *The Beast of Monsieur Racine* and *The Hat.* 6–9. (35 min.) (800) 543-7843.

THE VELVETEEN RABBIT   BLUE CHIP

(Random House $9.95) Margery Williams's classic tale about love and how it can make even a toy rabbit real is all the more enjoyable with Meryl Streep's narration. Illustrated with soft pastel and earth tones, this tale about a toy bunny who arrives at Christmastime is a good choice for any season. Closed captioned. 4–8. (25 min.) (800) 733-3000.

SPOOKS, MONSTERS AND WILD THINGS

Here are a few choices that might be just right for talking about and maybe conquering the imaginary spooks that sometimes worry kids. Most would also be great choices for Halloween.

MAURICE SENDAK LIBRARY

(Children's Circle $14.95) On this single tape you'll find some of Sendak's most memorable works. Probably the best known is the classic romp about naughty Max who is sent to his room without dinner and leaves home on an adventure to "Where the Wild Things Are." Also on this tape are the fantasy "In the Night Kitchen" and all four stories from "The Nutshell Library." Carole King sings on this stunning video. Also "What's Under My Bed and Other Creepy Stories." 5–8. (35 min.) (800) 543-7843.

> **TOY TIP:** Another way to "handle" monsters: Buy Max or one of the Wild Things, which come packed in a paperback book/toy combination from HarperCollins ($16.95).

THERE'S A NIGHTMARE IN MY CLOSET

(MCA $12.98) From Shelley Duvall's *Bed Time Stories* series, these are exactly wrong for bedtime, but they might be useful for viewing together with kids who worry about spooks under beds, inside closets or up in the attic. Based on Mercer Mayer's droll books, the video includes "There's a Nightmare in My Closet" (narrated by Michael J Fox), "There's an Alligator under My Bed" (narrated by Christan Slater), and "There's Something in the Attic" (narrated by Sissy Spacek). 5 & up. (25 mins.) (800) 727-2233.

FOLKTALES, LEGENDS, HEROES AND HEROINES FROM MANY CULTURES

The stories in this section are good choices for school-age children, who more clearly understand the difference between real and make-believe.

THE ANIMATED TALES OF SHAKESPEARE

(Random House $14.95 each) Like the old Classic Comics many of us grew up with, these animated videos make the Bard accessible to a new generation. Purists may object, but using a form familiar to kids is often a way to help them get started. Each video has its own look and tone. *Macbeth* has the darkness of a sinister superhero, while the art for *Romeo and Juliet* is romantic. Series includes *A Midsummer Night's Dream, The Tempest, Twelfth Night* and *Hamlet.* 10 & up. (30 min.) (800) 733-3000

BRER RABBIT AND BOSS LION   PLATINUM AWARD

(Rabbit Ears $9.95) Time was when all the creatures got along peaceably, but that was before one mean fat cat, Boss Lion, came strutting along. Danny Glover's brilliant narration of this African-American tale proves how the little guy can take on the high and mighty and come out ahead! Also *Anansi,* narrated by Denzel Washington; *Rumpelstiltskin*—Kathleen Turner spins the story thread; and *Jack and the Beanstalk*, with Michael Palin. 5 & up. (28 min.) (800) 541-9904.

DAVID AND GOLIATH

(Rabbit Ears $9.95) Young David, armed with just his slingshot and abiding faith, manages to defeat the giant Goliath. Highly stylized illustrations and limited animation give this a sometimes stiff look, but the music by Branford Marsalis and narration by Mel Gibson bring the stirring tale to life. From the *Greatest Stories Ever Told* series. Also *Jonah and the Whale.* 5 & up. (30 min.) (800) 541-9904.

FINN MCCOUL   PLATINUM AWARD

(Rabbit Ears $9.95) There's a giant portion of Irish blarney and brogue in Catherine O'Hara's wonderfully lively telling of this folktale from the Old Sod. Finn McCoul, a small-sized giant, manages to outwit a mountain-sized giant with a lot of help from his clever wife. A funny tale with the music of pipes, concertina and penny whistle. Also *King Midas,* narrated by Michael Caine. 5 & up. (30 min.) (800) 541-9904.

JOHN HENRY   PLATINUM AWARD

(Rabbit Ears $9.95) Denzel Washington narrates the tall tale of that steel-driving hero who pits himself against the steam drill. With music composed and performed by B.B. King, this is a winner! Also wonderful from the same series, *Follow the Drinking Gourd,* a story of the Underground Railroad narrated by Morgan Freeman. 6 & up. (30 min.) (800) 541-9904.

JOHNNY APPLESEED   PLATINUM AWARD

(Rabbit Ears $9.95) Who better than Garrison Keillor to tell the story of Johnny Appleseed who roamed the Ohio Valley planting apple orchards. With a Nashville-flavored soundtrack, this is a delight for eyes and ears. Also notable *The Song of Sacajawea,* the tale of the Shoshone woman who helped Lewis & Clark on their historic expedition. 7 & up. (30 min.) (800) 541-9904.

PECOS BILL   BLUE CHIP

(Rabbit Ears $14.95) A tall tale of a pioneer baby raised by coyotes who grows up to be a cowboy—the one who created the Great Salt Lake! Narrated by Robin Williams, complete with John Wayne imitations. The whole family will enjoy this one. Also *Annie Oakley,* narrated by Keith Carradine sounding like Will Rogers. 5 & up. (30 mins.) (800) 541-9904.

PEGASUS

(Lightyear $12.98) This heavenly myth, narrated by Mia Farrow, will add another dimension to stargazing. Doris Orgel's retelling of the myth of Pegasus, the magical winged horse, captures the excitement and adventure in an excellent introduction to the ancient Greek tales. 7 & up. (25 min.) (800) 229-STORY.

STREGA NONA AND OTHER STORIES

(Children's Circle $14.95) This wonderful video starts with a tasty tale of a magic pasta pot, a boy who was told not to touch it and what happens when he doesn't listen. "Tikki Tikki Tembo" is the tale of a boy whose name is so long it almost costs him his life. Next comes a totally absurd nonsense song, "The Foolish Frog," sung by Pete Seeger, that's guaranteed to inspire giggles. Finally there's the prize-winning African folktale "A Story, A Story." 5 & up. (40 min.) (800) 543-7843.

SNOW QUEEN   PLATINUM AWARD

(Lightyear $12.98) Sigourney Weaver narrates Hans Christian Andersen's tale of a brave young girl who seeks to rescue her friend from the distant, icy palace of the Snow Queen. A beautifully animated adventure. Also *Beauty and the Beast.* 5–12. (30 min.) (800) 229-STORY.

STORIES FROM THE BLACK TRADITION
PLATINUM AWARD

(Children's Circle $14.95) This five-story collection
includes surefire favorites "A Story, A Story" and "Why
Mosquitos Buzz in People's Ears," wonderfully narrated
by James Earl Jones. The brilliant art work is enhanced
by limited animation. Video also includes "Goggles,"
"Mufaro's Beautiful Daughters" and "The Village of
Round and Square Houses." 5 & up. (52 min.) (800) 543-
7843.

THE TIGER AND THE BRAHMIN   PLATINUM AWARD

(Rabbit Ears $9.95) Ben
Kingsley's narration of this
Indian folktale is marvelous.
A trapped tiger tricks a holy
man, the Brahmin, into opening the cage. As soon as he's
free the tiger threatens to eat
the Brahmin. The mysterious
raga composed and played by Ravi Shankar sets the right
tone. 7 & up. (29 min.) (800) 541-9904.

THE WILD SWANS ⭐ PLATINUM AWARD

(Lightyear $12.98) Sigourney Weaver narrates the sus-
penseful Hans Christian Andersen tale of eleven princes
who are transformed into wild swans by their evil step-
mother. It is their brave sister who breaks the spell and
saves them and herself. Closed captioned. 6–12. (30 min.)
(800) 229-STORY.

FEATURE-LENGTH FILMS

ALADDIN ⭐ PLATINUM AWARD

(Disney $24.99) A magic carpet ride! Disney's award win-
ning mega-hit is now ready to transport the family. There
are some scenes that may be frightening to young
preschoolers. This is a better choice for 5s & up,up,up.

ANNE OF GREEN GABLES   BLUE CHIP

(Wonderworks $29.95) Originally shown on PBS, this is a moving drama about the loving relationship of a spirited young girl who is orphaned and the unforgettable aunt and uncle she goes to live with, who are as unaccustomed to her as she is to them. Starring Colleen Dewhurst, this family classic is a two-volume set. Also *Anne of Avonlea*. Closed captioned. 8 & up. #11536. (199 min.) (800) 669-9696.

BACH AND BROCCOLI

(Family Home Entertainment $14.95) Fanny, an orphaned 12-year-old, is sent (with her pet skunk, Broccoli) to her bachelor uncle when her grandmother becomes too ill to care for her. Uncle John is more interested in winning a prize playing Bach on the organ than in becoming an instant father. Uncle John finally figures out what the real prizes in life are about. 7 & up. (96 min.) (800) 288-LIVE.

HOMEWARD BOUND: THE INCREDIBLE JOURNEY

(Disney $22.99) Imagine *Lassie, Come Home* with three loyal pets instead of one facing one obstacle after another on a journey home. Shot in live action, the stars of this feature are a big old dog (voice by Don Ameche), a young sassy boxer (Michael J. Fox) and a furry cat (Sally Field). Has some suspenseful scenes that might be scary for young kids. 6–9. (90 min.)

THE LITTLE PRINCESS   PLATINUM AWARD

(Public Media Video $29.95) This award-winning film is based on Frances Hodgson Burnett's endearing story of a poor little rich girl whose life changes radically when her father dies and she is left in the hands of a spiteful headmistress of a girls' school in Victorian England. 6 & up. (180 min.) (800) 262-8600.

THE LION, THE WITCH AND THE WARDROBE
PLATINUM AWARD

(Films Inc. Video. $29.95 2-tape set) Originally created for Wonderworks, this is the first of C. S. Lewis's trilogy *The Chronicles of Narnia*. Filmed in live action, the story begins in a castle where four children step into a wardrobe and are transported into a magic kingdom where the evil White Witch has cast a spell that must be broken. An enchanting treasure! Also *Bridge to Terabithia*. 8 & up. (174 min.) (800) 323-4222.

SARAH PLAIN AND TALL

(Republic $14.98) Glenn Close stars as a mail-order bride who journeys to the frontier and wins the love of a widower and his children. Based on Patricia MacLachlan's prize-winning book, this powerful film gives kids a glimpse of the past and connects them to the universal need for love that's shared by people in all times. 7 & up. (98 min.)

THE SECRET GARDEN

(CBS Fox $14.95) This is the BBC version of the classic story of an orphaned girl who goes to live with relatives. She and her bedridden cousin discover each other and a secret garden that transforms their lives. A special gift set with a diary is also available. 7 & up. (107 min.)

BLUE-CHIP FEATURE-LENGTH FILMS

These are widely available films that you'll find in the video store or library. They also are shown frequently on TV, but the video versions lack commercials—a real plus! Most of these are for early school years and beyond.

- The Sound of Music
- Mary Poppins
- Peter Pan (Mary Martin version)
- Chitty Chitty Bang Bang
- Willy Wonka and the Chocolate Factory
- ET
- The Wizard of Oz
- The Little Mermaid
- Beauty and the Beast
- Fantasia
- To Kill a Mockingbird
- Sounder
- The Red Balloon
- The Black Stallion

INFORMATION, PLEASE

TODDLERS AND PRESCHOOLERS

DOING THINGS   BLUE CHIP

(Bo-Peep Productions $19.95) Every video library should have *Doing Things!* With almost no talking or cutesy narrative, we watch kids and familiar barnyard animals go through the routine of the day—eating, washing and playing. There's something new to see each time you watch. The cast of kids is multiracial, and the music is fun but not intrusive. *Doing Things* leaves the talking to you and your kids. 2 & up. (27 min.) (800) 532-0420.

HERE WE GO: VOLUME 1 AND 2

(Kids Express $12.95 each) For transportation buffs, here are two videos narrated by Lynn Redgrave. Volume 1 takes viewers on such exciting vehicles as a blimp, hovercraft, steam engine, firetruck and ocean liner. Volume 2 focuses on a helicopter, dump truck, bike, bulldozer and high-flying tramway. (30 min). *Here We Go Again* transports kids on jets, police cars, tow trucks, trolleys, subways and more. Also *Meet Your Animal Friends.* 3–6. (60 min.) (800) 331-6197.

SEE HOW THEY GROW: PETS '94 PLATINUM AWARD

(Sony $9.98 each) Like the handsome DK books they are based on, each of these stylish videos zooms in on baby animals and how they grow. We were initially put off by narration coming from the animal's point of view, but our young viewers were captivated. Looks at four favorites—puppy, kitten, goldfish and parakeet. Also recommended in the series: *Farm Animals* and *Mini Creatures.* 2 & up. (35 min.) (800) 551-7200.

MOVING MACHINES   BLUE CHIP

(Bo-Peep Productions $19.95) For junior earth movers who love playing in the sand, this will be a hit. Shots move from real construction sites to kids building pretend roads in the sand with toy trucks. Zooms in on kids' fascination with building. One of a wonderful series that invites the kids to take part in the narration without the

sappy script typical of so many videos targeted for kids.
2 & up. (27 mins.) (800) 532-0420.

SESAME STREET HOME VIDEO VISITS THE FIREHOUSE
(Random House $9.95) Big Bird, Elmo and Gordon take a
tour of a firehouse and learn how firefighting equipment
works. A friendly introduction to fire prevention. Closed
captioned. 3 & up. (30 min.) (800) 733-3000.

COPING WITH REAL LIFE

HEY, WHAT ABOUT ME?
(Kidvidz $14.95) A good choice for your older child who
is about to have a younger sibling. The feeling, fears,
excitement and wonder of it all is shared by several
believable young experts, big brothers and sisters who
tell it like it is. Focuses on the positive aspects of becoming a family. 3–7. (25 min.) (617) 243-7611.

IT'S POTTY TIME
(A Vision $19.98) Developed by the Duke University Med-
ical Center, this "story" features kids of many ages getting ready to go to a party. Part of getting ready is going
to the potty! The bottom line is—no guarantees of success here. 2 & up. (25 min.) #2272 One Step Ahead (800)
274-8440.

PRESCHOOL POWER 1 AND 2
(Concept Video $14.95 each)These self-help videos for
preschoolers feature young children who demo such
useful skills as flipping their jackets on, tying shoelaces,
brushing teeth and other important ways of gaining independence and sense of "can do." Our testers loved
watching kids like themselves. Preschool 3 & 4 did not
test as well. 2 & up. (30 min.) (800) 333-8252.

SESAME STREET HOME VIDEO VISITS THE HOSPITAL
(Random House $9.95) Big Bird expresses a lot of the
anxiety kids may have about hospitals that they may not
be able to put into words. Big Bird discovers that the
hospital is not so scary after all. A good starting point for
discussing your child's fears about her own visit to the

hospital or that of a family member or friend. Closed captioned. 3 & up. (30 mins.) (800) 733-3000.

DON'T JUST SIT THERE!

ACTIVITIES FOR PRESCHOOLERS AND EARLY-SCHOOL-YEARS KIDS

SQUIGGLES, DOTS AND LINES

(Kidvidz $14.95) This video won't (and shouldn't) replace Ed Emberley's step-by-step drawing books. What it does offer is a variety of novel ways kids can use Emberley's drawing alphabet to decorate cookies and make greeting cards, costumes and original books. 5 & up. (30 min.) (617) 243-7611.

LOOK WHAT I MADE

(Intervideo $14.95) Next time somebody says, "There's nothing to do," turn this terrific video on. Amy Purcell, a friendly teacher, walks kids through such fascinating projects as making a piñata, floral bouquets, puppets and even a newspaper hammock, plus Japanese paper-folding. A great resource for grandparents! 6–60. (60 min.) (800) 366-3688.

MY FIRST ACTIVITY VIDEO

(Sony $14.98) Based on the handsome *My First Activity Book,* which shows kids step-by-step ways to make pasta jewelry, papier-mâché plates, fabric masks, plus melon- and pumpkin-carving and more. Also *My First Cooking Video.* Both will involve parental supervision. 5–11 (50 min.) (800) 551-7200.

MY FIRST MUSIC VIDEO

(Sony $14.98) Each of the ten activities on this tape shows kids how to make simple instruments with distinctively different sounds, including a soda-bottle water organ, an ice cream tub banjo, a South American guiro and an Australian didgeridoo, to name but a few. Goes well beyond the typical homemade rhythm instruments often suggested for preschoolers. For hard copy, see *My First Music Book* (Dorling Kindersley). 5–11. (50 min.) (800) 551-7200.

AN INTRODUCTION TO PUPPET MAKING

(BEI $14.95) Puppeteer Jim Gamble introduces kids to ways of making a variety of puppets, from tiny finger puppets to talking "book" puppets, rod puppets and, for the more ambitious and able, a marionette. This is a user-friendly tape that is most enjoyed by children 6 & up. (30 min.) (818) 784-3781.

101 THINGS FOR KIDS TO DO   BLUE CHIP

(Random House $9.95) For the new generation of Shari Lewis fans, this video is filled with crafts, tricks, riddles and puppet-making ideas. Not to be watched from beginning to end, this is a start, stop and do program that can cure cabin fever for 5–8. (30 min.) (800) 733-3000.

WILL YOU BE MIME?

(Krafty Kids $26.99) It doesn't have to be Halloween for kids to enjoy getting made-up and stepping into pretend roles. This unusual video comes boxed with washable, nontoxic face paint, directions for using it and inspiration for young performers. 4–10. (35 min.) (515) 276-8325.

SCIENCE ACTIVITIES

LOOK WHAT I FOUND—MAKING CODES AND SOLVING MYSTERIES

(Intervideo $14.95) Amy Purcell, the teacher you wish your child could have every semester, shows junior slueths how to do such fascinating things as make a periscope, record fingerprints, create secret codes and more. 5–12. (45 min.) (800) 366-3688.

LOOK WHAT I GREW!

(Intervideo $14.95) You don't need a backyard to grow the many windowsill gardens on this lively video. Learn how to make shrunken-head apple finger puppets, terrariums and other experiments. A show-and-tell with a clarity that is neither cutesy nor condescending. Some projects call for adult assistance. 5–12 (45 min.) (800) 366-3688.

MY FIRST SCIENCE VIDEO/MY FIRST NATURE VIDEO

(Sony $14.98 each) Clear how-to directions on how to make weather predictions, fingerprints, magic with colors, music, shadows, magnets and other simple kitchen-chemistry science experiments with easy-to-find materials. Based on the stunning DK book *My First Science Book*. Also *My First Nature Video*, for making a terrarium, sprouting seeds, trapping bugs, feeding birds, making leaf prints and more. 5–11. (45 min.) (800) 551-7200.

DINOSAURS

PATRICK'S DINOSAURS AND WHAT HAPPENED TO PATRICK'S DINOSAURS

(MCA $12.98) Patrick is awed by his big brother's knowledge of dinosaurs. But his imagination has a way of running away with itself and scaring him. An artful blend of information and fiction narrated by Martin Short, based on Carol and Donald Carrick's books. 5–8. (25 min.) (800) 727-2233.

WHATEVER HAPPENED TO THE DINOSAURS?

(Golden $12.98) Kids visit real scientists who share their theories. The big concept here is that we don't always have absolute answers to our questions. 6–10. (30 min.) (800) 236-7123.

ECOLOGY

MY FIRST GREEN VIDEO

(Sony $14.98) Here are 13 activities for kids to do that deal with environmental issues. Clear step-by-step directions show kids how to test for pollution and acid rain, grow a garden and get involved in hands-on ways that are meaningful for kids. 5–11. (50 min.) (800) 551-7200.

RAINFOREST

(PBS Home Video Pacific Arts $20) For armchair travelers, here's a spectacular journey through the tropical rain forest, where many of the most exotic plants and creatures live in a fragile ecosystem. 8 & up. (58 min.) (800) 776-8300.

THE ROTTEN TRUTH

(Children's Television Workshop $14.95) Without being preachy this video answers a lot of questions about what happens to garbage once it leaves your house. 6 & up. (30 min.)

SPORTS

JUGGLETIME

(Jugglebug $19.95) Combining action, learning and fun, Professor Confidence shows how to juggle. Lively music, humor and three scarves are all included. Truly for beginners. 5 & up. (30 min.) (800) 523-1776.

LITTLE LEAGUE'S OFFICIAL HOW TO PLAY BASEBALL

(MasterVision $19.95; with book $29.95) Aspiring Little Leaguers will love this detailed how to throw, pitch, catch and field video. Kid-to-kid demos with friendly expert coaches. 7 & up. (70 min.) (800) 322-2000.

TEACHING KIDS SOCCER

(ESPN Home Video $19.99) Head coach of U.S. Soccer Federation's national team gives parents advice on how to help young players build skill and confidence. Also *Teaching Kids Swimming* and *Teaching Kids Tennis.* (75 min.) (800) 662-ESPN.

HOLIDAYS

AMAHL AND THE NIGHT VISITORS
($29.95) Teresa Stratas stars in Menotti's opera about a poor boy and his mother, who welcome the Wise Men into their home. 7 & up. (52 min.) #AMA01.
(800) 262-8600.

CHRISTMAS CRACKER

(Smarty Pants $14.98) Includes four short pieces: "Christmas Cracker" is a witty cartoon about a tree trimmer who takes a spaceship to find a perfect star for his tree. In "The Great Toy Robbery" Santa's sack is stolen; fear not, the good guys (accidentally) win. "The Energy Carol" stars Ebenezer Stooge, who wastes plenty until the Spirits of Energy Past, Present and Future arrive. A wordless telling of the Nativity, with animated cut-out figures and lyrical music, finishes this Yuletime celebration. 4 & up. (30 min.) (216) 221-5300.

CHRISTMAS STORIES
(Children's Circle $14.95) Ezra J. Keat's luminous illustrations for "The Little Drummer Boy" are accompanied by the St. Paul Choir School. Also a memorable story, "The Clown of God," by Tomie de Paola. "Morris's Disappearing Bag" and "Max's Christmas" are amusing and quirky tales by Rosemary Wells. 3 & up. (30 min.)
(800) 543-7843.

HOW THE GRINCH STOLE CHRISTMAS
(Random House $9.95) Who better than Walter Matthau to narrate the tale of the grumpy, cold-hearted curmudgeon whose ways are changed by the spirit of giving and love in the Christmas season. 4–8. (26 min.)
(800) 733-3000.

SHALOM SESAME CHANUKAH

(Children's Television Workshop $19.95) From the Israeli version of *Sesame Street,* this lively video celebrates the Festival of Lights and includes a funny send-up of "Wheel of Fortune" called "Dreidel of Fortune," starring Lavana White. The Count is doing his thing in English and Hebrew. 3–8. Comet International. Also, for Passover: *Jerusalem Jones and the Lost Afikoman,* and *Aleph-Bet Telethon.* (800) 428-9920.

Noteworthy Video Catalogs:

Finding some of the videos listed in this section will be as simple as going to the nearest toy supermarket, video store or children's book/specialty shop. If there are none in your area, you may prefer to shop by phone. These are some sources for quality videos:

- *Music for Little People:* Quality video, audio, musical instruments and other gift items. (800) 727-2233
- *Coalition for Quality Children's Videos:* A select list of prize-winning videos that are made chiefly by smaller companies and are frequently hard to find. (800) 331-6197
- *Home Vision:* Distinctive films for adults and children, many of which are difficult to find in small video rental shops. (800) 262-8600

4 ★ AUDIO

Great Music & Stories

The children's music market is experiencing a boom, with many major new companies joining the competition. There are great choices for both music and stories. Unfortunately, we found many of the new entries to be very cutesy, preachy, over-produced and, in many cases, condescending to young listeners. Our list reflects our preference for real music and good stories. Our ultimate test was whether we could stand being in a car with it or whether someone in the driver's seat or car seat screamed, "Turn it off!"

We also recommend that you share *your* favorite music, whether it be contemporary, folk, jazz, classical or show tunes. If you're enjoying the music, chances are it will be contagious.

We have listed the prices for tapes first and then for CDs, if available. Large music stores carry major companies like MCA, Disney, CBS, A&M, RCA Victor, etc. We have provided numbers to help locate titles from smaller recording companies that sell directly or through catalogs.

MUSIC

LULLABIES AND SONGS FOR THE VERY YOUNG

BABY'S MORNINGTIME

(Judy Collins, Lightyear $9.95) In her own soothing style, Judy Collins sings 26 poems from Kay Chorao's glorious *Good Morning Book* of songs and rhymes by poets like Robert Louis Stevenson, A. A. Milne and good old Mother Goose. Music to share with your baby any time of day. Video also available. (800) 229-7867.

BEASTIES, BUMBERSHOOTS AND LULLABIES

(Mike and Carleen McCormack, Alacazar $8.98/$11.98) This is a lovely collection of classics, including "Twinkle, Twinkle, Little Star," "Teddy Bears Picnic" and "The House at Pooh Corner." The vocals, and the collection of guitar, bassoon, cello, electric bass, English concertina and keyboards, give this a real musical quality that is a pleasure to listen to. (800) 541-9904.

LULLABIES FOR LITTLE DREAMERS

(Kevin Roth, Random House $9.98) This was a favorite with our testers. "Little Boy Blue," "Star Light, Star Bright," "Roll Over," "Hush, Little Baby" and other traditional lullabies are right on target for bedtime. Comes with a paperback book that new parents will appreciate right away and enjoy sharing later on. (800) 733-3000.

LULLABY MAGIC

(Joanie Bartels, Discovery $9.98) On one side Bartels sings contemporary and traditional lullabies that are designed to help set the mood for going to sleep. The other side has all-instrumental versions of the same songs. (800) 451-5175.

STAR DREAMER: NIGHTSONGS AND LULLABIES

(Priscilla Herdman, Alacazar $8.98/$11.98) Herdman's voice is so clear and friendly you wish she could come over, sit in the rocking chair and sing a few tunes. (800) 541-9904.

'TIL THEIR EYES SHINE—THE LULLABY ALBUM
🟊 PLATINUM AWARD

(Rosanne Cash, Carole King, Gloria Estefan, et al. CBS
$10.98/$16.98) Some of today's leading female recording
artists sing a collection of lullabies, with a portion of the
profits to benefit the Voiceless Victims program, which
aids children of war and poverty.

MUSIC FOR MOVING, SINGING & DANCING

A CHILD'S CELEBRATION OF SONG

(Music for Little People $9.98/$12.98) A hit parade of children's songs sung by well-known artists. "Puff (The
Magic Dragon) ," by Peter, Paul and Mary, "This Old
Man," by Pete Seeger, "Over the Rainbow," by Judy Gar-
land, "The House at Pooh Corner," by Kenny Loggins and
many more. 2 & up. (800) 727-2233.

BETHIE'S REALLY SILLY SONGS ABOUT ANIMALS
🟊 PLATINUM AWARD

(Discovery $9.98) "Codfish Ball" and "Ivana the Iguana"
are just two of the truly silly songs sung by this welcome
new addition to children's music. Bethie's zippy, retro
'40s style appeals to both kids and parents. (800) 451-
5175.

BIG BIG WORLD

(Bill Harley, A&M $8.98/$12.98) Upbeat, fun-to-move-to
music with lyrics that deal with a range of issues from
divorce to cleaning your room and saving the planet.
Harley has heart and a sense of humor. 5 & up.

CAMELS, CATS, AND RAINBOWS

(Paul Strausman, A Gentle Wind $8.95) Toddlers on up
will enjoy "You Are My Sunshine," "The Ants Go March-
ing" and other songs, including "Peanut Butter," which
have a sense of humor without being condescending. If

you've wished you knew all the words to a bunch of fun songs, played guitar, and had a group of kids to sing along, this one's for you! 3 & up. (518) 436-0391.

CAR SONGS

(Kimbo $10.95) This could make leaving home fun or at least ease the miles and frequency of "Are we there yet?" Twenty-two great sing-along favorites, such as "Wheels on the Bus," "Bingo" and "John Jacob Jingleheimer Schmidt." All ages. (800) 631-2187.

DANCIN' MAGIC

(Joanie Bartels, Discovery $9.98/$14.98) Get ready to boogie! Older toddlers and preschoolers will be doing "The Hokey Pokey," "The Peppermint Twist," "Rockin' Robin" and other get-up-and-dance tunes. 2 & up. (800) 451-5175.

> **TOY TIP:** 10" Drum and Beater (Music for Little People $12.98) This drum on a stick makes a terrific sound and is decorated with a drawing of six kids from around the world. (800) 727-2233.

DAN CROW LIVE

(Sony $8.98/$13.98) You can tell that this popular children's artist has fun in concert. This is a witty collection of songs that will make everyone want to sing along. Also enjoyed by our testers: Dan Crow's *The Word Factory* (Sony $8.98/$13.98), with such songs as "I'm a Pronoun," "Preposition Blues" and "Dirty Words." 4 & up.

DEEP IN THE JUNGLE

(Joe Scruggs, Shadow Play $9.95) Scruggs mixes up original tunes with adapted versions of classics like "Old MacDonald," "The Eensy Weensy Spider" and "Put Your Thumb in the Air." Another favorite tape with young listeners is *Bahamas Pajamas* (Joe Scruggs, Shadow Play $9.95). 2 & up. (800) 274-8804.

FOR OUR CHILDREN

(Disney $11.98/$19.98) Superstars including Bruce Springsteen, Elton John and Sting sing their versions of kids' classics to benefit the Pediatric AIDS Foundation. Fun for the whole family.

HELLO EVERYBODY!

(Rachel Buchman, A Gentle Wind $8.95) An upbeat collection of traditional and original songs that your toddler will sing, dance and play along to. 2 & up. (518) 436-0391.

LITTLE RICHARD: SHAKE IT ALL ABOUT

(Disney $10.98/$15.98) The title says it all! Little Richard brings his high-powered style to 12 classic tunes, including "The Hockey Pokey," "On Top of Spaghetti" and "Twinkle, Twinkle." It's fun and such a natural that you wonder why he didn't do it years ago. 2 & up.

PUT ON YOUR GREEN SHOES ✹ PLATINUM AWARD

(Sony $13.99) An all star album with artists such as Willie Nelson, Tom Paxton, Tom Chapin, Kevin Roth, Richie Havens, Dr. John and others making great green music dedicated to healing the planet. 4 & up.

SHARON, LOIS AND BRAM GREAT BIG HITS

(A&M $8.98/$12.98) This popular trio offers some of the best-produced children's music today. Our preschoolers loved moving to this hit parade of 31 favorites, including "Pop! Goes the Weasel," "She'll Be Comin' Round the Mountain" and "Tingalayo." Also top-rated: *Mainly Mother Goose* (A&M $9.98). 2 & up.

SINGABLE SONGS FOR THE VERY YOUNG

(Raffi, MCA $10.98/$15.98) Raffi remains on top with our testers who loved singing along to "Down by the Bay" and such holiday classics as "Must Be Santa" and "My Dreidel." Also recommended: *Baby Beluga* (MCA $10.98/$15.98), which includes "Day O" and "Kumbaya." 2 & up. Also see Videos section.

FOLK TUNES FOR
ALL AGES

DOC WATSON SINGS SONGS
FOR LITTLE PICKERS

(Alacazar $8.98/$11.98) A wonderful
collection of traditional folk songs, including "John
Henry" and "The Crawdad Song," with guitar, harmonica,
harp and Doc Watson's engaging voice. (800) 541-9904.

PETE SEEGER'S FAMILY CONCERT

(Sony $8.98/$13.98) Nothing could be better than this
combination of Pete Seeger and 12 favorites, including
"Skip to My Lou," "Coming Round the Mountain," and
"This Land Is Our Land." A winner you won't mind listening to again and again.

PETER, PAUL AND MOMMY, TOO ⭐ PLATINUM AWARD

(Peter, Paul and Mary, Warner $9.98/$15.98) In concert
this beloved trio sings such classics as "Puff (The Magic
Dragon)" and "I Know an Old Lady Who Swallowed a Fly."
A must for any children's audio collection. This is the
sequel to the highly recommended *Peter, Paul and
Mommy* ($9.98/$15.98). Also see Videos section.

PLAY YOUR INSTRUMENTS AND MAKE A PRETTY SOUND

(Ella Jenkins, Smithsonian Folkways $9.50) Generations
of kids have grown up singing songs with Ella, the ultimate songsmith for the young. Classic folksongs with
plenty of repetition and easy sing, clap and tap-along fun.
Also recommended: *You'll Sing A Song and I'll Sing a Song*
($9.50). (800) 443-4727.

RHYTHM AND RHYMES

(Josh Greenberg and Bill Vitek, A Gentle Wind $8.95) Fun,
lively and great for the car or for just enjoying around
the house! "Brother John" is jazzy and sassy. Everyone in
the family will enjoy this collection of classics. (518) 436-
0391.

TICKLES YOU!

(Rosenshontz, Lightyear $9.95) This duo's upbeat style
got our testers tapping their feet and moving. Opening

with a silly ditty about "Sam the Tickle Man," the tape
includes both original and traditional songs. (800) 229-
7867.

Multicultural Music

AFRICAN-AMERICAN FOLK RHYTHMS
(Ella Jenkins and the Goodwill Spiritual Choir, Smithsonian Folkways $9.98) If you're looking for an introduction
to African-American spirituals, look no further. "Wade in
the Water," "A Man Went Down to the River" and many
more. (800) 443-4727.

I GOT SHOES 94 PLATINUM AWARD
(Sweet Honey in the Rock, Music for Little People
$9.98/$12.98) Once again this spirited quintet of African-
American women sings a powerful group of spirituals
and African folk songs a capella. Tape includes such
favorites as "Little David Play on Your Harp," "Freedom
Now," and several counting songs. Also, for a great collection of freedom songs, *All for Freedom*. (800) 727-2233.

JOINING HANDS WITH OTHER LANDS
(Kimbo $11) Here's a multicultural potpourri of songs to
celebrate our diversity. There's one for Chinese New
Year, "Birthdays Around the World," "Many Ways to Say
Hello," and others in English and Spanish. 4–8. (800) 631-
2187.

LE HOOGIE BOOGIE: LOUISIANA FRENCH MUSIC
FOR CHILDREN
(Michael "Beausoleil" Doucet et al., Rounder
$9.98/$11.98) Looking for something different that will
brighten everyone's spirits? Try a musical tour of Cajun
country that will be sure to make you get up and dance.
Wonderful! (800) 443-4727.

RAINBOW SIGN
(Rounder $9.98/$11.98) If you are looking for a selection
of contemporary folk singers, this is a great choice. Tom
Chapin, Beausoleil, Arlo Guthrie, Pete Seeger, Sweet
Honey in the Rock and many more sing to benefit Grass-
roots Leadership, a nonprofit organization dedicated to

promoting community harmony in the South. (800) 443-4727.

SHAKE IT TO THE ONE THAT YOU LOVE

(adapted by Cheryl Warren Mattox et al., JTG $9.98) A taste of jazz, reggae, gospel and rhythm and blues in this set of 26 songs from African, African-American, Creole and Caribbean cultures. Songbook and instructions for how to play ring, line and clapping games included. (615) 329-3036.

SUNI PAZ/ALERTA SINGS CHILDREN'S SONGS IN SPANISH AND ENGLISH

(Smithsonian Folkways $9.98) A wonderful collection of children's songs in Spanish and English from Latin America, the Caribbean and the United States. (800) 443-3727.

WESTERN THEMES

If you're planning a cowboy party, there are more choices for music than you might think! *The Cowboy Album* (Kid Rhino $7.99/$11.99) is a terrific medley of songs, including "Home on the Range," "Back in the Saddle Again," "Rawhide" and "Happy Trails," sung by such stars as Roy Rogers and Gene Autry. Also top-rated is *Riders in the Sky* (Rounder $9.98/$11.98) (800) 443-4727 and *Horse Sense for Kids and Other People* (Music for Little People $9.98/$12.98) (800) 727-2233.

COUNTRY FOR KIDS

(Disney $10.98/$16.98) Twelve of today's leading country singers, including Mary Chapin Carpenter, Emmy Lou Harris and Glen Campbell, sing classic and original tunes for kids.

MUSIC FROM BROADWAY AND HOLLYWOOD

A CHILD'S CELEBRATION OF SHOWTUNES
(Music for Little People $9.98/$12.98) A wonderful intro to some of the best-known show tunes from *Oliver!, The Sound of Music, The King and I, Peter Pan* and *Fiddler on the Roof,* with the added bonus of having them sung by the original casts, including Mary Martin, Zero Mostel and Julie Andrews. A real treat! (800) 727-2233.

ALADDIN/BEAUTY AND THE BEAST/THE LITTLE MERMAID
(Disney $9.98/$15.98) Our testers loved listening to these wonderfully rich scores from Disney's latest run of mega–box office hits. Disney enthusiasts will also want to consider *The Music of Disney* ($35.98/$49.98), a 3-part set of 78 classic Disney tunes dating back to 1928. Some will be of more interest to collectors than to kids. Comes with a 60-page book giving the history of the music. A wonderful gift!

BING CROSBY'S GREATEST HITS   BLUE CHIP
(MCA $12) Both young and old rated this collection tops! Includes "Too-Ra-Loo-Ra-Loo-Ral," "Ac-cent-tchu-ate the Positive," "Swinging on a Star," "White Christmas" and "You Are My Sunshine."

PETER PAN   BLUE CHIP
(Mary Martin et al., RCA $9.95/$17) This is the original cast from the 1954 Broadway production and simply the best! No one sings "Never-Never Land" like Mary Martin!

INTRODUCING THE CLASSICS

BERNSTEIN FAVORITES   BLUE CHIP
(Sony $7.98/$14.98) Children's Classics: "The Carnival of the Animals," "The Young Person's Guide to the Orchestra" and "Peter and the Wolf" are all part of this wonderful introduction to classical music.

FIEDLER'S FAVORITES FOR CHILDREN   BLUE CHIP
(RCA $5.95) Baby boomers remember this spirited conductor. One side includes a collection of dances from

such composers as Tchaikovsky and Strauss. The other side includes nursery rhymes and show tunes, including "Whistle While You Work" and a medley from *The Sound of Music.*

HUSH
(Yo-Yo Ma and Bobby McFerrin, CBS $9.98/$17.98) Our testers enjoyed the musical union of this world-renowned cellist and contemporary vocalist performing works by Bach, Vivaldi and Rachmaninoff. Pieces range in style from "The Flight of the Bumblebee" to "Hoe-down."

THE CLASSICAL KIDS COLLECTION
(The Children's Group $9.98/ $16.98) If you're looking for a way to introduce your kids to classical music, this series fits the bill. In Vivaldi's *Ring of Mystery*, Katarina meets the great composer, who is also the music direc-tor at the orphanage she is sent to in Venice. The excit-ing story is rich with mystery, suspense and Baroque music. Others in the series: *Beethoven Lives Upstairs, Mr. Bach Comes to Town* and *Mozart's Magic Fantasy.* (800) 668-0242.

CLASSICS FOR KIDS
(BMG $8.50) Give them some scarves or rhythm instru-ments as they move to such familiar gems as the *March of the Wooden Soldiers, Mother Goose Suite, Carnival of the Animals, Sleeping Beauty, Sorcerer's Apprentice* and more, played by James Galway, the Boston Pops and the Philadelphia Orchestra. All ages.

PETER AND THE WOLF WITH UNCLE MOOSE AND THE KAZOO-O-PHONIC JUG BAND
(Dave Van Ronk, Alacazar $8.98/$11.98) Van Ronk does a jug band version of "Peter and the Wolf" that's pure fun, as well as other favorites such as "Swing on a Star" and "Teddy Bears' Picnic." A romp! (800) 541-9904.

PETER AND THE WOLF AND TUBBY THE TUBA
(Caedmon $11) Carol Channing performs these two clas-sics with the Cincinnati Pops Orchestra. Both stories

introduce kids to the instruments of the orchestra through playful stories that have entertained children for generations. Channing's distinctive voice and performance make this a two-sided treasure. Other "Peter and the Wolf's" of interest: Sting (Polygram $14.99 CD), David Bowie (RCA $9)—no kidding!—and Itzhak Perlman (EMI $14.99 CD).

> **BOOK TIP:** *Lives of the Musicians: Good Times, Bad Times (And What the Neighbors Thought)* (by Kathleen Krull, Harcourt Brace HBJ $18.95). Vignettes from the lives of 16 famous composers, Mozart to Woody Guthrie.

HOLIDAY SONGS

BILLBOARD'S GREATEST CHRISTMAS HITS 1935–1954
BLUE CHIP
($7.98/$12.98) Classic holiday hits sung by the original artists including Bing Crosby, Gene Autry, Nat King Cole and the Andrew Sisters.

CHANUKAH, A SINGING CELEBRATION
(Cindy Paley, $10.98) Songs that celebrate the Festival of Lights are sung by kids and adults in both Hebrew and English. Music for Little People. (800) 727-2233.

JOANIE BARTELS' CHRISTMAS MAGIC
(Discovery $9.98) A cheerful collection of holiday classics sung by this popular children's recording artist. Favorites including "Jingle Bells," "Have Yourself A Merry Little Christmas," "Frosty The Snowman" and "Rudolph the Red-Nosed Reindeer." (800) 451-5175.

STORIES: AUDIO/ BOOK SETS

Illustrated by Margot Apple

Most storybooks pub- lished in audio form have already been well received as stand-alone books. Add music, sound effects and a well-known narrator, and a good thing just gets better! These combined forms of media can do a lot to promote positive atti- tudes and kids' appetites for books and reading. Here are some of the best tickets to pleasurable and independent storytimes.

PRESCHOOL SETS

ALL-TIME FAVORITE CHILDREN'S STORIES
(Smarty Pants $2.98 & up, tape only) Talk about retro, these classics, such as *The Little Engine That Could* and *Tubby the Tuba,* are narrated by stars of yesteryear like Kate Smith and José Ferrer. Good choices for car trips. 5 & up. (216) 221-5300.

ANGELINA BALLERINA AND OTHER STORIES
(by Katherine Holabird, performed by Sally Struthers, Caedmon, $11 tape only) Angelina is a little mouse who could not concentrate on anything else but her love of dancing. Struthers's engaging reading is right on target. Word-for-word recordings so kids can read along if you buy the books. 4 & up.

ARTHUR'S BABY
(by Marc Brown, Little, Brown $7.95) Arthur, the endear- ing aardvark, is none too happy with the news of a new baby in the family. The story opens with a zippy song and is narrated by the author. Also packaged in tape/paperback combos: *Arthur's Tooth* and *Arthur's Eyes.* 4–8.

BLUEBERRIES FOR SAL

(by Robert McCloskey, Puffin $6.95) In this classic mix-up, a mother bear and cub get separated as do a mother-and-child duo. All's well that ends well. This no-frills paper and audio set has no big-name stars but beginning readers can follow the text or flip the tape for lively activity songs related to bears and berries. The Puffin series includes *The Story of Ping*, *Ferdinand* and other classics. 3–7.

THE CAT IN THE HAT (EL GATO ENSOMBRERADO)
✯ PLATINUM AWARD

(by Dr. Seuss, Random House $6.95) Now both book and tape of this classic beginner book are done in English and Spanish. Children can follow the word-for-word text in either language as they listen to the tape. Also new: a bilingual version of *Are You My Mother?* 3–7.

CHICKA CHICKA BOOM BOOM

(by John Arahambault/illus. by Bill Martin Jr., Simon & Schuster $19.95 book & tape) Long before they're ready for the alphabet, kids love playing around with letters, and that's exactly what this rhythmic verse does. Ray Charles does two readings followed by a rap version done by kids. 3 & up.

GOOD NIGHT MOON   ✯   PLATINUM AWARD

(by M. W. Brown, HarperCollins $7.95 book & tape) This just might be the ticket for dreamland! There's a musical version on one side and a reading of Brown's best-loved book with page-turn signals on the other. Won't replace a real live reading, but on nights when you can't "read it again," this may do. 2 & up.

KING BIDGOOD'S IN THE BATHTUB

(by Audrey and Don Wood, Harcourt Brace $19.95 book & tape) Unlike most tapes that are word-for-word tellings, this picturebook has been enlarged into a musical production as the characters do their best to get the King out of the tub. Deliciously silly, detailed illustrations! 4–8.

MARY WORE HER RED DRESS

(adapted by Merle Peek, Clarion $7.95 book & tape) Adapted from a folksong, this sing-along story is a color concept book that ends with a birthday celebration— always a sure hit for preschoolers! A fun song to play with everyone in the family. 3–6.

THE RUNAWAY BUNNY

(by M. W. Brown, HarperCollins $7.95 book & tape) A musical adaptation and a read-along version of this classic bunny tale of independence and dependence. The music has the simplicity of a folksong and preschool kids enjoy chiming in. 3–7.

SHEEP IN A JEEP

(by Nancy Shaw/illus. by Margot Apple, Houghton Mifflin $7.95 book & tape) Five sheep in a jeep get stuck in the mud, get rescued and end up in a happy heap! With zany illustrations, bouncy rhymes and a tape with page-turn signals. 2 & up.

WINNIE THE POOH STORYTIME GIFT SET
⭐ PLATINUM AWARD

(Disney $14.99) Pooh fans will enjoy the music and adventures on this three-cassette set. Wonderfully narrated by Christopher Plummer. 3 & up.

EARLY SCHOOL YEARS SETS

ANTARCTICA

(by Helen Cowcher, Farrar Straus/Soundprints $19.95 book & tape) Cowcher's stunning illustrations of Antarctica and some of its inhabitants come to life with authentic animal sounds. Narrated by Red Grammer. Also *Tigress* and *Rainforest*. (800) 228-7839.

FROG AND TOAD TALES

(by Arnold Lobel, Caedmon $11 tape only) Five well-loved tales of friendship are narrated by the author. This set of tales is sold without the books, which you'll find in most stores and libraries. Especially good read-along choices for new readers. (800) 331-3761.

MAURICE SENDAK AUDIO COLLECTION

(Caedmon/HarperCollins $25 tape only) This four-cassette set is a Sendak fan's dream come true, with "Where The Wild Things Are," "Really Rosie" and "Higglety Pigglety Pop!" narrated by Tammy Grimes and brought together with the music of Mozart and Carole King. 5 & up.

MIRANDY AND BROTHER WIND

(Knopf $17 book & tape) Cicely Tyson's lilting voice and the high-stepping cake walk music match the rollicking pace of this Southern tale about a girl who manages to make the wind her dancing partner. A Caldecott Honor Book by Patricia McKissack with spirited watercolors by Jerry Pinkney. 5 & up.

MISTY OF CHINCOTEAGUE

(by Marguerite Henry, Caedmon $9.95 tape only) Paul and Maureen have their hearts set on making Phantom, the wild mare, their own. Others have tried to capture her, and now they are faced with a double challenge of how to pay for the the mare and her colt as well. Narrated by Daisy Eagan. 7–12.

PINOCCHIO READ-ALONG COLLECTION

(Walt Disney $15.98 book & tape) Looking for a great birthday gift? This set fills the bill. Young readers can follow along in a 24-page word-for-word storybook with page-signal cues. Tape is well paced and includes some music from the soundtrack. Also *Aladdin* and *Beauty and the Beast* sets. 5 & up.

THE STORY OF BABAR AND BABAR AND FATHER CHRISTMAS

(by Jean de Brunhoff, performed by Louis Jourdan, Caedmon $11 tape only) If you are a Babar fan, you will love

Jourdan's reading of these two Babar classics in his wonderful French accent. 5 & up.

SEASONS OF THE RED FOX

(by Susan Saunders/illus. by JoEllen Bosson, Soundprints $16.95 book & tape) Without an overload of information, here is a lively account of the red fox's first year of life. From the Smithsonian Wildlife Collection. (800) 228-7839. 4–8.

STREGA NONA

(by Tomie de Paola, Simon & Schuster $7.95 book & tape) Strega Nona has a magic pasta pot, but look out when Big Anthony doesn't know how to control it! Narrated by Dom DeLuise. A Caldecott Honor Book. Side 2 is "The Fisherman's Wife," which would be easier to follow if it came with a book. 5 & up.

SWAN LAKE

(as told by Margot Fonteyn/illus. by Trina Sahart-Hyman, Harcourt Brace $19.95 book & tape) Anyone who has seen Swan Lake or is about to for the first time should experience this exquisitely produced tape and beautiful book. Fonteyn's memorable telling lingers in the listener's memory. Excerpts of André Previn with the London Symphony. 7 & up.

SYLVESTER AND THE MAGIC PEBBLE

(by William Steig, narrated by Peter Thomas, Simon & Schuster $8.95 book & tape) When Sylvester the Donkey finds a magic pebble he also discovers that one must be careful about what he wishes for! A gem of a story! 5 & up.

WE ALL HAVE TALES SERIES

(Rabbit Ears $9.95–$19.95) Using the art and audio from their outstanding videos, Rabbit Ears has packaged them in storybook/audio sets. The pace of some work better in this format than on the screen. Stories and music are done by well-known performers. For example, *King Midas and the Golden Touch* is told by Michael Caine, with music composed by Ellis Marsalis and featuring Yo-Yo

Ma. These are not easy-to-read books. They are basically video scripts turned into book form. They come in full size or mini-book/tape combos or tape only ($7.98). Great gifts!

These are just a few favorites from this highly recommended series:

- *Brer Rabbit and Boss Lion,* told by Danny Glover ✷ Platinum Award
- *Jack and the Beanstalk,* told by Michael Palin
- *Koi and the Kola Nuts,* told by Whoopi Goldberg
- *The Tale of Mr. Jeremy Fisher,* told by Meryl Streep
- *The Tiger and the Brahmin,* told by Ben Kingsley, with music by Ravi Shankar

YERTLE THE TURTLE

(by Dr. Seuss, Random House $14 book & tape) John Lithgow narrates the tale of Yertle, an ambitious amphibian. Then there's "Gertrude McFuzz," a bird who wants fancier feathers, and "The Big Brag," about two braggarts who are put in their place by a tiny worm. 5 & up.

AUDIO EQUIPMENT

- For the youngest listeners we recommend Mattel's Easy Touch tape player ($31), with all controls safely locked away except the easy-to-use on/off buttons.
- For threes and up, Playskool's ($40) and Fisher Price's ($45) players have equal sound quality. Both have nondetachable sing-along microphones, a safety hazard for kids under three.
- Sony's My First Radio/Cassette recorder ($59.95) is the heaviest of the bunch but its more grown-up design will appeal to kids 4 and up.

Resources: Alacazar's Kiddie Cat (800) 541-9904 and Music for Little People (800) 727-2233 are two wonderful sources for children's audio and video. You'll also find select titles in many fine toy catalogs.

5 ★ COMPUTER SOFTWARE/ CD-ROM

★ ★ ★ ★ ★ ★ ★ ★ ★ ★ ★ ★ ★ ★ ★ ★ ★

The science fiction of our youth has become our kids' computer reality. From toddlers to teens, children are receptive to the interaction between user and machine. These technologies are not substitutes for books or toys or a good run in the park, but they are important supplements to growth in the computer age.

Before you buy a program, be sure that it will run on your equipment. Unfortunately, some of the latest super graphics and sound technology will not work on older systems. Check the box carefully to make sure that you have enough hard-disk space, memory and the right kind of sound card, monitor and printer.

TOOLS FOR CREATIVE EXPRESSION

Programs that enabled our testers to create finished projects that could be used off-line were the biggest hits. Kids loved producing great-looking results using these applications, whether they were paintings, drawings, crafts projects or stories. This recommended software builds computer familiarity and self-confidence.

FOLLOW THE READER

(Disney $49.95) Disney's follow-up to Mickey's ABC's. Early readers can create their own animated stories by selecting action words from scrollable lists. Stories can be saved and replayed like a movie or sent to the printer to be colored in with crayons and pens. This program mixes works, graphics and sound into an effective exploration for early readers. Format: IBM. 5–8. (818) 841-3326.

KIDPIX   BLUE CHIP

(Brøderbund $59.95) You can't buy a better software package for your whole family than KidPix, a fun-filled multimedia art exploration program with a sense of humor. It is chockful of clever goodies that invite computer and artistic exploration. Paint brushes leak, drip and blow bubbles, and there are dozens of simulated rubber stamps and drawing tools. Younger users will appreciate the mystery eraser, which scratches off the white "background" of the screen to reveal a pre-drawn picture underneath. The program reminds us a little bit of Disneyland. Every bit of it has been engineered with children in mind. Around every corner is a new delight. 3 and up with parental help. Format: IBM, MAC. A Windows version is available, but not recommended. (415) 382-4400.

KIDPIX COMPANION

(Brøderbund $39.95) KidPix owners can make a good thing better with the KidPix Companion, which adds new menu choices to KidPix. There are 112 new rubber stamps, a slide-show maker and coloring-book-style outline pictures ready to be colored in. Format: IBM, MAC. 7 & up. (415) 382-4400.

KIDCUTS

(Brøderbund $59.95) Kidcuts is an electronic activity book, a 21st-century evolution of an age old kids' favorite. Use Kidcuts to create paper planes, hats, cutout figures and other play accessories. Rather than gluing the child to the screen for hours on end, Kidcuts uses the computer as a springboard for off-line creative play. Format: IBM. 4 & up with parental help. (415) 382-4400.

KIDWORKS II

(Davidson & Assoc. $59.95) Kidworks II may be the first multimedia publishing system for kids. The program integrates a wacky drawing program (similar to KidPix) with a simple word processor that bring pictures and stories together. The computer will even read the story aloud. One of the nicest touches is the ability to add rebus picture symbols to the stories. 7 & up. Format: IBM. (800) 545-7677.

THE PRINT SHOP DELUXE

(Brøderbund $44.95) This program produces high-quality greeting cards, signs, stationery, banners, calendars, gift tags and posters. The latest version comes with 30 different fonts and over 300 graphics. Format: IBM/Windows. 10 & up. (415) 382 4400.

ENVIRONMENTS FOR LEARNING

"Environments for learning" is our name for software in which children are presented with a "virtual reality" for learning by exploration. The emphasis here is on discovery and creativity.

MCGEE/MCGEE AT THE FUN FAIR/MCGEE VISITS KATIE'S FARM

(Lawrence $29.95 IBM/MAC; $39.95 Apple/Amiga) In these three programs picturebooks come alive for young children. The programs work without written words. Think of these as electronic pop-up books. Kids enjoyed exploring with McGee at his home, at the park and with Katie at the farm. These programs are available individually or in a triple pack. 2 & up. (800) 421-4157.

MICKEY'S ABC'S ✹ PLATINUM AWARD

(Disney $29.95) Step into the world of Mickey Mouse and his pals in this gorgeous program featuring Mickey at home and at a fair. When children press a letter a pleasant voice speaks the letter's name and then Mickey goes to the object that starts with that letter. The computer speaks the name of the object and then displays an amusing animation. Because there are no wrong answers, children are encouraged to explore without frustration. 3 & up. Format: IBM. (818) 841-3326.

RODNEY'S FUNSCREEN ⭐ PLATINUM AWARD

(Activision $49.95; CD–ROM $59.95) A multimedia extravaganza for preschoolers! Five sound-packed, color-filled games stimulate exploration and learning. The hit of the package is Barber Joe, a clever painting program that lets kids draw hairstyles on Jane, Joe and Woof the dog. Baby boomers will wax nostalgic for the old days when we did the same thing with a magic wand and magnetic shavings, but this program is more fun. There is a concentration game that develops memory skills, a letter recognition game and a counting game. Highly recommended. 4 & up. Format: IBM/MAC. (800) 477-3650.

THE PLAYROOM

(Brøderbund $49.95) Virtual reality for three- to six-year-olds. There is real education going on behind the scenes of this creative playroom. Clicking on objects in the room launches short animations and learning games. Be sure to check the box to see if your hardware can support this program. 3 & up. Format: IBM. (415) 382-4400.

THE TREEHOUSE ⭐ PLATINUM AWARD

(Brøderbund $59.95) Brøderbund has done it again, with another magical room for exploration. This time the setting is a treehouse overlooking a pond that kids will enjoy making their own. The graphics and music are first-rate, and the activities are interactive and fun. Using the silly sentence theater, kids form funny sentences from pictures that are acted out. A wonderful synthesizer can be used to play supplied songs or to introduce kids to musical notation as they write their own songs. Dozens of other good-humored learning activities await your child inside the Treehouse. Top of the list. 6 & up. Format: IBM. (415) 382-4400.

KIDDESK ⭐ PLATINUM AWARD

(Edmark $39.95) If you and your kids share a computer, you need to install Kiddesk immediately! It provides a graphic menu chockful of handy desk accessories for kids. Best and most important of all, it sits as a security program between your valuable programs and the younger members of your family. The program can be configured so that kids never have access to the possibly destructive DOS prompt. Adults can bypass the program and drop to the DOS prompt by use of a password. All ages. Format: IBM/MAC. (206) 556-8484.

TURBO SCIENCE

(Sierra-on-Line $49.95) To solve these fun science problems kids have to apply information that they look up in a supplied book about energy, chemistry, magnetism, and air and water pressure. 9 & up. Format: IBM. (800) 743-7721.

SPACE ADVENTURE/DINOSAUR ADVENTURE
⭐ '94 PLATINUM AWARDS

(Knowledge Adventure $79.95 and $49.95) If you are going to give a computer to an older kid, these are the programs to load on first. Creativity and technical excellence meet in Knowledge Adventure's newest multimedia extravaganzas. These programs have text, beautiful graphics and amazing sound effects. Click on the animated graphics to reveal information or take you to another picture. One child said that this is what books must be like on the Starship Enterprise! Be forewarned: These programs take nearly 10 megabytes of disk space and really need a sound card to get the full effect. Most highly recommended. Kids five and up will enjoy the music, pictures and special effects, though older readers will get the most benefit. (800) 542-4240.

ZUG'S DINOSAUR WORLD

(ZugWare $34.95) Our testers couldn't get enough of this program, which features a dinosaur coloring book, concentration match game, dinosaur identification game and animated story maker. 4–9. Format: IBM. (310) 793-0610.

ROCK AND BACH STUDIO

(Binary Zoo $59.95) Kids create their own music videos and learn a bit about music history and theory. 7 and up. Format: IBM. (800) 521-6263.

CARMEN SAN DIEGO   BLUE CHIP

(Brøderbund $39 & up) Carmen San Diego has become a conglomerate. Kids can search for her in America, Europe, Time and the World. The series is available for IBM, MACs and Apples in most formats ($39.95–$79.95), though the new CD–ROM deluxe version is presently available for IBMs only ($79.95). 10 & up. (415) 382-4400.

DRILL AND REVIEW SOFTWARE

"How do you get to Carnegie Hall?" goes the old joke. "Practice," the punch line, reminds us that some things can be learned only by repetition, review and memorization. Flash cards and work-sheets were the precursors to drill and problem-solving software, and this type of tool still has a place in contemporary learning. If our category "Environments for Learning" is characterized by open-ended exploration, these programs stress getting at the "right" answer.

Drill-and-review programs give kids incentives to study reading, math and spelling. The best use a "spoonful of sugar" approach to facilitate learning. Some display a brief animated sequence after getting a certain number of correct answers. Others, notably the Treasure and Super Solver™ series from The Learning Company, mix arcade gaming with drill repetition to encourage kids to keep working.

MILLIE'S MATH HOUSE   94   PLATINUM AWARD

(Edmark $49.95) Six quality math games for younger kids develop counting, concentration and shape and pattern recognition through creative activities. 3–6. Format: IBM/MAC. (206) 556-8484.

READER RABBIT'S READY FOR LETTERS

(The Learning Co. $59.95) Kids explore Grandma and Grandpa's house and discover five major activities that emphasize early reading skills. Word and letter recognition and concepts (like "over" and "under") are developed in activity rooms in the house (Mix and Match Bed-

room, ABC Bathroom, Picture Parlor, Grandpa's Workshop and Grandma's Kitchen). The graphics are snappy
and colorful, and our testers liked that the program
"talked" on appropriately equipped machines. Younger
kids will need assistance at first. 3–5. Format: IBM. (800)
852-2255.

NEW MATH BLASTER PLUS

(Davidson and Assoc. $49.95 IBM; $59.95 MAC/Windows)
Davidson has updated its classic math package with
arcade-quality graphics that make these drills snappy
and entertaining. The program covers addition, subtrac-
tion, multiplication, division, fractions, decimals and per-
cents. The program keeps track of the student's learning
and even prints out graphic certificates to mark
progress. We wish we had had this solid mix of fun and
math when we were learning our basic skills. 6–12. (800)
545-7677.

TREASURE MATHSTORM

(The Learning Co. $59.95) Treasure MathStorm is part of
a trilogy (Treasure Cove and Treasure Mountain are the
others) of arcade-like games that develop academic
skills. These are richly illustrated full-color programs
that feature sound-card support. The Treasure series is
designed to make kids think they are playing, while in
fact they are doing drills. And it works! To free Treasure
Mountain from the icy spell of the Master of Mischief,
kids have to solve math and time-telling problems. The
problems get progressively harder as the program tracks
your child's performance. Highly recommended for 6–8.
Format: IBM. (800) 852-2255.

SUPER SOLVERS OUTNUMBERED

(The Learning Co. $49.95 IBM; $59.95 MAC) Proves that
practicing math problems need not be tedious. To stop
the Master of Mischief from his insidious plot to make
television boring, children must solve number, logic and
math-word problems. Our panel of kid testers rated this
program highly. Comments like "You really need to know
your math facts to play this game" suggested that they
felt good about their ability to meet the challenge. 6–9.
Format: IBM/MAC. (800) 852-2255.

SUPER SOLVERS SPELLBOUND

(The Learning Co. $49.95 IBM; $59.95 MAC) It takes a lot to make learning how to spell fun, but the Learning Company has done it! Kids use word search, criss-cross and flash-card activities to win the spelling contest. The graphics and sound support are state of the art. 7–9. Format: IBM/MAC. (800) 852-2255.

MYSTERY AT THE MUSEUMS

(Binary Zoo $59.95) Tracking down missing treasures of the Smithsonian Museum is the plot device for 16 different creative problem-solving puzzles. 7 & up. Format: IBM. (800) 521-6263.

CD–ROM AND MULTIMEDIA TECHNOLOGY

CD–ROMs look just like audio CDs but require a special player called a CD–ROM drive. CD–ROM's promise is in its ability to hold thousands of pages of text, graphics, sounds and even mini-movies on a single disk. The drawback is price. These programs have strict hardware requirements that can be expensive. All, of course, require a CD–ROM disk drive. But there may be additional costs, such as a sound card (look for one with Soundblaster support), additional memory and (because many programs copy material from the CDs to the hard disk) more disk storage.

GRANDMA AND ME 🌟 PLATINUM AWARD

(Brøderbund $54.95 IBM; $39.95 MAC) This program, like others in Brøderbund's Living Book series of interactive, animated books, is state of the art. The package includes a paperback book as well as the CD–ROM disk. Music, animations, sound effects and talking characters bring books to life. Preschoolers will enjoy being read to and watching the videos with some adult supervision. Older children can explore the pictures interactively. Little Critter's day at the beach with Grandma is humorous and touching. The animation and voices enhance this story about balancing independence and security. The program can read the story and interact with the user in

English, Spanish and Japanese, which means that it can be used in multi-lingual settings as well as with kids who are learning a second language. 3 & up. Format: IBM/MAC. (415) 382-4400.

ARTHUR'S TEACHER TROUBLE ✸ PLATINUM AWARD
(Brøderbund $54.95 MAC; $59.95 Windows) Based on Marc Brown's picturebook of the same name, this is the story of Arthur, his third-grade teacher and the school spellathon. Each page bursts with images that come to life by clicking the mouse. Our testers loved the good-natured sense of humor of the text and illustrations. Program operates in English and Spanish. 5 & up. Format: Windows/MAC. (415) 382-4400.

THE SAN DIEGO ZOO™ PRESENTS THE ANIMALS!
(Software Toolworks $119.95) This is a gorgeous program, a multimedia must-have. Comparable to a beautiful coffeetable book about animals and zoo life, but better! It comes to life with animations (some of which are narrated), sound clips, pictures and a bold, colorful design. There are many ways to explore: Take a guided tour of an exhibit, examine the animals by habitat or use the alphabetical index. The trip to the animal nursery, which features movie clips of the zoo's youngest stars, was a huge hit. We wish the pictures and info could be printed out. Format: IBM-DOS; Windows and MAC versions are promised. (415) 883-3000.

WORLD ATLAS
(Software Toolworks $77.95 IBM; $99.95 Windows; $89.95 MAC) Geography reports are a fixture of the third and fourth grades, and our testers were able to produce really special results using this program. The 240 maps are supplemented by almanac-style data as well as great charts and graphs. The Windows version displays the national flag and (on sound-card equipped machines) plays the national anthem and pronounces the name of each country. The maps are not as beautiful as the traditional one depicted on the box, but this program was a tremendous hit with the kids, who appreciated the wealth of data and the ease with which it could be sent to paper or other programs. (415) 883-3000.

BEST IN ITS CATEGORY: THE NEW GROLIER MULTIMEDIA ENCYCLOPEDIA 🏅 PLATINUM AWARD

(Software Toolworks $395.95) Kids voted this the best electronic encyclopedia, and we agree. In the past, design limitations made using CD–encyclopedias less useful than print versions. That has changed with the introduction of this product. Encyclopedias tend to compete based upon numbers of articles, photos and the like, but that's only part of the equation: The data must be legible, accessible and readily exportable to print or other programs. This product scores on all counts. It is good-looking, readable in all screen resolutions and loaded with great graphics and sound clips. Be aware, however, that only text is directly exportable to other programs or to print. To copy or print photos requires the use of a third-party screen-capture program. 8 & up. Reviewed format: Windows. Other formats available: MAC/IBM. (415) 883-3000.

COMPTON'S INTERACTIVE ENCYCLOPEDIA

(Compton's New Media $395.00, Upgrade $149.95) Compton's has revised and renamed its CD–based encyclopedia, improving on it and lowering its price at the same time. The single CD–ROM disk contains over 15,000 pictures, sound clips, some animations and the informative text that has been a Compton's trademark for generations. However, the graphics, photos and animations were smaller, darker and grainier than the Grolier's, and the interface is not as clean. Still, Compton's provides a space-saving electronic format that many will find appealing and familiar. 8 & up. Format: IBM/MAC. (800) 532-3766.

LIFE AFTER ARCADE: GETTING VALUE FROM SEGA AND NINTENDO

You can't ignore video games. Your children will want them and probably already have them. The trick is finding cartridges that give value to their play. Mix these programs into your child's diet of Mario and Sonic to turn that brain drain into a brain gain.

THE MIRACLE PIANO TEACHING SYSTEM

(Software Toolworks $299–$419 depending on format) Learning to play the piano and mastering a video game take similar skills and effort. Both take weeks of practice, memorization and repetition of keystrokes. It took the Miracle Piano Teaching System to bring these activities together into a self-paced beginner's introduction to reading and playing music. This is by far the highest use a video-game machine has ever been put to. From the first lesson the emphasis is on making music, playing real songs. Reading skills are necessary, as is a certain amount of self-disipline. Available on Sega Genesis, Super Nintendo, Nintendo game machines, IBM and MAC. 8 & up. (415) 883-3000.

MARIO PAINT 🌟 PLATINUM AWARD

(Nintendo $59.95) This package includes painting software and a mouse for the Super Nintendo system. Kids can draw their own pictures or fill in pre-drawn coloring book style graphics. Scenes can be animated along with original or preselected musical scores. Creations can be saved on a VCR, though there is no paper output. A big hit with our testers, young and old. Format: Super NES. 8 & up. (800) 255-3700.

> James Oppenheim, computer consultant, attorney, president of the CPU computer users group and father of two, wrote our computer chapter byte-by-byte.

6 ★ USING ORDINARY TOYS FOR KIDS WITH SPECIAL NEEDS

* * * * * * * * * * * * * * * * *

On these pages are products that are both entertaining and useful to children with special needs.
We suggest ways to adapt and use many of these
products for optimal learning and play opportunities, and some need no adaption at all. This section
has been prepared in conjunction with the National
Lekotek Center, a nonprofit organization that provides toy lending-library services and play-centered
programs for children across the country.

Products selected for these pages have received
our Special Needs Adaptable Product (SNAP)
Award. It's our hope that bringing attention to
these products will serve kids *and* motivate manufacturers and publishers to become more aware of
this audience of children, who, like all children,
need quality products.

All of the toys recommended have been used
with success by children with special needs. Many
are especially easy to activate and provide interesting sensory feedback. For children who are visually
or hearing impaired, learning to make effective use
of their other senses is essential. Similarly, those
with motor impairment need products that respond
and motivate active exploration. While the accent
here is on meeting such needs, we also recognize
that children enjoy playing with products that are
like their siblings', cousins' or neighbors'. By adapt-

ing ordinary toys we can help put their play lives into the mainstream.

Most toys have more than one use and will provide various kinds of feedback for children with different kinds of disabilities. Although we have used headings for infants, toddlers and preschoolers, age guidelines are blurred since conventional age labels will be less meaningful for children with significant developmental delays.

INFANTS AND TODDLERS

All the toys in this section were selected because they provide plenty of sensory feedback. Some of the best toys for infants and toddlers need little or no adapting.

• •

Basic Gear Checklist for Infants and Toddlers

★ ★ ★

✔ Mobile
✔ Musical toys
✔ Crib mirror
✔ Fabric rattles
✔ Teethers
✔ Balls
✔ Fabric blocks
✔ Soft huggables
✔ Manipulatives
✔ Bath toys
✔ Floor toys
✔ Infant seat

Reviews of top-rated basics are in the Infants and Toddlers sections. Here we have focused on products that are easy to activate and that are loaded with sound, light, texture or motion, as well as those that can be adapted.

BOOM BOX
(Fisher Price $16.99) A boom box for tots! This toy offers
a range of manipulative challenges from fine-motor to
whole-handed activities for kids with motor difficulties.
Unlike many musical toys that require the ability to turn
a knob, this is easily activated by pushing a bright-red
plunger. (800) 432-5437.

DISNEY COLOR SPIN   BLUE CHIP

(Mattel $10) This is a wonderful
toy for kids who have low muscle
tone and motor difficulties. Small
colorful balls spin when the large
roller ball is stroked. One of our
favorite toys, it is both visually appealing and has terrific
auditory feedback. Use suction cups to keep it on a table
top or wheelchair tray. (800) 524-8697.

WATCH ME TALK MIRROR SNAP AWARD
(Mattel $27) This sound-activated mirror that records
and plays back a child's voice will be of interest to
babies as well as older kids with autism or language
delays. The mirror and verbal feedback may spark interest and increase the possibility of further communication. The mirror also comes with a phone for pretend.
Will appeal to kids who cannot push buttons on a tape
recorder. (800) 524-8697.

LIGHTS AND SOUND PIANO   PLATINUM AWARD
(Fisher Price $30) Kids with sensory disabilities love this
piano, with its three easy-to-activate colorful light-up
keys and great auditory musical feedback. You can glue
textures or braille dots to each key to add tactile dimension. A child with language delays can be encouraged to
sing along with songs. (800) 432-5437.

LISTEN AND LEARN BALL
(Texas Instruments $25) Touch one of the many pictures
on the ball's faceted surface and you'll hear a related,
appropriate sound. It's a toy that children of varying
ages and levels of development will enjoy independently.
Comes with animal sounds or nursery rhymes and in
Spanish, French and English. (800) 842-2737.

MUSICAL DREAM SCREEN

(Playskool $30) A slow-moving scene provides visual and auditory stimulation. Designed on a slant, this toy works on the floor or on a wheelchair tray. (800) 752-9755.

MY EASY SHAPE 'N STIR POT   BLUE CHIP

(Playskool $7) The three shapes on the lid of the pot are raised so kids with visual impairments can get tactile feedback for sorting. Kids can be given an added sorting clue if you put the same type of sticker on all of the circle blocks and near the circle slot. Use for pretend play and games of filling and dumping. (800) 752-9755.

POP 'N' GO TRAIN

(Tomy $4.99) Push the conductor's head and send the little engine zooming. For kids who are becoming mobile, it builds "can do" power, motivation to crawl and lessons in cause and effect. (714) 256-4990.

POP-UP BUNNY

(Fisher Price $13) This bunny-in-the-box toy plays peeka-boo. Sound is activated by the slightest touch. Without any special adaptions this toy gives both visual and auditory feedback, empowering children to make things happen. (800) 432-5437.

SOUND BOX PUZZLE

(Battat $13.50) Three see-through cylinders are combined to make a shape-sorter with just three shapes that "whistle" as they slide down one of the three tubes. Also Sound Tube Rattle ($5) with just one cylinder and nonremovable shape. Great for visual tracking. (518) 562-2200.

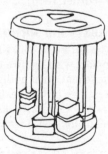

SQUEEZE BLOCKS

(Chicco $17) This set of pastel, soft-vinyl blocks provides plenty of sensory feedback. Blocks are lightly scented and squeak when pressed. They also have embossed objects to feel, count and name. Great to toss, taste, stack and knock down. (800) 336-8697.

• •

ACTIVITY TIP:
Play a little game of Hide-and-Seek the Sound.
Cover one of the blocks with a blanket and press to
make it squeak. Ask the child, "Where is it?"

• •

WRIST AND ANKLE HOT TOT RATTLES ✹ **SNAP AWARD**
(Eden $6.50) Soft-fabric rattles are attached to baby's
wrist or feet for more feedback. All babies are fascinated
to discover their limbs, and these add-ons can help them
refine more purposeful motions. (212) 947-4400.

PRESCHOOL AND EARLY SCHOOL YEARS

As children grow they need a
rich variety of playthings to
match their expanding interests
and abilities.

• •

*Basic Gear Checklist for Preschool and
Early School Years*

★ ★ ★

✔ Construction toys
✔ Toys for pretend (dolls, trucks, puppets)
✔ Art materials
✔ Puzzles, games and manipulatives
✔ Sand and water toys
✔ Big muscle toys
✔ Musical toys
✔ Electronic toys
✔ Tape player and tapes

Age ranges are purposefully broad; products
need to be selected on the basis of your child's particular needs. Many basic toys reviewed in the
Preschool and Early School Years sections will be
of interest and need no special adaptation. Here we
have focused on products that lend themselves to
adaptation.

SOUNDS AND SIGHTS TOYS

ROUND BELLS

(Battat $26) The bright-colored bells are arranged in a ring and make a pleasing sound when they are struck. If the child cannot grasp the beater, attach it to her hand with a large fabric ponytail holder or put Velcro on a stick and a mitten. (518) 562-2200. Little Tikes Xylophone ($20) can be adapted the same way. (800) 321-0183.

• •

SHOPPING TIP:

A Round Bells that is operated with a simple electronic switch can be purchased from Toys for Special Children. (914) 478-0960.

• •

SESAME STREET BUSY POPPIN' PALS

(Playskool $15) This classic pop-up toy with five characters hiding behind little doors can be adapted for different needs. Braille dots or textures can be glued to the numbers on each door for tactile cues. Stickers of characters can be glued to each door to reinforce visual memory for kids with developmental delays. (800) 752-9755.

SEE 'N SAY

(Mattel $11) A satisfying toy that produces auditory feedback with a new easy-to-pull lever. Comes with animals, colors or nursery rhyme pictures and corresponding sounds, words and songs. Kids like the repetition and magic of a talking machine. (800) 524-8697.

MANIPULATIVES AND TRACKING GAMES

BUSY BALLS

(Playskool $19) At last, a marble run with extra-large balls for visual tracking and hands-on fun. Adults may need to stack

ramps. To adapt, use a puppet as the second player—
who playfully snatches or stops the ball. For outdoor fun,
pour water down the tracks! Or put numbers on balls
and guess which will land first. (800) 752-9755.

BEADS ON WIRE TOYS

(Anatex/Educo/Playskool $12 & up) This great tracking
toy has colorful beads that can be turned, pushed and
counted. Anatex and Educo offer equally handsome
wooden versions. Playskool's plastic model is less expensive. Anatex (800) 999-9599/Educo (800) 661-
4142/Playskool (800) 752-9755.

DELUXE BUSY GEARS

(Playskool $39) These large
gears are ideal for visual tracking. For added visual interest,
glue pictures or animal figures
to gears. For a child who has
difficulty grasping, adapt handles with a piece of Velcro
as a hand strap. Designing gear patterns helps kids with
learning disabilities to develop problem-solving skills.
(800) 752-9755.

MOTOR TRACKS 🌟 SNAP AWARD

(Kapable Kids $45.95) Large 13 × 13 board has a cut-out
track and giant wooden knob that slides along the path-
way. Enhances eye-hand coordination, visual tracking,
problem-solving, and can be used with two hands to
develop fluid arm movements. One is designed like a
maze, another with an amoebalike form. (800) 356-1564.

STACK AND DUMP TRUCK

(Parents Child Development $22) This truck with its high
handle is easy to grasp, roll and dump for kids with limited motor control. Cover colored circles and squares
with fabric textures to add sensory cues for kids with
visual impairments. (201) 831-1400.

TUMBLING RACERS

(Fisher Price $ 11) A well-designed visual tracker with
big-kid appeal. Set cars at the top and watch 'em race

down the track and onto the floor or table. Give your racers sports caps, a number to don that's also on one of the cars and a flag and bell for the finish line. (800) 432-5437.

PUZZLES AND MORE MANIPULATIVES

FLYING WHEELCHAIR PUZZLE

(Wind River $16.80) Kids with special needs will enjoy finding images of kids like themselves on a 15-piece puzzle with a child in a wheelchair or a 13-piece puzzle with a child who has foot braces and hand crutches. Pieces are slightly raised above puzzle frame for ease of handling. A four-piece shape puzzle with finger holes is also a good choice for beginners. (800) 743-9463.

GEOMETRIC PUZZLE BOARD

(Environments $21.25) This 9" square puzzle has five brightly colored shapes with jumbo handles for easier grasping. #275-013. (800) 342-4453.

• •

SHOPPING TIP:

To adapt a standard wooden puzzle, pinch holes can be drilled for grasping or dowels can be glued on. Any lumberyard will cut dowels to fit your child's needs.

• •

FORM FITTER

(Playskool $6) Great for tactile discrimination. The textures on each side and shape can be enhanced using glued dots, fake fur, small pom-pom balls, etc. Use shapes with Play-Doh for added concept reinforcement. (800) 752-9755.

• •

SHOPPING TIP:

Sensory feedback is important to kids with visual impairments who are eventually going to learn to read Braille. Look for toys that help to develop their sense of touch or add cues they can "read" with fingers, ears and nose.

••

LETTER AND NUMBER PUZZLES

(Wandix $49.99 & up) Kids will find success with these big 6" foam squares with A–Z letters and 0–9 numbers. Handling bumpy-textured letters gives kids a "feel" for the letter shapes. (The plastic has a strong odor that fades with time.) For a less-pricey toy, buy the letters of your child's name. 12" ($6 each) or 6" ($1.49 each). (800) 385-6855.

SOFT STUFF MR. POTATO HEAD

(Playskool $13.99) For kids who found the old peg-in-the-hole hard to use, this all-fabric body with Velcro features is ideal. To make choices simpler, place features on a flat box with a felt surface or try a game of "Name That Part" as they are pulled out of a bag and placed on the potato. (800) 752-9755.

••

ACTIVITY TIP:

Make your own play board by gluing colored felt on the lid and sides of a sturdy box. Use board for sticking on cut-out shapes, letters and animals backed with Velcro. Box can be used to store pieces.

••

TELL BY TOUCH

(Constructive Playthings $16.95) Ten round textured knobs fit into ten matching textured slots on a puzzle board. A playful way to develop tactile discrimination that makes it especially attractive for a child with vision impairments. #MTC-917. (800) 832-0572.

• •

ACTIVITY TIP:
Make your own touch 'n' match game. Create matching pairs of cards with varying textures (terry cloth, satin, wool, foil and sandpaper). Use for rummy or concentration games.

• •

CONSTRUCTION TOYS

Building invites creative thinking and decision making. Color, counting and size concepts are built in (we couldn't resist). Best of all, blocks offer a win-win opportunity because there is no right or wrong way for them to be used. Visually challenged kids can learn their shapes by rubbing the textured blocks on cheeks or hands. For shopping info about blocks sets, see the Preschool and Early School Years sections.

How to adapt blocks:

• Add strips of sticky-backed Velcro tape to standard unit wooden blocks or Mega Blocks for a more stable base for building. To build two-handed skills, have child play at pulling block apart and putting them together.

• Use colorful plastic Duplo and Lego blocks for color-matching, counting and size discrimination concepts for a child with learning disabilities.

• Magnetic blocks can be made more user-friendly by using them on a cookie sheet. (Battat $12.95). (518) 562-2200.

• Krinkle Blocks are stimulating to the touch and make great sounds when "zipped" across the edge of any surface. Pulling the blocks apart will develop strength in fingers. (Battat $23 set of 80). (518) 562-2200.

- Tinkertoys' new large colorful plastic pieces are easier to handle than the old wooden sets. For a child who has trouble connecting the rods, a wad of Play-Doh will provide an easier target.
- Textured foam blocks are ideal for kids with visual challenges. Block Party (Discovery $24.98 for 37-piece set) (Not for kids who still mouth things.)

PRETEND PLAY

Pretend play is not just great fun. It's the way kids develop imagination and creative-thinking skills, and try on roles of being big and powerful. Pretending also brings the world down to the child's size and understanding. It's a way to develop communication skills and an outlet for expressing feelings and fears.

HOUSEKEEPING EQUIPMENT

For descriptions of toy kitchens, plates and other pretend props like vacuum cleaners and gardening tools, see reviews in the Toddler section. Here are a few props of particular interest:

MAGIC BURNER STOVE

(Fisher Price $20) This two-burner stove top is small enough to use on a wheelchair tray. Plastic utensils can be tied to the stove top, and pretend pots can be Velcroed to the burners. (800) 432-5437.

KIDS KITCHENETTES

(Today's Kids $30) Small-scaled for kids who are unable to stand. (800) 258-8697.

• •

ACTIVITY TIP:
To enhance pretend play, add water for pouring, play-dough, dried cereal, etc. Most kids love the messiness of it all, which motivates ample touching and exploration that strengthens fingers and hands as well as language and curiosity.

• •

WOODEN FRUITS AND VEGETABLES
(Plan Toys $18) These cleverly crafted two- to three-segmented wooden fruits and veggies are ripe for dramatic play possibilities for kids who are learning shape, color and part and whole concepts. The chunky wooden knife is a safe way to introduce functional use of a cutting tool. (212) 689-3590.

• •

ACTIVITY TIP:
For sniffing, tasting and touching, present real fruits in parts or wholes. Put pieces in a bag. Child must name fruit without visual cues.

• •

TRANSPORTATION TOYS

BUSY DRIVER
(Playskool $20) A dashboard for pretend. Great auditory feedback from the horn, steering wheel and gear shift. The many manipulative switches are excellent for promoting two-handed play. (800) 752-9755.

REMOTE-CONTROL VEHICLES
Choose either Playskool's **Remote Control Car** ($30) or Nikko's amazing **Air Nikko Jet** ($38) ✹ SNAP Award, which has jet sounds and lights. Single-button control is easy to

master. These toys are half the price of many switch toys seen in specialty catalogs. Both are especially satisfying choices for a child in a wheelchair or with physical challenges. (800) 752-9755.

SPIN-AROUND TRAIN

(Playskool $23) For kids who love trains but can't manipulate a loose train on a track, this train is attached to the track and activated with a simple push on the "switch-like" plunger. Fits easily on a wheelchair tray. (800) 752-9755.

WOODEN TRAIN SETS

(Brio or T. C. Timber $50 & up) Trains are ideal for pretend play and language reinforcement. These sets have magnetic couplings that will be easier for many kids to handle. For kids who can't fit tracks together, adapt by mounting to a play board. A tabletop makes this toy accessible for a child in a wheelchair. Brio (800) 558-6863/ T. C. Timber (800) 359-1233.

• •

SHOPPING TIP:

A play mat with a printed roadway is a play environment that's always ready and does not need to be put together. Cars and trains don't need to fit in grooves, so less dexterity is needed.

• •

PUPPETS

Few toys provide a better way to get kids to express their feelings. Without the need to move themselves, kids in wheelchairs or beds can take on pleasingly active roles through the puppets. For top-rated puppets and stages, see the Preschool and Early School Years sections.

How to Adapt a Puppet:

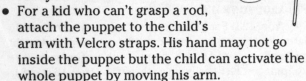

- Fill the puppet with a styrofoam cone. Push a wooden dowel into the cone and your puppet is ready for action!

- For a kid who can't grasp a rod, attach the puppet to the child's arm with Velcro straps. His hand may not go inside the puppet but the child can activate the whole puppet by moving his arm.

- Place puppets over big plastic soda bottles that can be moved around like dolls.

- Attach a magnet to stuffed finger puppets or Little People–type figures and use them on a metal cookie sheet.

- Velcro puppets with changeable features have wonderful play value. See Pick a Puppet (Creative Education of Canada $14). (800) 982-2642.

MEDICAL PRETEND PROPS

For kids with chronic medical needs, pretend props can help them prepare for treatments or work through some of the feelings and fears about them.

CABBAGE PATCH KIDS BABYLAND CHECK-UP CENTER
(Hasbro $25) When it's time for a check-up, this play center includes an X-ray, heart monitor, stethoscope and other instruments. Can be used with 10" to 16" dolls. Also Cabbage Patch Dental Center ($32). 3 & up. (800) 752-9755.

DOCTOR'S KITS
See Comparison Shopper in Preschool section.

DOCTOR AND NURSE PUPPETS
(Poppets $20 each) A zany-looking pair of humanoids— but definitely nothing like your family doctor! (800) 241-1161.

HOSPITAL SYSTEM AND DENTAL OFFICE
(Playmobil $10 and up) Role-playing with mini-medical
equipment and doctors, nurses and patients helps kid
feel more in charge of visits to doctor, dentist or hospital. Parents may need to assemble, but kids can use them
as props for dollhouse or block play. (908) 274-0101.

• •

VIDEO TIP:
Sesame Street Home Video Visits the Hospital (Random House $9.95). Closed captioned. (800) 733-
3000.

• •

DOLLS & DOLLHOUSES
Many wonderful dolls and soft animals are
described in the Toddlers, Preschool and Early
School Years sections. The dolls below will be especially interesting for children with special needs.

HAL'S PALS 🏅 **SNAP AWARD**
(Hal's Pals $59 & up) There is something especially
grand about having a doll that, like you, has hearing aids,
leg braces or a wheelchair. Boys and girls will be thrilled
with these 19" fabric dolls that have Cabbage Patch–like
faces and easy on/off clothes.

- Hal Doll is a one-
  legged downhill
  skier
- Ballerina Pal is a
  darling red-haired
  dancer with hear-
  ing aids
- Winning Pal rides in his wheelchair
- Outdoor Pal, an African-American girl, is visually
  impaired and comes with a "guide" dog and cane
- Party Pal has leg braces that peek out beneath
  her party dress.

The designer of Hal's Pals will mix and match
boy/girl, activity and disability to make a doll that's
especially right for your child. (303) 726-5400.

PRESS 'N' DRESS DOLL  SNAP AWARD

(Pockets $30) Dressing dolls can be difficult, but not with this 13" flat fabric doll that's like a paper cut-out. She comes with six outfits that are backed with Velcro for easy changing. Wardrobe, stand and doll all store in a zip-up carrying case. A beautifully made toy for pretend play. Childcraft. (800) 631-5657.

LITTLE TIKES PLACE/WHEELCHAIR AND RAMP
SNAP AWARD

(Little Tikes $70) This big open dollhouse is ready for dramatic role-play. Chunky furniture is easy to manipulate, and so are the family figures. Wheelchair and Ramp ($9) A chunky miniature wheelchair and ramp set makes Little Tikes Place accessible in a new and memorable way for many families. Great idea! (800) 321-0183.

GAMES

Games are entertaining ways for kids to develop social skills, as well as counting, matching and color concepts.

BED BUGS

(Milton Bradley $10) This classic game encourages fine motor skills, hand/eye coordination and color recognition. Each child has a pair of colored tongs to match their bed bugs. To make the game easier, use pom-pom balls that can be purchased in any color or size instead of the small bugs that come with the game. (413) 525-6411.

CANDYLAND

(Milton Bradley $7) To adapt this (and other boardgames) for kids who can't manipulate small pieces: 1) Mount play pawns on top of big caps from plastic milk jugs. 2) Glue thick washer-shape magnets (from hardware store) into cap bottoms. 3) Make a photocopy of the playing board, color it and cover with clear Contact paper; then attach it to a cookie sheet. If child can't hold cards, adult can do so, or make a die with a foam rubber square block with color dots stuck on. (413) 525-6411.

RING AROUND A ROSY GAME

(Ravensburger $16) The object of this charming game is to match the little figures by color and position of their hands. For stability and ease of handling, glue small magnet strips under the figures' feet and play the game on a cookie sheet. Try the domino-style match game or simplify by taking turns matching pairs two by two. (201) 831-1400.

TEXTURE DOMINOES

(Chaselle $18.95) Here are 28 wooden dominoes that are matched by touch. Each domino has two textures. A terrific game choice for children with vision impairments. (800) 543-7411.

ART SUPPLIES

Art materials are more than fun. They provide a great way to motivate kids to develop dexterity and express feelings without words, and they give tons of sensory feedback. Creative exploration, without lots of right or wrong rules, also gives kids a wonderful sense of "can do" power.

Special Art Tools:

- **Sure Grip Crayons** (Battat $6.95) A set of 12 "bulb-shaped" plastic crayons fit easily in the palm of the hand. (800) 448-4115.
- **Fruity Markers** (Alex $4) Ten scented, broad-tipped markers will give extra sensory stimulation along with bright juicy colors. (201) 569-5757.

- **Double-Hand Training Scissors** (Galt $2.95) One set of holes is for the child, the other for an adult to help the child learn to cut. (800) 899-4258.

- **Stirex Scissors** (Galt $8.95) These have a flexible spring bar and allow for a whole-hand grip rather than the typical thumb-and-finger grip. (800) 899-4258.

- **Big Handle Paint Brushes** (Alex 3 for $10) These extra-large brushes with handles shaped like bulbs help kids with fine motor difficulties to paint. (201) 569-5757.

• •

ACTIVITY TIP—ADAPTING CRAYONS, MARKERS, GLUE-STICKS AND BRUSHES:

For an easier grip, use a foam hair curler over the drawing tool. Or wrap a crayon with a small piece of Velcro and then have the child wear a mitten. The Velcro will stick to the mitten, allowing the child to color without dropping the tool.

• •

- **Tempera Paint Markers** ($10.75 set of 4) Bypass brushes altogether! Pour paint into refillable bottles that are easy to grasp and use for dabbing and drawing. #232708 Chaselle. (800) 543-7411.

- **Sponge Painters** (Alex $3) ✴ SNAP Award For bold strokes kids will love this set of three foam painting tools. Great for painting with water, too. (201) 569-5757.

- **My Paper Craft Kit** (Alex $25) Kids of all ages and abilities will enjoy the feel, sound and sight of tissue, foil and other paper. The glue stick and glitter pen are great for kids with limited arm/hand function. Secure paper with tape to writing surface. (201) 569-5757.

- **Stamp Kits and Stencil Kits.** Although we like kids to create their own pictures, stampers and stencils can be extremely satisfying for older

kids who want realistic
results. To adapt stampers
for kids with fine motor difficulties, glue a dowel handle to the back of each
stamp . Our testers loved
Talking Stamps (All Night

Media $12 each) with the sound and image of
cow, train or frog. (415) 459-3013. For a wonderful variety of sets, see the Early School Years
section.

- **Play-Doh** (Playskool $5 & up) An ideal material
  for pounding, poking, twisting and molding. A
  rolling pin is great for pretend. For kids who are
  reluctant to get their fingers into the action,
  wrap the ball of dough around a small surprise.
  (800) 752-9755.

- **Krazy Klay—It's Scented!** (Great Kids $8.75)
  You can add another sensory dimension with
  this five-tub set that comes in primary or fluo-
  rescent colors with lemon, grape and bubble-
  gum scents. #KC19257. (800) 533-2166.

- **Magna Doodle Deluxe Set** (Tyco $20) Like Etch-
  a-Sketch but easier to use, with a drawing stylus
  instead of dials to turn. Erase with a simple pull
  of the lever. Set the board on a slanted tray for
  kids with visual challenges. Set includes stamps
  and stencils. (800) 367-8926.

• •

ACTIVITY TIPS:

Smelly Art: Add a few drops of scented oil or spices
to homemade dough for extra sensory stimula-
tion. (See Preschool section for dough recipe.)

Dab a Dab a Do Sponge Art: Sponges are easy to
grab and motivate artistic and messy art explo-
rations. Cut your own sponges or buy a pre-made
set.

Marble Painting: Place a piece of paper in a shallow
box. Dip a spoonful of marbles in tempera paint

and place them in the box. Tip box to produce a marvelous marbles masterpiece. Great for kids with limited motor control.

Make a Slanted Play Board: For kids who need a slanted surface to work on, cut the sides of a cardboard box at a slant and it's a ready for Play-Doh, coloring and other projects.

• •

BIG MUSCLES/PHYSICAL PLAY

Toys that challenge children to use their big muscles help them develop gross motor coordination, a sense of their own place in space, independence and self-esteem. Physical play also lends itself to social interaction and opportunities for pretend. See earlier sections for such basics as balls, sand equipment and other great products that need no adapting.

WHEELED TOYS

PUSH TOYS

We looked for the most stable push-about toys for beginning walkers. Our favorite choices: Little Tikes' plastic **Push 'n' Go Rider** ($20) is easy to straddle and low to the ground. (800) 321-0183. Galt's wooden **Wagon/Walker** ($80) is more expensive but can also be used for carting treasures about. Add rattles or a bike horn to the hand bar. Can also double as a doll carriage. (800) 899-4258.

EASY RIDERS

ROCKING ROCKET

(Little Tikes $40) This bright-red rocket is wonderful for whole-body action. Kids can rock front to back or side to side. With a key to turn, a horn to honk and gear shifts on the wings, there are sounds aplenty to enhance dramatic play. (800) 321-0183.

MINI VAN

(Little Tikes $85) This blue van can be used to develop upper- and lower-body coordination. A seat belt with Velcro closing can be added to the high-backed seat for those who need extra support. (800) 321-0183.

••

ACTIVITY TIP:

Open a car wash with a pail of water and sponges, or alternate driver and traffic cop roles with a whistle and stoplight made of paper.

••

TRIKES AND BIKES

Your child may be able to ride a trike or bike with little or no adaptations. You'll find our guidelines for buying and descriptions of top-rated wheeled toys in the Preschool and Early School Years sections.

How to Adapt a Wheel Toy: Adapting a bike may involve adding an easily made belt of Velcro. Other kids may need a trunk-support seating system, foot harnesses or a hand-driven trike. Two companies that specialize in adapted riding toys and supplies are J. A. Preston Corp. (800-631-7277) and Flaghouse Inc. (800-221-5185).

••

SHOPPING TIP:

Battery-operated ride-in cars that can be activated with a touch of a button will provide a thrilling ride for kids who are unable to pedal a ride-in toy. Use only with supervision.

••

BALLS

Large balls invite gross motor and social play. Three notable sets with added sensory feedback:

Boom Ball (Cadaco $20) comes with two rackets that make a "boom" sound when you hit the ball. A great choice for older developmentally delayed children. Use large balls that are easier to hit.

Grip Ball ($12.99) Ball and disc-like paddles, covered with Velcro, will help kids with limited hand control catch a ball. The paddle slides easily over a child's hand.

Bumble Ball (Ertl $14.95) ❀ SNAP Award A 3" soft ball with knobs that vibrate and jump. Put it in a paper bag for a playful adaptation. (800) 553-4886.

SAND FUN

For kids who can't get down on the ground to play in the sandbox, why not bring the sand up to them? Put a small sandbox on a picnic table and voilà! A child in a wheelchair can now dig in!

MUSIC AND AUDIO FEEDBACK

Many electronic and musical toys are especially helpful because they provide easy-to-activate feedback.

EASY TOUCH TAPE PLAYER
PLATINUM AWARD

(Mattel $30) This terrific tape player provides great stop-start visual controls in red and green. An excellent cuing system for a child with learning disabilities. For a child with visual impairment, adapt by gluing textures to buttons. (800) 524-8697.

PLAYBACK KEYBOARD

(Fisher Price $18) Kids can play tunes by following the color-coded notation. They can also record and play back their songs. Fosters skills in listening, rhythm and song. Add textured or Braille dots for a child who is visually challenged. (800) 432-5437.

BARNEY ANIMAL KEYBOARD 💥 SNAP AWARD

(Playskool $35) This versatile keyboard plays notes and makes animals sounds. It speaks and sings in Barney's voice. The big colorful keys are easily pushed with a fist or palm of the hand. An animal guessing game of "What am I?" helps develop auditory, memory and language skills for a child with speech/language delays. (800) 752-9755.

SESAME STREET ALL-STAR BAND

(Golden $34.99) Push a button and Sesame Street characters talk. Push another to select the tune and instruments you want to hear. The keyboard allows kids to play along. Add textured paste-ons to buttons for a child with visual limitations. Can be used at varying developmental levels, from those who are just working on cause and effect to those who are developing sequencing skills. (800) 558-5972.

SUPER SPEAK AND SPELL

(Texas Instruments $55) An excellent tool that reinforces letter recognition, phonics, spelling and word pronunciation with both auditory and visual cues. For a child with a visual impairment, this can be adapted by adding Braille dots to keys. By drawing an enlarged version of the keyboard on paper, a child with limited finger-pointing skills can make independent choices on the larger board. Letter selections can then be entered for the child. Also **Super Speak and Math.** (800) 842-2737.

BOOKS

For years, children with special needs were essentially invisible in picturebooks. Today publishers are issuing more books that reflect feelings and issues faced by children who are physically or mentally challenged.

BABY AND TODDLER BOARD BOOKS

ME AND MY DAD AND ME AND MY MOM
(by Debby Slier, Checkerboard Press $2.95 each) Two chubby little board books with photos of babies doing typical things with their parents. Photos include some children with Down syndrome. Also *Me and My Grandma and Me and My Grandpa.*

WHAT HAPPENS NEXT?
(by Cheryl Christian, Checkerboard Press $4.95) A first little mystery book for toddlers. Shows two clues, such as a little girl in pajamas with her clothes on the bed. What happens next? Open the flap and the little girl is dressed. Fun for guessing games! Photos include a child with Down syndrome. Also *Where's the Puppy?*

FRIENDS AND FAMILY

ALEX IS MY FRIEND
(by Marisabina Russo, Greenwillow $14) A warm story of friendship between two boys, one of whom is a dwarf and uses a wheelchair after an operation. 5 & up.

FAIR AND SQUARE
(by Nan Holcomb, Turtle $6.95) Kevin, who has a physical disability, is upset when he wins a game in which others had to move for him. Given access to a computer, he is ecstatic. When he plays a game, win or lose, he feels it's fair and square. 6 & up.

FRIENDS IN THE PARK
(by Rochelle Bunnett/illus. by Carl Sahlhoff, Checkerboard Press $7.95) Colorful photos capture the fun kids of mixed abilities share at the park. The accent is on the joy they share together at play rather than on their differences. 4–8.

MAMA ZOOMS
(by Jane Cowen-Fletcher, Scholastic $14.95) "Mama's got a zooming machine and she zooms me everywhere." In this

playful story a small boy tells how he and his mom pretend to ride a race horse, a sailing ship and a space ship. What a surprise to discover that Mama's zoom machine is a wheelchair! 3–6.

MY BUDDY

(by Audrey Osofsky/illus. by Ted Rand $14.95) A school-age child with muscul dystrophy tells about his special relationship with Buddy, his dog. 5–10.

PATRICK AND EMMA LOU

(by Nan Holcomb, Turtle Books $6.95) Three-year-old Patrick, who has cerebral palsy, steps out with his new walker and takes an embarrassing fall. His six-year-old friend, Emma Lou, who has spina bifida, helps him over his upset. 3–7.

WHERE'S CHIMPY?

(by Bernice Rabe/photos Diane Schmidt, Whitman $13.95) Misty, a little girl with Down syndrome, does not want to go to bed without her toy monkey, Chimpy. With help from Dad she solves the mystery of the lost monkey by recalling the events of the day. A warm, charming story. 3–7.

SIBLINGS

I HAVE A SISTER—MY SISTER IS DEAF

(by Jeanne W. Peterson/ illus. by Deborah Ray, Harper-Collins $12.95) A young girl describes her little sister, who loves to do all the things little sisters love to do. A warm, affirmative book about the special bond between sisters. 4–8.

PRINCESS POOH

(by Kathleen Muldoon/illus. by Linda Shute, Whitman $13.95) Patty Jean is jealous of the attention her big ten-year-old sister gets. Patty dubs her sister's wheelchair

a throne and her sister Princess Pooh. One day Patty
goes off with that royal seat and discovers it's not all
roses. 6–10.

KIDS COPING IN MAINSTREAM CLASSROOMS

THE BALANCING GIRL

(by Bernice Rabe/illus. by Lillian
Hoban, Dutton $12.95) Margaret,
who goes to a mainstream class,
may need a wheelchair to get
around, but that does not stop her
from becoming a heroine at the
school carnival. Also *Margaret's
Moves.* 6–9

FIELD DAY

(by Nick Butterworth, Bantam $2.99) This annual school
event is almost spoiled by showers. Karen, who runs a
race with crutches, does so well kids in her class want to
try them too. 5–9.

SOMEBODY CALLED ME A RETARD TODAY . . . AND MY HEART FELT SAD

(by Ellen O'Shaughnessy/illus. by David Garner, Walker
$13.95) With simple but moving words, this book says a
lot, both to a child who is mentally challenged and to
children of all abilities who go to school in mainstream
classrooms. In this upbeat book, the child who tells the
story affirms (with reinforcement from a loving family)
her belief in herself. A good book for all kids! All ages.

HARRY AND WILLY AND CARROTHEAD

(by J. Caseley, Greenwillow $13.95) Harry was born with-
out a left hand. When he starts school the kids are curious about his arm prosthesis. Harry not only proves him-
self, he turns out to be a good friend to a kid called
Carrothead. 5 & up.

A VERY SPECIAL CRITTER

(by Gina and Mercer Mayer, Golden $1.95) When Alex, a
floppy-eared critter, arrives at school in a wheelchair the

other critters are curious. This is as much for classmates as for kids with special needs. 3–6.

INSPIRATIONAL BOOKS

BRAVE IRENE

(by William Steig, Farrar Strauss & Giroux $12.95) Although she must face many difficulties, Irene has the courage to stay the course. An inspiring story for kids who often need to go the extra mile.

CLEVERSTICKS

(by Bernard Ashley/illus. by Derek Brazell, Crown $10) Everyone seems to be good at something, except Ling. Then he finds one thing he can do that everyone else wants to learn. Not specifically about a child with special needs, it does speak to feelings many will recognize. 4 & up.

HOW IT FEELS TO LIVE WITH A PHYSICAL DISABILITY

(by Jill Krementz, Simon & Schuster $18) A powerful collection of first-person accounts by 12 kids from ages 6 to 16 with a variety of disabilities. They share their feelings with courage and honesty. 7 & up.

HOWIE HELPS HIMSELF

(by Joan Fassler /illus. by Joe Lasker, Whitman $13.95) Howie, a boy with cerebral palsy, wants to be able to move his wheelchair on his own. A hopeful book that reinforces a positive sense of "can do." 4–8.

LEO THE LATE BLOOMER

(by Robert Kraus/illus. by Jose Aruego, Windmill $4.95) It seems everyone has learned to read and write before Leo. But, fear not, "in his own good time" Leo blooms! 4–8.

WE CAN DO IT!

(by Laura Dwight, Checkerboard Press $7.95) A photo essay features young children with varying special needs and focuses on their "can do" pride. Dwight's photos capture active kids with friends and family, at home and preschool.

WHY DUCKS SLEEP ON ONE LEG

(by Sherry Garland/illus. by Jean and Mou-Sien Tseng, Scholastic $14.95) In an ancient folktale from Vietnam, three ducks are unhappy because each has only one leg. But the members of this resourceful trio (with help along the way) seek and find a golden solution. 4–8.

FOR THE VISUALLY CHALLENGED

A CANE IN HER HAND

(by Ada Litchfield/illus. by Eleanor Mill, Whitman $13.95) Told in the first person, this is the story of a young girl whose sight is failing. With help from her family, her doctor and a teacher, she learns how to cope and use a cane. 6–10.

A GUIDE DOG PUPPY GROWS UP

(by Caroline Arnold/photos by Richard Hewitt, Harcourt Brace $16.95) A photo essay that follows the training of a golden retriever as a "guide dog" for the blind. 6–9.

REDBIRD

(by Patrick Fort, Orchard $19.95) A vinyl book in Braille and bold black type about a small plane that's trying to land. Pictures are raised so they can be felt and/or seen. Constructed with key words and pictures labeled in isolation and then used in context on the facing page. All ages.

• •

SHOPPER'S TIP:

A neat novelty for a child learning to read Braille is a plastic placemat with the Braille alphabet imprinted on it. From Straight Edge. (800) 331-8697.

• •

THE SEEING STICK

(by Remy Charlip and Demetra Maraslis, HarperCollins/ Crowell $13.89) A modern fantasy set in ancient China about the Emperor's daughter, who is blind, and a wise old man who uses a "seeing stick" to help her learn to see. 4–8.

COPING WITH HEARING IMPAIRMENTS AND INTRODUCING SIGN LANGUAGE

Every day more than 500,000 Americans use American Sign Language to communicate. Few other subjects have so caught the imagination of artists and publishers. You'll find great choices here for kids of every age.

ANIMAL SIGNS

(by Debby Slier, Checkerboard $4.95) Bright photos of a single animal per page. Inset drawings show kids signing the name of each animal. Also *Word Signs*. 1–4.

THE HANDMADE ALPHABET

(by Laura Rankin, Dial $13.95) Hands of all sizes, ages and ethnic groups are used in this witty hand alphabet, all done in American Sign Language. Handsome in more ways than one! 4 & up.

HANDTALK BIRTHDAY

(by Charlip and Miller/photos by George Ancona, Aladdin paper $4.95) Mary Beth's friends plan a surprise birthday party. Ancona's full-color photos show readers signs and numbers that people with hearing impairments use. Also *Handtalk*. 5 & up.

I'M DEAF AND IT'S OKAY

(by Lorraine Aseltine et al./illus. by Helen Cogancherry, Whitman $11.95) A school-aged boy is struggling with the reality of needing hearing aids and being deaf. 6–9.

MANDY

(by Barbara Booth/illus. by Jim Lamarche, Lothrop $14.95) When Grandma loses a silver pin, Mandy braves a stormy night to find it. Both story and magnificent painting illuminate the world of a child with a hearing impairment and her courage. 5–9

SESAME STREET SIGN LANGUAGE FUN
(Random House $10) An intro to sign language for kids. Actress Linda Bove and the Muppets illustrate concepts such as opposites, action words and feelings. Prepared with the National Theatre for the Deaf. 4 & up.

• •

VIDEO TIP:
Sign-Me-a-Story video (Random $14.95) Linda Bove teaches kids some signs and then performs non-scary versions of Red Riding Hood and the Three Bears. We wish there were many more! Closed captioned. (30 min.) (800) 733-3000.

• •

SILENT LOTUS
(by Jeanne M. Lee, Farrar Straus $14.95) The story of a Cambodian girl who cannot hear or speak but finds a way to express herself as a court dancer. 5–8.

WHERE'S SPOT?
(by Eric Hill, Putnam $13.95) Exactly like the original lift-the-flap book but with an illustrated sign-language translation on each page. 2 & up.

RESOURCES

Books: Most bookstores will order any books listed here from major publishers. Here are the phone numbers for several smaller publishers they may not regularly deal with or know about. Checkerboard Press (414) 639-8182; Turtle Press (814) 696-2920; Albert Whitman (800) 255-7675.

Videos: Many of the titles in the Videos section will be enjoyed by all children. In fact, many are closed captioned.

Descriptive Video Service (DVS), for visually impaired audiences, adds between-the-scenes narrations to TV and videos. For info about DVS television, write to DVS, WGBH, 125 Western Ave., Boston, MA 02134. To order DVS videos, such as *Dumbo* and *Anne of Green Gables* ($15–20), call (800) 736-3099, ext. 31.

Additional resources: A number of useful catalogs are targeted directly for the special needs market. Many contain useful adaptation devices. Browsing the catalogs below can help you find some great products as well as ideas for adapting more widely available toys.

- Achievement for Children and Adults with Special Needs (412) 444-6400
- Bell-Special Products (414) 642-7337
- Flaghouse (800) 221-5185
- Jesana Ltd. (800) 443-4728
- Kapable Kids (800) 356-1564
- Lakeshore (800) 421-5354
- Toys for Special Children (914) 478-0960

OTHER PUBLICATIONS OF INTEREST:

- *Exceptional Child* magazine is dedicated to parents and caregivers of children with special needs. Published nine times a year. (800) 247-8080.
- *Parenting* magazine has a monthly feature for families with special needs. (800) 234-0847.
- *Pre-K Today* is published monthly for early childhood teachers and has one page in each issue directed to special needs. (800) 544-2917.
- *Oppenheim Toy Portfolio,* in cooperation with Lekotek, includes a feature in every issue on adapting toys, as well as new books and videos of special interest. Published quarterly. (800) 544-TOYS.

Two national organizations that provide toy lending library services and play-centered programs for children with special needs and their families. To locate the center nearest you, contact:

- National Lekotek Center, 2100 Ridge Avenue, Evanston, IL 60201, or call (800) 366-PLAY.
- USA Toy Library Association, 2530 Crawford Avenue, Suite 111, Evanston, IL 60201, or call (708) 864-3331.

Top-Rated
Mail-Order Catalogs

For busy families mail-order catalogs are a time-saving way to shop. This list includes companies that feature many of the products we recommend.

CHILDREN'S CATALOGS

These catalogs offer a variety of toys, puzzles, games, and outdoor equipment. Some also have selected books, videos, and audios.

Back to Basics Toys	(800) 356-5360
Childcraft	(800) 631-5657
Constructive Playthings	(800) 832-0572
FAO Schwarz	(800) 426-8097
Great Kids Company	(800) 533-2166
Hand in Hand	(800) 872-9745
HearthSong	(800) 325-2502
Lilly's Kids	(804) 430-5555
One Step Ahead	(800) 274-8440
Reader's Digest Kids	(800) 458-3014
Right Start Catalog	(800) 548-8531
Sensational Beginnings	(800) 444-2147
Toys to Grow On	(800) 542-8338

SCHOOL CATALOGS OF INTEREST

Chaselle, Inc.	(800) 543-7411
Community Playthings	(800) 777-4244
Environments	(800) 342-4453
Learning Resources	(800) 222-3909

SPECIALTY CATALOGS

Chinaberry (books)	(800) 776-2242
Educational Insights	(800) 933-3277
Lego Shop at Home	(203) 763-4011
National Geographic	(800) 638-4077
Nature Company	(800) 227-1114
Pleasant Company (dolls)	(800) 845-0005
T.C. Timbers (wooden toys)	(800) 359-1233

AUDIO AND VIDEO CATALOGS

Alacazar's Kiddie Cat	(800) 541-9904
Coalition for Quality Children's Videos	(800) 331-6197
Home Vision	(800) 262-8600
Music for Little People	(800) 727-2233
Signals WGBH Educational Foundation	(800) 669-9696
Wireless	(800) 669-9999

Safety Guidelines

Many people assume that before toys reach the marketplace they are subjected to the same kind of governmental scrutiny as food and drugs. The fact is that although the government sets specific safety standards, there is no agency like the FDA that pre-tests and approves or disapproves products.

The toy industry is charged with the responsibility to comply with federal safety standards, but they are self-regulating, which means it s not until there are complaints or reports of accidents that the Consumer Product Safety Commission (CPSC) enters into the picture. The CPSC is the federal government agency charged with policing the toy industry—but not until the products are already on the shelf!

What does all this mean to you as a consumer? Basically it means "Let the buyer beware!" Both small and large manufacturers have run into problems with small parts, lead paint, strangulation hazards and projectile parts.

The CPSC releases useful recall warnings that are posted in most major toy stores and manufacturers are required to release recalls to the wire services. The CPSC also has a hotline if you want further information about a recalled product or want to report one that perhaps should be recalled; you can call (800) 638-CPSC. The CPSC also publishes a safety handbook that you can request.

To protect your child, here is a safety checklist to keep in mind when you're shopping for playthings:

For infants and toddlers:

- Dolls and stuffed animals. Select velour, terry or nonfuzzy fabrics. Remove any and all bows, bells and doodads that can be swallowed. Stick to dolls with stitched-on features rather than buttons and plastic parts that may be bitten or pulled off.
- Crib toys. Toys should never be attached to an infant's crib with any kind of ribbon, string or elastic. Babies and their clothing have been known to get entangled and strangled by such toys.
- Soft but safe. Be sure that soft toys such as rattles, squeakers and small dolls are not small enough to be compressed and possibly jammed into a baby's mouth.
- Heirlooms. Antique rattles and other treasures often do not meet today's safety standards and can be a choking hazard.
- Wall hangings and mobiles. Decorative hangings near or on the crib are interesting for newborns to gaze at but pose a safety hazard once a child can reach out and touch. They need to be removed when an infant is able to touch them.
- Foam toys. Avoid foam toys that can be chewed on and swallowed, and that present a choking hazard.
- Push-and-straddle toys. If you're looking for your child's first push toy, make sure it's stable and that your child can touch the ground when sitting on the toy.
- Toy chests. Old toy chests with lids that can fall do not meet today's safety standards. They can severely injure and even entrap small children. New chests have removable lids or safety latches. We recommend open shelves and containers for safe and easy access instead of the jumble of a deep toy chest.
- Age labels and small parts. When you see a toy labeled "Not for children under three," that's a

warning signal! It usually means there are small parts. Such products are unsafe for toddlers— no matter how smart they may be! They are also unsafe for some threes and fours who frequently put things in their mouths.

- Batteries. Toys that run on batteries should be designed so that kids are locked out of the batteries and child-proofed so that only an adult can get into the batteries.
- Quality control. Run your fingers around edges of toys to be sure there are no rough, sharp or splintery, hidden thorns. Check for products that can entrap or pinch little fingers.

For Older Children:

- Eye and ear injuries. Avoid toys with flying projectiles. Many action figures come with a number of small projectile parts that can pose a safety hazard if pointed in the wrong direction and that certainly pose a danger if there are younger children in the house.
- High-power water guns. Doctors report many emergency room visits from children with eye and ear abrasions caused by the trendy high-powered water guns.
- Burns. Avoid toys that heat up when used. Many of the toy ovens and baking toys become hot enough to cause burns.
- Safety limits. Establish clear rules with kids for sports equipment, wheel toys and chemistry sets.
- Adult supervision. Avoid toys labeled "Adult supervision required" if you don't have the time or patience to be there.

For mixed ages:

Families with children of mixed ages need to establish and maintain safety rules about toys with small parts.

- Older children need a place where they can work on projects that younger sibs can't get hurt by or destroy.
- Establishing a work space for the older sib gives your big child the privilege of privacy along with a sense of responsibility.
- Old toys need to be checked from time to time for broken parts, sharp edges or open seams. Occasionally clearing out the clutter can foster heightened interest in playtime. It also brings old gems to the surface that may have been forgotten.

Subject Index

Brand Name and Title Index

Note: Toys and equipment are listed under the manufacturer or distributor. The following codes are used for titles of works: (A) = Audio tapes; (B) = Book; (C) = Computer software/CD-ROM; (M) = Magazine; (V) = Video.

●●●●●●●●●●●●●●●●●●●●●●●●●●●●●

**Receive your subscription to
Oppenheim Toy Portfolio Newsletter
Full Year $12
The exclusive quarterly consumer
guide to the best toys, books,
videos, audios, computer software and
special needs products**

Name ——————————————————

Address ——————————————————

City/State/Zip Code ——————————————

Send check to: OPPENHEIM TOY PORTFOLIO, INC.,
40 East 9th Street, New York, NY 10003, or call
(800) 544-TOYS.